School Link to the Workforce

by
Victor H. Bolado, Ed.D.

DORRANCE PUBLISHING CO., INC.
PITTSBURGH, PENNSYLVANIA 15222

ISBN # 0-8059-3360-3

Library of Congress Catalog and Card Number 92-075292

Printed in the United States of America

First Printing

Dedication

This book is dedicated to the youth of America, including Victoria Lee, Ian Carmichael, and Johnathan Dudley, as well as to Anel's and Carlos' and Suzy's children.

Other Books by Victor H. Bolado

GLOSSARY OF AERONAUTICAL TERMS
Copyright © 1972 by Victor H. Bolado
Library of Congress Catalog Card Number: 75-187117
All Rights Reserved
ISBN 0-03-080088-9
Air University Press
Montgomery, Ala. 36122-5522

MANAGEMENT TERMINOLOGY
Copyright © 1981 by Victor H. Bolado
Library of Congress Cataloging in Publication
Data HD30 15.B64
ISBN 0-89962-034-5
Todd and Honewell, Inc.
Great Neck, New York 11021

Contents

Every man who knows how to read
has it in his power to magnify
himself, to multiply the ways in
which he exists, to make his life
full, significant, and interesting.

Aldous Huxley

Illustrations

Preface

Our Future may be beyond our
vision, but it is not beyond
our control. It is in our own hands.

Robert F. Kennedy

Several forces strongly motivated me to write this book. One was a lifelong preoccupation with values, many of which originated within my own family—my parents, my sisters, and my brothers. Values are operating projections that direct the course of mankind. Expressed values must be part of an educational system, and they should be practiced by the faculty and the student body. No youth should leave school without knowing the governing values of his or her culture. If you do not know where you came from, it is difficult to know where you are going. Values must be considered an essential part of our society.

Another strong motivating force was and is education. In the old days, we were concerned with memorizing numbers, lists, rules, and principles. Today we are faced with the use of concepts, and how concepts apply to rigorous analysis and predictions. In addition education is part of our social values, an important part. Central to education, now and then, are the crucial choices that youth face in the current social and economic competitive environment. Some of the least important choices include the extreme pursuit of materialistic gain and the ability of man to destroy each other.

Yet another strong force has been my experience in developing an educational curriculum. Curriculum, as is generally accepted, is limited to educational objectives. My own belief is that governing cultural values should reflect the basic foundation of an educational curriculum.

Considering these three motivating forces as a basis, and considering what the well-known music philosopher Bob Dylan has said: "The times, they are changing," this text is concerned with what I firmly believe to be the nation's priorities for the 1990's and for the twenty-first century—values (ethics and morality), education, and formal training.

Values

Parents introduce them, the schools teach them, the churches preach them, and the courts pronounce judicial decisions on their own terms. Values are not taught, they are "caught"; caught from examples. Children do not do what you tell them to do, they do what you do. (See Figure 4.)

We are talking about ethics, morality—and the monster that threatens to destroy our society—corruption. Ethics is often confused with morality. It is hardly possible to speak of one without implying the other. Ethics is associated with rules and standards of conduct, values and honesty, right and wrong, good or bad behavior. Morality also refers to rules and guidelines. Morality means conformity to ideals of conduct—a standard of what is right and good. Ethics is not necessarily related to religion, but rather is a working social principle. Ethics and morality must apply to society, to a group, and to the individual to be effective. The Golden Rule is fundamental to ethics and morality: Do unto others as you would like them to do unto you.

The far-too-long period of value-free schooling has resulted in great mistakes and dishonesty and the greatest number of perversities, especially among our youth. It has weakened our society excessively. Teaching values must be part of the school curriculum, including the study and application of ethics and morality, which must coincide with what has been taught by grandparents, parents, church leaders, and peers. It is important that we proceed in principle.

Honesty and ethical behavior are essential to preserving our freedom and avoiding extreme government centralization. If unchecked government regulations and centralized authority thrive on corruption and dishonesty. The political process was made for man, not man for the political process. The Declaration of Independence clearly states that our Government derives its "just powers from the consent of the governed," and that "whenever any form of Government becomes destructive of these ends, it is the right of the people to alter or to abolish it...." You need not be a political scientist to note the extreme abuses of power that exist in the executive and congressional branches of Government. Throughout the years there has been a continuous expropriation of the peoples' power by Washington politicians. No dishonest Government will ever benefit the people. Survival depends on mutual and public trust.

The preservation of a free society depends on, to a great extent, an ethical and moral foundation. Lest we forget the original magistrate founders of our Republic were all clergymen. Ethics is lifeblood of a free society, which can tolerate only so much adulteration. We must remember that freedom of the strong is usually lost from within, not from without.

It is not enough to seem content in the belief that as long as we observe below-standard ethics, we should not feel responsible for the conduct of others. By accepting responsibility, reacting in the right manner, and practicing day-to-day ethics, we can help stabilize society. Mankind requires coherence.

Professor Robert Cooley Angell, regarded as one of the great social scientists, wrote in his book *Free Society and Moral Crisis* as follows: Every group that is to any degree self-governing has something in the nature of moral order. People cannot work together without overt or tacit standards of conduct corresponding to their common value.

Dishonesty is so widespread, from the mainstream to the special interests of the Congress of the United States, that at times we seem to grow accustomed to it. We begin to accept the lack of values as "situation normal." Special interests have swayed many of our politicians to the extent that they are publicly corrupt. Unfortunately with little respect for themselves, they are "exempt from dishonest behavior by law," their own enacted laws. Some of these self-exempt laws which, of course, are inflicted on you and me, include:

- Social Security
- National Labor Relations Act
- Fair Labor Standards Act
- Civil Rights Act
- Freedom of Information Act
- Occupational Safety and Health Act
- Equal Employees Opportunity Act
- Privacy Act
- Rehabilitation Act
- Ethics In Government Act

These representatives of the people lead an exclusive lifestyle of power and luxury similar to kings and queens of the eighteenth and nineteenth centuries, with free access to swimming pools, golf courses, tennis clubs, four private health clubs with massage parlor facilities—all at taxpayers' expense.

That's not all. These people have totally ignored the ever-increasing, catastrophic national debt. Instead they have voted themselves a generous and unheard of pay increase during a recession. Read on.

There are the congressional check-writing and post office scandals. A great number of congressmen (in excess of three hundred) and former congressmen (four are currently members of the president's Cabinet, such as the secretary of defense and the secretary of labor) overdrew hundreds of thousands of dollars from the congressional bank. These people conveniently exempt themselves from the law. Apparently no law can be found that can legally prosecute them; nonetheless the justice department is investigating the matter.

Then there is the White House credit union scandal. Members of the executive branch cannot account for losses of millions of dollars, according to the General Accounting Office. This scandal, in the president's backyard, not only parallels the congressional scandal, but appears to be more serious.

On several occasions the vice president and the former transportation secretary (now the president's Chief of Staff) used government aircraft to attend golf tournaments, all at taxpayers' expense, according to the General Accounting Office. When these representatives of the people were "caught," they simply stated that they would reimburse the Government at "commercial aircraft rates." This is an insult to the American people. The cost of commercial aircraft is merely several hundred dollars from Washington to California, or points West. This is peanuts compared to the cost of operating government aircraft. Government aircraft, mostly four-engine type, costs the taxpayer approximately $4 thousand per hour, per engine—another simple, but abusive reason why the government is so expensive to operate. It is not the cost of Government that is expensive to operate; it is the way the Government mismanages the money that is expensive.

Another common mismanagement of taxpayers' hard-earned money is the excessive use of servants and large staffs by the government. A good example is the White House, where some one hundred employees serve the president and his wife. It is not difficult to see why the Government today spends 40 percent of its income. A great portion of the expenditure is on servants and large staffs. With these styles of expenditures, little, very little is left for the welfare and benefits of the people.

Both Democratic and Republican Party members viciously attack prominent and nonprominent members of each other's party. It is no longer an honor to be called to public office. Human respect is being totally ignored. It is now common for politicians to use dirty tricks, falsify records, lie, and apply callous conduct and cruel, unbecoming comments in political campaigns. The idea seems to be to destroy reputations rather than to lend consent. Nominees to high positions have become a harrowing rite of character assassination and, of course, degradation. Almost all political appointees, prominent or not, are victimized by vicious lynchings.

It is time we bring back decency, courtesy, and respect for each other when dealing with public servants. The Golden

Rule must be fully restored. The wheels of an honest, decent, fair, democratic-principles concept will then be lubricated, and the public will be better served.

The wise words of one of our greatest presidents, Abraham Lincoln, spoken on April 30, 1863, can serve as an awakening for us all today:

We have been the recipients of the choicest bounties of heaven. We have been preserved these many years, in peace and prosperity. We have grown in numbers, wealth and power, as no other nation has ever grown. But we have forgotten God. We have forgotten the gracious hand which preserved us in peace, and multiplied and enriched and strengthened us; and we have vainly imagined, in the deceitfulness of our hearts, that all these blessings were produced by some superior wisdom and virtue of our own. Intoxicated with unbroken success, we have become too self-sufficient to feel the necessity of redeeming and preserving grace, too proud to pray to the God that made us! It behooves us, then, to humble ourselves before the offended Power, to confess our national sins, and to pray for clemency and forgiveness.

In the last ten years, this Administration, together with the last Administration, has tripled our country's national debt, to the tune of $3.6 trillion (1991 figures). As late as December 1928, Federal Government spending amounted to only 3 percent of the national income. Today it is 40 percent. Taxpayers' money is not well accounted for today, nor is it well managed. The huge national debt does not include more than $500 billion needed to clean the mostly dishonest dealings of the savings and loan scandal. This scandal is a needless, careless, unethical, fraudulent debt that must be paid by the innocent—the American people.

And guess who is charged with paying our huge national debt in the not-too-distant future?—the very children whose financial support for education has been denied by the Congress and the president. What makes this excessive and national debt so exuberant is the fact that our schools and children have been totally ignored, financially, for years. We have no advanced educational or technical training program. We are competing with countries that have not only foreseen the huge, dynamic technological changes, but that have planned adequately for them. We have not.

The behavior of congressmen, the president, and his Cabinet and staff, represents the moral state of the nation, which can have an extreme adverse effect on our society because morality is easier to acquire when inspired by example, rather than when presented as a behavioral principle. The common people—you and I—on the other hand, have a choice. We can be honest and free, or we can be corrupt, policed, and tried in a court of justice.

The good news, of course, is that most Americans are morally honest and believe in our heritage of ethical principles.

Were we not ethical in the majority, we would not be able to maintain order. Corruption is in the minority in the United States, and it is up to each of us to ensure that dishonesty is contained in the minority. The less corruption and crime, the better the future will be for our children. Only honesty and positive ethics will preserve our hard-earned freedom.

Upon leaving what was then, and what today continues to be, the highest office in our land, George Washington, in 1796, stated: Of all the dispositions and habits which lead to political prosperity, religion and morality are indispensable support. In vain would man claim the tribute of patriotism who should labor to subvert these two great pillars.

Is there a new work ethic in the horizon that can give direction to curriculists—a work ethic in which job satisfaction, the feeling of contribution, cooperation, and innovation take precedence over money, the income earned? If so let us develop a plan to incorporate it into the school curriculum under values.

Our problem is that many of us are waiting for the other teacher—the principal or the dean or anyone else—to make a move. Instead all of us must take the initiative in our own hands and adhere to a good, honest code of ethics. We must strive for a better school system, for a better society, and for a better America.

Education and Formal Training

Our national lack of preparation in education and formal training has caused some very serious economic circumstances. The United States has been on an economic and moral decline for at least the last three decades. We have been lead astray by faith in adversarial competition. In 1980 our country imported approximately $31 billion in mostly high-technology products, symbolizing Japan as a developed nation. During the same period, the United States exported $19 billion to Japan in mostly raw materials, such as lumber, grain, soybeans, coal, and scrap metals, symbolizing an exporting, underdeveloped country. The important point to remember is that the Japanese merely used most of our technology, improved its quality, and then sold these products right back to us.

Without doubt technology *is* the future. The United States developed the computer and the initial software, as well as the atom bomb, among a great number of "critical" high-technology inventions. Even though we remain strong in science, our inability to follow through in technology and quality has placed the United States a distant follower in world production The Council on Competitiveness, warns us: "Unless the nation acts immediately to promote its position in critical generic technologies, the United States competitiveness will erode farther, with disastrous consequences for

American jobs, economic growth, and national security." This implies a serious need to increase the amount of technical literacy on our part, which translates into more and better education and formal training. In 1985, 12 percent of all United States college students elected engineering as their major. In 1991 it was less than 6 percent. In 1980, 60 percent of our engineering majors were from foreign countries. In 1991 it was 82 percent. The United States continues to value creativity and innovation, but we are almost totally disregarding production. Unfortunately money (economy and growth) is not in innovation and creativity, but in production. To be effective economically, development must be linked to industry and, ultimately, to production.

American genius rests not in its ideological fervor, but in its pragmatism, in its ability to listen, to learn, to research and experiment, and to move forward and succeed. However we have failed to plan and to prepare our youth the way their previous generation was prepared. Our lack of commitment to an educated and well-trained citizenry is the number-one problem facing the United States today. The time to begin to enhance our educational and training readiness is now.

National policy on education must be put into effect. The United States must regain and retain its high-technology stature. A new policy is necessary to avoid gross mistakes in educational and economic planning. Our educational and formal training system must be revitalized. Our present educational standards reflect our society and our lack of workforce preparation.

A large number of high school graduates who go into the workforce are working side by side and are being trained by workers who were never trained themselves. These youngsters are following unintelligible instructions from nontrained fellow workers. Employers looking for eighth-grade-level skills cannot find them in high school graduates. We must remember: Today's graduates are tomorrow's leaders. Their education will affect all of society.

Experts say that many of our present-day social problems would be eliminated through education. Talk about reverse cost-effectiveness within our educated society—today more than 80 percent of all United States prisoners are high school dropouts. More people are incarcerated in our country than in any other.[*] In 1992 there were 1.2 million prisoners, each costing the taxpayers $20,000 annually. During 1991 more than 2 million youngsters were arrested for various crimes in the United States and high school dropouts cost the United States Treasury over $240 billion in lost earnings and tax revenue.[**] The real question is whether we can afford not to implement a broad-based policy to improve our education and formal training.

[*]Source: Department of Justice, Washington, D.C.
[**]Treasury Department, Internal Revenue Service, Washington, D.C.

*All who have
meditated on the art
of governing
mankind are
convinced that
the fate of empires
depends on the
education of youth.*

Aristotle

As part of the 1990 State of the Union Message to the Congress and to the American people, President Bush set these National Educational *Goals* in January 1990 to be accomplished by the year 2000:

- Every child starts school ready to learn.
- Raise the high school graduation rate to 90 percent.
- American students at the fourth, eighth, and twelfth grade levels can demonstrate competence in core subjects.
- Every American adult must be a literate worker and citizen.
- Every school must offer a safe and drug-free environment to make learning possible.

In over two years, here is what a few states (seven, to be exact) have done in response to the president's education proposals:

ARKANSAS—The state legislature has passed the Quality Act. The Act includes creating, by 1991, a math and science high school where gifted students can live and learn. The Act also includes adopting a 1 percent state sales tax to fund reforms. The state also has schools of choice.

CALIFORNIA—An educational overhaul has begun with improving school standards for learning materials and forming partnerships with businesses and colleges for special programs. The state now is embarking on a new assessment system for students.

KENTUCKY—the state adopted an eight-part plan in 1990 to improve education. The plan will be phased in during the next five years, and it includes creating primary schools, in which students, ages six to eight, will work in the same classrooms and advance at their own pace.

NEW JERSEY—Under the 1990 Quality Education Act, limits have been set on how much school districts can increase yearly spending. Poorer districts are allowed higher limits, and thirty districts have been designated as having special needs and are being given extra state aid.

NEW YORK—The New Compact for Learning supports a new testing and assessment system for the state's 3 million school children and sets goals for the year 2000. Under the plan each district must adopt site-based management, in which parents, teachers, and administrators work on planning and operations.

OREGON—The Oregon Educational Act for the Twenty-First Century was signed into law in July 1991. It gives school districts until 1995 to design new approaches to learning. Under the Act students will have to qualify for a certificate of initial mastery at about age sixteen. Then students continue on in high school while taking college courses, working on apprenticeships, or doing internships.

WASHINGTON—A task force has selected thirty-three model education projects with common themes such as shared decision making, environmental consciousness, at-risk students, and global awareness.

In the spring of 1992, two years after the president's National Educational Goals were announced, very few, if any, improvements can be seen. National two-year presidential Commission Reports continue to be repressive. Late 1991 academic reports clearly show our educational report cards to be at 1970 levels. This is way below and behind world educational quality standards. All present education panaceas, such as year-round school classes, magnet school programs, and vouchers have not even scratched the surface of the critical education problems we face as a nation.

Paul Copperman, noted education analyst, has stated : "For the first time in the history of our country, the education skills of our generation will not surpass, will not equal, will not even approach those of their parents." This will certainly hamper the abilities of our youth to compete with other countries in world-class education and world-class economic advancement.

The nation's faith in its public schools is fading fast. In late fall 1991, Florida's Commissioner of Education announced a proposal to have two private companies manage an entire public school system, from cafeterias to classroom instruction. The contract is to commence in the fall of 1992.

Florida's reaction to the school reform movement reflects troubling national reality. In 1991 there were 5.1 million students attending private schools in the United States. Here are some interesting statistics. Overall 95 percent of parochial school students graduate from high school compared with 69 percent from public schools. In the last ten years, 83 percent of Catholic school graduates attended college compared with 52 percent of public school graduates. Strict educational discipline and hard work does it. There is an ancient Spanish proverb which states: "No positive dream ever comes true until you wake up, get out of bed, and go to work." The choice here is clear—discipline or face disintegration.

Curriculum

Massive rejuvenation of our school curriculum, with quality measures to meet the requirements of the workplace, is essential. Perhaps a study or at least a comparison with one of our world education and economic competitors would help some. Four significant fundamental disparities could be looked into. First, the Japanese basic high school curriculum contains 250 contact class hours (approximately 25 percent) more than ours. (See also Figure 3). Second, teacher selection in Japan is second to none. Strict selection, continuous testing, and strict observation is ongoing throughout the teaching career. Rejection is approximately 50 percent in the first year. Third, the Japanese literacy rate is 20 percent higher than that of the United States. Japan has the world's highest literacy rate today. Fourth, the average secondary school pupil in the industrial nations averages 216 more assigned annual homework hours than do pupils in the United States.

Unlike all other industrialized countries, the United States does not have a policy to help noncollege-bound youngsters make the transition from school to the workforce. To make matters worse, few teachers know anything about careers or jobs. Most teachers are judged by their superiors on how well they prepare students for college. The result is that teachers, generally, do not stress the importance of job preparation in their classrooms.

While most teachers are busy preparing students for college, almost half of the students graduating from high school do not go into college. The 1990 graduating seniors in the United States totaled 2.6 million. Of this graduating group, more that 1 million youngsters did not go into college. Here is the important and challenging question: What are these 1 million-plus noncollege-bound youth doing after graduating from high school? For sure the majority of these American youngsters are now unemployed, and will remain unemployed for long periods of time. Some will go into low-paying, part-time jobs; however upward mobility has become a vanishing dream for these young men and women. Other young men and women have been walking the streets and the malls with nothing but temptation on their minds. While still others, most unfortunately, have joined gangs, and many times these few antisocials become involved in crimes of all sorts. The reasons?

There is no preparation or connection between the school and the job. Some plan and preparation must be established, a system whereby students can begin preparing for a job while they are still in the formal classroom. This preparation plan must develop students' skills and enable them to step right into a decent, reasonable-paying, stable job. We need to tailor our educational management style to a realistic economic world—not as we want it to be necessarily, but instead as it realistically must be. The economic picture is no longer traceable to events in the United States. In today's global economy, most of the changes in our buying power are generated abroad.

No matter what statistics you examine today, from 1980 to 1990, the earnings of U.S. workers who have only a high school education decreased approximately 10 percent, while the income of the college graduate increased more than 10 percent during the same period. There is a whopping difference of more than 20 percent in the amount of possible earnings that noncollege graduates might have received had they prepared themselves. (See Figures 1 and 2.)

We are speaking here about a major national crisis. The global economy is reserving its rewards in pay for the well educated and the well trained. Global industry today looks for personnel who are inventive, who are creative, who are thinkers, and who can solve problems on the spot. This is a very select group, who are mostly college graduates or professionally well-trained personnel. The name of the present and future global game is obvious—top-paying jobs are available for the educated and the well trained; minimum wages and part-time jobs, for almost all other workers.

Industry and our Federal Government are looking into some solutions, but we may be looking in the wrong direction. Two negative cases in point: First the New York Life Insurance Company now processes most of its claims, not in New York City or New York State or the United States, but instead in Ireland. The reasons? Ireland has more highly qualified workers, personnel who can perform a better job qualitatively. Also Irish workers cannot only do a better job, but they can do it for 25 percent less than United States' wages, provided qualified workers were available. Second case in point: Once the U.S. Congress has passed the president's proposal for a United States-Mexico-Canada North American Free Trade Agreement (NAFTA) and the present barriers fall, Mexican and Canadian workers' pay will increase while U.S. workers' pay will decrease. NAFTA is not a win-win prospect, but a win-lose proposition, with Mexico set to gain jobs and production output, mostly at the expense of the U.S. workers, especially the low-skilled workers, according to the U.S. International Trade Commission. Unless major changes are included in NAFTA on U.S. job-protection safeguards, safety, and the environment, the treaty falls short of benefiting the United States. It is interesting to note, also, that the majority of U.S. workers involved in NAFTA are either high school graduates or school dropouts. Thus provided the Agreement is signed, U.S. workers may very well be competing with well-trained workers from Canada and Mexico, where school dropout rates are considerably lower than they are in the United States.

To be able to maintain an edge on global education and the global economy in the twenty-first century, the United States must capitalize on its most important resource—its youth. The decade of the 1990s will determine whether our nation will be competitive in the twenty-first century. It is up to our present generation to rally behind our youth generation. All of us must be involved and we must be involved now. Children are the living message we send to a time that we will not see—an investment in the future of America for years to come. Only a society that cherishes its youth deserves to thrive.

Most school curriculum reforms focus on preparation for college and for higher education. Nothing on the existing or changing curriculum includes or encourages noncollege-bound students whose only desire is to work hands-on in a technical, service, or other specialized field. We are talking about students whose performance is more predictive and more productive without books and paper. These youth may have the skills to become highly productive workers and leaders given the opportunity.

This group of youngsters makes up 40 percent of all high school graduates, and this is the group that is being ignored as future skilled workers. A cumulative total of some 20 million—yes, 20 million—youngsters are in this category, in 1991. This large group of mostly unskilled labor and unemployed has been called the "uneducated group," and the "unskilled labor force." Yet there are some 82 million jobs in the United States that do not require a four-year college degree, although requirements do demand some formal skills. Among the professions that do not require a college degree are machine operators, assemblers, retail clerks, health service technicians, and construction workers. Formal skills required for these jobs vary.

Here is where the curriculum experts are needed. Students need to be permitted to exercise and express their curiosity and innovative ideas. The concept of education should be to create a whole human being. Education must be built from the fingertips to the brain, with students being constantly involved. Today's curriculum is much too rigid. It conforms to school and to administrative policies and rules, but the student's interest is not taken into consideration. Let students remain inquisitive throughout school. Let them inquire about the connection among the academic subjects, and about the application of subject matter to common, daily living experiences. All school curriculum must focus on the student. The curriculum must be student-centered.

National surveys indicate that most educators believe that they are doing a superb job in preparing high school students. However some 90 percent of the business leaders state that high school graduates are not ready for either the workplace or society. The claim is that there is, in most of today's high school graduates, an absence of values that employers seek. There is lack of commitment, maturity, self-discipline, motivation, responsible attitude, and there remains that serious obstacle, the inability of today's youth to conform to the continuous evolving workplace. Both industry and business leaders recommend that future employees he encouraged to develop these qualities prior to seeking employment:

Self-development	Dependability
Self-concern	Dedication
Self-image	Imagination

A high school diploma, long considered the single most powerful predictor of success in the labor market, is now not quite the minimum requirement for entry into the workforce. This high school diploma notion may have been true in an expending economy with a simple technical basis. The bastion of American high school graduates working in steel, automobile, and machine tool industries have lost market share at home and abroad. Today the requirement for technology, advanced skills, and competencies—plus the ability to think flexibly and creatively about new high technology, ongoing research, and emerging problems and their solutions—makes it necessary for the individual and society to adapt to a world of endless wrenching change. With such skills and competencies could come the earnings that make it possible to benefit from a decent living, and to contribute responsibly to the community. Unfortunately today a high school diploma will not suffice.

Although a college degree is an important step in developing the talent and professional abilities of American young men and women, college preparation in secondary schools must not ignore students who, for a variety of reasons, do not go to college. This group of noncollege-bound students is being cut off from their professional growth, many through no fault of their own.

Is the American economic dream still alive, and is it still shining? (This is when the United States dominated the world economy.) The economic dream is still alive, but it is not shining as it used to; it is not shining as it should be. An urgent need exists for reorganizing and for radically reevaluating the professional preparation of our youth, not only for today but for the future of a successful workforce.

Global education and the global economy are not in the horizon. Both have clearly arrived. High-speed communication and high-speed transportation have brought competitor after competitor to barely a few blocks from our market doors. There is no turning back. Today whoever can do the job faster, least expensive, better, and can be professionally well prepared will take over great portions of the global markets. All economic trends are not necessarily dark, yet. The United States capital still plays an important role in the financial markets of many foreign countries. A lot of misconception exists about the Japanese acquiring excessive amounts of American businesses and real estate. In fact other countries, such as Great Britain, own more than twice as many American businesses and much more real estate than Japan. Also Canada, Germany, the Netherlands, and some other countries own more property in America than the Japanese. But that's not the entire story. U.S. industry and business still own far more foreign property and businesses than all foreign countries combined own in the United States. This is economically healthy for the United States and the countries concerned. In addition the volume of imports and exports involving the United States today totals more than $1 trillion a year. Still economic experts claim that the United States should be much farther ahead, economically. Room for improvement remains.

Once worldwide famous for its skilled workforce and ingenuity, the United States was at the lowest level in the summer of 1991 compared with all other industrial countries. Official education reports from the high school classrooms across America indicate, unequivocally, that the majority of secondary school students cannot pass a simple fractions/decimals/interest test. Most of these students (176,000 students took the test) can add, subtract, and multiply. However the great majority of students tested could not apply their math problems and answers to common sense, everyday living experiences. Almost one-fourth of high school students graduating in 1991 could not read or write properly. The SAT (Scholastic Aptitude Test) scores for 1991 were the lowest in history in the United States. To make things even worse, if that is possible, during the normal nine-month school year in 1990-1991, one student dropped out of high school every six seconds. Almost one-third of our youngsters drop out before finishing high school. In comparison only 8 percent do so in Germany, and only 6 percent in Japan.

We, in the United States, have set educational quality standards of our own, and as far as our own standards are concerned, our schools appear to be in excellent standing. The president's own proposals for setting "National Standards" fall along the same school of thought. These are all false pretenses on our part. The president has been ill-advised. American educational standards are antiquated. We are operating based on educational standards of our own making, forgetting the unusually high advancement in education in other countries. The difference is so great that were we to compete with such countries as Germany, Japan, France, and even with less industrialized countries, such as Taiwan, Hong Kong, and Singapore, we would "flunk" our tests. The underlying objective in our educational standards should be quality of time, not quantity of time. More of the same does not necessarily result in quality. Or does it? (See Figure 3 for comparison purposes.) Spending more money is not necessarily the answer either. Japan spends 50 percent less per student than we do in the United States, and both Japan and Germany pay their teachers a higher salary than we do in the United States.

We *need* to, and we are really forced to, set world-class standards—not "National Standards." Our standards for education in support of the global economy have already been set—unfortunately not in Washington, D.C., but in faraway places, abroad. From automation to automobiles, from computers to research, from think tanks to supercolliders, we must plan, we must operate, and we must compete with Germany, Japan, Hong Kong, Taiwan, and many other countries by setting world-class quality standards. American educational standards are no longer considered valid. We cannot afford to limit our educational standards to those in Minnesota, Mississippi, or mid-America. We must prepare ourselves to compete with a worldwide education system. Our long unemployment lines should awaken us, and they should make us well aware of where we stand on world-class standards of quality in the global economy. We have no choice. Our schools must meet and they must surpass world-class quality educational standards if we wish to survive. It is that serious. We must look at ourselves in the context of a worldwide education and economic revolution—changes will then be most evident.

Everyone has a stake in the educational reform movement—educators, parents, business, and the Government must all raise their expectations. Improved measures for education and formal training is one of the keys. We must set higher standards for our schools and students. Our complacency is dangerously obvious. We have to work harder, longer, and mainly, more forceful. What goes on in the classroom is not only the business and responsibility of the teacher; it is also the business and responsibility of parents, community groups, leaders, and all of us. We must all get and remain involved.

Today in a highly competitive economy, which depends to a great extent on technology, prosperity is offered to those with advanced skills and education. For those with less skills or no skills at all, it is a scramble to get jobs that are neither steady nor well-paying. Certainly their pay is insufficient to support themselves or a family above the poverty level. For the most part, these workers with less skills try hard to find a place in society, but what they find is less than what most of them deserve.

Because of shortages of skilled, professionally trained labor, companies are exporting production jobs in great quantities to low-wage countries, or are de-skilling jobs through automation in order to remain competitive. It is no wonder that industry, business, and management, who are directly affected by education and formal training, demand to have the last word or judgement as to whether recent graduate-employees are prepared for society and the workplace. This is where close cooperation between business and industry with educators is most essential.

America has long accepted literacy as a paramount aim of our school curriculum. However we must realize that literacy is not simply a skill. Literacy requires a large amount of information. Cultural knowledge is most essential in the development of reading, writing, and proper speaking skills. Competent readers must possess cultural literacy, which gives them the general background information that enables them to comprehend, to get the point of the story or the gist of the book being read. Students learn if information is meaningful and they are able to associate it with or relate it to their existing knowledge and experience. We have been taking our literacy competence for granted, and on our way we have let our youth down. Youngsters have difficulty relating because they have not learned their reading, writing, and proper speaking skills that are gained from the basic foundation. Simply reading, writing, and speaking, without being able to establish the relation to the ordinary daily living environment, completely fails to fulfill the fundamental civic responsibility of an informed citizen. Our students, as readers, as writers, and as oral users of the language, must be prepared to assume a starting point from which they can comprehend, in detail, what they wish to focus on for their own individual future. A citizen's vocabulary must contain a foundation for literate national communication. Unless citizens can deliberate and communicate with one another, at the same level, people in a democracy cannot be entrusted to make important decisions. Survival without a sense of mission, and ignorance of shared purposes, ideals, and values can indeed be the forerunner of extinction. A nation is an organism, and like an organism it can weaken and die. An informed citizenry was emphasized from the very beginning of our country by the Founding Fathers. During an educational debate before the Continental Congress, Thomas Jefferson stated:

If a nation expects to be ignorant and free
in a state of civilization,
it expects what never was and never will be.

Educators, parents, community leaders, and representatives of business and industry, working together, must invest heavily in efforts to raise the level of basic learning and set definite goals way before the year 2000. A good possibility exists that we have not improved our educational standards because we have not determined what has to be done.

Two examples of the president's 1990 National Educational Goals may be mentioned to support this argument. These two goals are:

1. Every child starts school ready to learn.
2. Every American adult must be a literate worker and citizen.

These proposed goals, as others, are much too vague and are subject to many interpretations. It is no wonder that the states' education systems have not improved two years after the president offered his Educational Goals. A *specific* transformation effort must include much parental involvement (the family is the most important institution for learning, parents being extremely important role models), community support, and some assurance from the business and industry sectors for youth employment. Volunteerism is a basic ingredient of our democratic form of Government. If we care enough about our youth, let us all get involved. The compensation is clearly obvious. We cannot sincerely help our youth without helping ourselves. Volunteer work is a must in this entire and continuous effort.

In 1830, during his visit to the United States, Frenchman *Alexis de Tocqueville said:

The health of a democratic society may be measured by the quality of functions performed by private citizens.

The challenge is to balance society's needs with a genuine responsiveness to the needs of others, our youth.

Educators must begin working on plans for a curriculum with a dual channel to "salvage students" who are college-bound, as well as to prepare students who do not plan to go or cannot go to college. In the case of students not planning to go or who cannot go to college, vocational training alone is not sufficient. These students require and deserve more than that; they deserve an opportunity to be part of an education and training plan that can interrelate with a predictive individual future goal. The plan may include apprenticeship, internship, preemployment training, and actual on-the-job training. Combined these concepts can expose the student to an adult-type society as a citizen, in preparation for the workforce. A long-term relationship with a caring adult can change a young person's life. I personally witnessed this phenomenon during my brief duties as Scoutmaster, mentor, and again as commander of young troops in the United States Air Force. Every student learns what they live.

Another important curriculum topic in global education and the global economy is the study of foreign languages and their culture. Language does not only reflect a culture, but it also influences the behavior of that specific culture. In Spain they say: "Cada lengua representa otro ser humano y otra cultura." (Each language stands for an additional human being and an additional culture.) Living abroad for a number of years, I have experienced this to be true. Also I have found that many students abroad commonly study as many as five languages during their course of study at school. On the other hand, of the few American students studying foreign languages, it is rare to find one student studying more than one language. The American Council on the Teaching of Foreign Languages lists foreign languages as one of the six important academic areas of a school curriculum. Our need in the United States for global communication in all fields is enormous. Yet less than 15 percent of all high school students were enrolled in foreign languages in 1990. The figures

---

*Tocqueville, Alexis Charles Henri Maurice Clerel de (1805-1859) (Britannica)

are even lower in most colleges. Also most of our competitors speak our language fluently, while most of us do not, embarrassingly, understand, much less speak their language. In 1990 approximately 35 percent of our secondary school students studied one foreign language (none in elementary school). Knowing a foreign language can be a terrific business advantage and an important means of social communication. Foreign language enrollment in the United States should be mandatory, a required subject. The study of foreign languages and their culture is as essential to the core curriculum as mathematics, English, and the sciences. Study should begin in the elementary schools, and should be continued on through high school and college.

Still formal education and formal training are the key words in our overall goal. However education and training, no matter how formal and extensive, are worthless without proper planning and preparation. Careful, well-identified planning and preparation are vital to the accomplishment of our goal.

A suggested aggressive education scenario follows:

1. *Career specialist.* Each high school administrator appoints a teacher, giving this teacher an additional duty as career specialist. Among other duties a career specialist assists the secondary school principal with the school-to-work preparation. A career specialist may also represent the school administrator at community workforce meetings.

2. *Planning.* A planning director, with a designated Steering Committee and a Scholarship Committee, develops an annual plan, to include resources, funds, materials, staff, and required periodic meeting schedules. The plan also includes specific strategies for accomplishing definite, identifiable goals by the Planning Committee, for each student graduate. For composition of Planning Team members, see item 4 below.

3. *Public report.* The Steering and Scholarship Committees, with approval from the planning director, jointly prepare, publish, and issue an annual progress report, to be made public. Parents who have children at the specific high school will receive a copy of this report.

4. *Planning Team.* Planning Team members consist of the following, or representatives thereof. At the initial meeting, a chairman or chairwoman will be appointed by the members of the Planning Team, for a period of two years. The planning director may chair the Planning Team.

Parents (No representatives permitted, except under unusual circumstances, and only upon approval from the planning director.)

High school teachers
High school administrator (principal)
College and university administrators
Community volunteer groups
Private industry
Civic leaders
Ethnic leaders
Chamber of Commerce
Job placement agencies
Religious leaders
Vocational schools
Technical schools
City government
County government
Neighborhood organizations
Other invitees by planning director

5. *Ongoing review (evaluations).* The Steering Committee, with guidance from the planning director, sets up a periodic review schedule to measure objectives and goals of the Planning Team.

6. *Accomplished goals.* If specific identifiable goals and/or objectives have not been met on time, according to established schedule, an Evaluation Team (composed of members of the Planning Team, Steering Committee, and Scholarship Committee, appointed by the chairperson of the Planning Team) assesses the delays and discrepancies, and recommends new strategies, in writing, with solutions for each goal or objective, to the chairperson, Planning Committee.

7. *Accountability.* Once the Planning Team is in full operation, the public will be concerned with, and will expect many answers. A few of the important items the public will be concerned with follow:

- Does the specific secondary school curriculum for noncollege-bound students include subject matter and supporting elements that will produce students who are able to perform effectively in the training workforce once graduated?

- Do the specific high school graduates know, and can they begin to perform according to, what the diploma implies?
- Do students obtain the identifiable knowledge and experience that will enable them to function effectively in the community, as well as in the initial training, in preparation for the workplace?
- Does the institution make adequate efforts to help the student succeed through counseling and remediation, or is it largely a front to collect tuition fees and let students drop out at the first sign of difficulty?

Curriculum plans, together with professional adult guidance from the community (mentors, perhaps, who can support the student with personal attention as role models and encouragement as part of the student's motivation), could be an excellent starting point. It takes an entire village to educate a single child.

Curriculum reforms are a must. The curriculum must be revised to reflect not only present-day scientific, technological concepts and civic standards, but also must outline better means of communication, with predictive quality at world economic and culture levels, as well as implement a dual-type approach to secondary schools. The dual-type approach must distinctly separate the college-bound student from the noncollege-bound. However the noncollege-bound channel must also include academics as well as formal training, beginning with the third year of high school.

Among the industrialized nations, Germany's dual school system is probably the best-known plan. In Germany teenage students are sorted out by tests and channeled either into university preparation or into a national vocational program. This concept, with perhaps some changes to suit our needs, could be initiated in the United States. One deviation to the German system could be one in which students could keep their options open to go on to college at some future date.

Another deviation, and a very important one, is that of including high school dropouts in the identical plan that is proposed for the noncollege-bound student. We must accept more flexibility in allowing young people over eighteen to return to school. We must encourage "dropping in" as much as we try to prevent students from dropping out. We must make every effort to try a variety of new ways to create more "bridges" to prepare these youngsters who do not take the usual academic road to success. If necessary dropout students could be channeled into a strictly On-the-Job Training program (OJT). There is no truly acceptable substitute for learning by doing. On-the-job training, broadly defined, provides the most direct route to useful employment that our economic system can offer to those who are not headed for full-time postsecondary education. The conscientious trainee acquires genuine respect for work, earns pocket money, and simultaneously learns self-discipline. OJT has been a powerful force in two of our principal economic competitors, Japan and Germany. OJT has a deservedly rich history in nations that share many of our own values. Also OJT is a key pathway to skills acquisition for most young workers in manufacturing, construction, mining, transportation, utilities, and similar fields. In Germany, Switzerland, and Austria, OJT covers almost all occupations requiring high-level skills, and employers participate willingly in training costs as a regular part of their employee recruitment program. In 1977 only .3 percent of the entire U.S. civilian employee workforce participated in OJT. During the same period, Switzerland, Germany, and Austria participation in OJT was over 6 percent. In Japan it was even higher, 12 percent. OJT should be seriously considered for noncollege-bound students. OJT is specific enough to qualify apprentices to enter highly skilled occupations, yet broad enough to serve as a foundation either for advancement to higher skill levels in the same occupation or for further training in a related occupation.

Yet another alternative to the dual school system is the one proposed by the National Center's Commission on the Skills of the American Workforce.[*] This workable system could easily be implemented. It requires both coordination and close cooperation between education, American industry, and business management. It is a four-step program:

1. High school student must acquire basic academic skills by age sixteen, usually at the end of the second year of high school.
2. Student who decides on a vocational course of study continues two to four more years of schooling together with on-the-job training. Length of time depends on the skills required for different occupations. Community colleges and technical schools provide most of the longer-term training.
3. Graduate receives a professional technical certificate based on standards set by a national education training board.
4. Youth enters the workforce.

[*] *The Forgotten Half: Pathways to Success for America's Youth and Young Families.* The William T. Grant Commission on World, Family, and Citizenship, Washington, D.C., 1988.

To assure that young men and young women acquire fundamental academic skills, this program calls for all students, by age sixteen, to pass an examination, demonstrating "an ability to read, write, compute, and perform at world-class standard levels." Student centers would be set up to help dropouts and those students who fail the test. Youth who favor the vocational path would spend two to four years in a work-study program, working part-time and attending classes at high schools, community colleges, and technical schools. By continuing academic subjects, students may transfer into four-year colleges at any time, if they so desire.

Upon graduation these students would be certified in one or more skills by a national board, (composed of business, labor, and government members) who would set national standards for occupational skills. Local boards would be set up to manage the school-to-work transition as a cohesive system.

Education and formal training remain the noncollege-bound high school graduate's and the high school dropout's fundamental and reliable pathway to success. Knowledge and high skills open doors to current employment opportunities that would otherwise remain closed. More important yet is the fact that education and formal training competencies are the means through which personal and societal gains are achieved.

The focus of American education must be on student population needs, and curriculum content, with less emphasis on narrow, predetermined goals that reflect only the past. This emerging trend will necessitate information on needs from diverse opinions, both from inside and outside education with greater influence by new technologies.

There is a rapidly changing reward structure in the world of work. Education, formal training, and preparation in the attainment of high skills pay off handsomely, for the individual and for society. The more years of education and formal training completed, the greater one's employability and annual income. What all this amounts to is that we now have a five-tiered education/reward structure[*], which follows. (See also Figures 2 and 3.)

1. Four or more years of college generally leads to the best remuneration and highest status employment—what most Americans equate with "success."

[*]*The Forgotten Half: Pathways to Success for America's Youth and Young Families.* The William T. Grant Commission on World, Family, and Citizenship, Washington, D.C., 1988.

2. Some postsecondary education, even without a degree, leads to a significant improvement in earnings over mere high school completion.
3. A high school diploma, long considered the single most powerful predictor of success in the labor market, is no longer valid. A high school diploma no longer guarantees being able to support a family at decent living standards.
4. High school dropouts are unlikely to be considered for employment much above minimum wage, except in geographic areas characterized by severe labor shortages and relative economic prosperity. Their future among the working poor is bleak.
5. School dropouts who disconnect from society and succumb to lives of crime, addiction, chronic unemployment, and dependency are headed for personal disaster with its attendant social costs.

The center of the teaching enterprise is not simply having a battery of skills and knowledge that is sufficient. Rather it is knowledge and skills as appreciated and enjoyed—which is to say—as they are valued, intrinsically and instrumentally and not just the day-to-day classes to meet a reasonable mastery of the academic skills or a requisite score on a comprehensive achievement test. Students are in urgent need of learning other things than the three Rs, the basic skills they learn in school. They require other skills as well, what I call "home/family-built value skills," the attitudes and basic values that determine the students' acceptance and adjustment in the classroom, as well as success in their societal future. Although reinforced by the teacher in school, no one is born with these value skills. (See Figure 4.)

This text lends itself to, strongly emphasizes, and is written with an academic-study-to-workforce training program with youth in mind. In particular Chapter VIII, "Instructional Systems Development," offers a plan, with options, wherein the learning outcome can be limited to the requirements of a job or skill.

The overall dual concept of this text is, first, to pinpoint the weak linkage that now exists between the school and the workplace; and second, to prepare an instructor or teacher to expose students to acquire the necessary skills to prepare themselves to perform a job, through formal education and formal training.

VICTOR H. BOLADO, Ed.D.

Acknowledgments

For the many hours she spent criticizing, questioning, and commenting upon some segments of this manuscript, I sincerely thank Marina Concepción.

I readily acknowledge the many contributions many of my former students have made through their classroom questions, their long-range vision, and their support. I have been most encouraged by their desire to succeed. These students are well aware that the only way to succeed into significance in our society, and the world at large, is to acquire a valid formal education or to be well trained as a professional specialist. Their contributions are incalculable and my gratitude to them is inexpressible.

To these students, as well as to the less fortunate students who, for one reason or another, have not had an opportunity to complete their education or their formal training, I dedicate this book.

*The evil that is in the world always comes of ignorance,
and good intentions may do as much harm as malevolence,
if they lack understanding. On the whole men are more
good than bad. That, however, isn't the real point. But
they are more or less ignorant, and it is this that we call
vice or virtue; the most incorrigible vice being that of an
ignorance that fancies it knows everything and therefore
claims for itself the right to kill. The soul of the murderer
is blind; and there can be no true goodness nor true love
without the utmost clear-sightedness.*

Albert Camus, The Plague

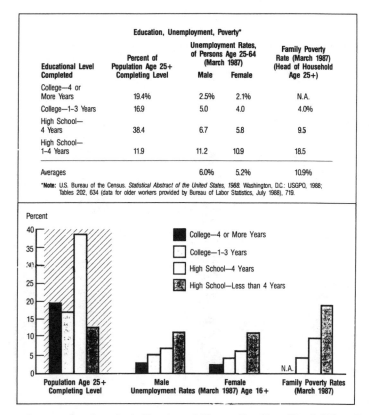

Education, Unemployment, Poverty*

Educational Level Completed	Percent of Population Age 25+ Completing Level	Unemployment Rates, of Persons Age 25-64 (March 1987)		Family Poverty Rate (March 1987) (Head of Household Age 25+)
		Male	Female	
College—4 or More Years	19.4%	2.5%	2.1%	N.A.
College—1-3 Years	16.9	5.0	4.0	4.0%
High School—4 Years	38.4	6.7	5.8	9.5
High School—1-4 Years	11.9	11.2	10.9	18.5
Averages		6.0%	5.2%	10.9%

***Note:** U.S. Bureau of the Census. *Statistical Abstract of the United States, 1988.* Washington, D.C.: USGPO, 1988; Tables 202, 634 (data for older workers provided by Bureau of Labor Statistics, July 1988), 719.

*The Forgotten Half: Pathways to Success for America's Youth and Young Families. The William T. Grant Commission on World, Family, and Citizenship. Washington, D.C., 1988.

Figure 1

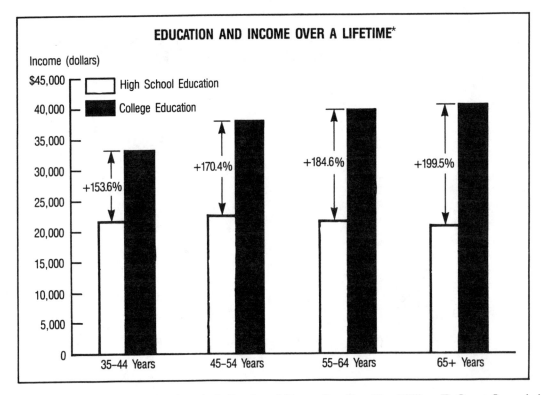

EDUCATION AND INCOME OVER A LIFETIME*

*The Forgotten Half: Pathways to Success for America's Youth and Young Families. The William T. Grant Commission on World, Family, and Citizenship. Washington, D.C., 1988.

Figure 2

Does a Longer School Year Improve
Academic Performance?

Average math scores of 13-year-olds on an achievement exam administered to students around the world in February 1992.

	Days Spent in School	Score
CHINA	251	80
SOUTH KOREA	222	73
SWITZERLAND	207	71
FORMER U.S.S.R.	210	70
FRANCE	174	64
ISRAEL	215	63
Canada	188	62
Great Britain	192	61
United States	180	55
Jordan	191	40

Source: International Assessment of Educational Progress Exam, Educational Testing Services, Washington, D.C., February 1992.

Figure 3

HOME/FAMILY-BUILT VALUE SKILLS

CARING—   regard for others, feel concern and interest in others
COOPERATION—   work together with others, joint effort for mutual benefits, collaboration, teamwork
TEAMWORK—   working together as a team, coordinated effort
COMMON SENSE—   practical judgment, sound opinion of ordinary people
LOVE—   esteem, admiration, common interests, brotherly concern for others, (without love a family will disintegrate, without love a country may perish)
DEDICATED—   loyal, devoted, dependable, faithful
COMMUNICATION—   establish commonness with others, listen
CONFIDENCE—   belief in one's own ability, trust in self, reliance, firm belief
MOTIVATION—   influencing one's own self to do, to accomplish
EFFORT—   a serious and conscious attempt to accomplish, attempt to succeed
INITIATIVE—   creative, ability to think and act without being urged
PERSEVERANCE—   steadfast, determined, not giving up on a job
AMBITION—   strong desire to succeed, to achieve, the drive to get ahead, eager to demand effort, zeal, aspiration
TRUTHFUL—   honest, corresponding with fact and reality, correctness, factual, true, reliable, trustworthy
HONEST—   trustworthy, sincere, fair, morality, principles, straightforward, faithfulness, honor, integrity, freedom from lying, stealing, cheating, free from deceit
DILIGENT—   industrious, hardworking, persevering, steady, earnest, energetic application and effort, thorough
FORTITUDE—   courage, strength of mind, guts, moral strength, spirit, resolution, determination, tenacity, endurance, nerve
RESPONSIBILITY—   trust, accountable, obligation, ability to come through, an awareness of how you fit into a job
RESPECTFUL—   considerate, polite, mannerly, attentive, accommodating, genial, personable, courteous, dutiful regard
PROBLEM SOLVING—   search for ideas, develop ideas, find solutions

Figure 4

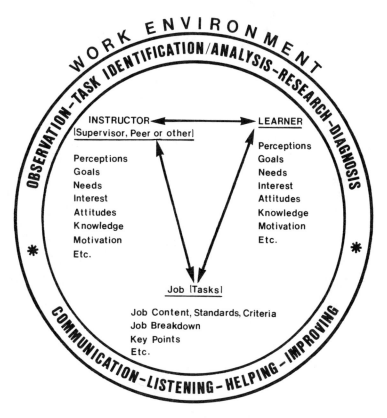

Figure 5

Chapter I
Introduction

The wiser you are, the more you believe in
equality, because the difference between what
the most and least learned people know is
inexpressibly trivial in relation to all that is unknown.

John F. Kennedy

For too many years, those in the business of educating the next generation's teachers have held to the theory that teaching has been more an art than a science—that is, a skill or art that must be absorbed on the job, rather than an entity that defines skills and specific processes that may be learned. Traditional teacher education curricula have focused on the history of education, educational theory, and the like. Too much attention has been paid to the theoretical and not enough to the practical. In the traditional programs, the first useful experience was the student teaching, or practicum, course. Little in the courses preceding the student teaching experience actually prepared novice teachers for what would happen when they actually stepped into the classroom for the first hour on that first day.

This lack of preparation and knowledge—and an unreal set of expectations—caused many to bolt and run, searching university catalogs for potential new avenues to their post B.A. or B.S. lives. In short classroom realities proved to be markedly different from what groups of aspiring teachers were told by their instructors—many of whose last sojourn in a primary or secondary classroom was their own!

One bright-eyed, eager young woman laboriously prepared lecture notes and a series of questions and answers for her first day of teaching. Assured that she had done her "homework," she triumphantly marched into class and began her lesson. To her utter horror, what she had planned for a full fifty-minute class took fifteen minutes. What to do next?

1

This example is illustrative of, but by no means isolated to, the problems and issues surrounding the traditional teacher training programs as they currently exist in many U.S. colleges and universities and, for that matter, in many parts of the world.

This text addresses the questions posed in the teacher education/training situation. Throughout the text every instructional thought stresses the relation to the overriding question: How can we prepare ourselves as teachers/instructors to better expose our students to learning? Clearly the dynamics of the classroom experience and the maximizing of time allotted for instruction are of paramount importance to the concerned teacher/instructor. To this end we proceed to examine a unique blend of teaching methodology and management strategies.

The first portion of this text discusses an awareness of the teachers' importance and contribution to the community, in the role as an educator; teachers' acceptance of their responsibilities of par excellence commensurate with their community role as professionals; a common sense challenge, if you will, that is expected and a challenge built on prestige, with an ethical foundation; and values that, without doubt, will enhance the quality of education.

The second part of the text carefully explains to teachers/instructors how to go about their task. Modes of learning are succinctly defined in terms of the learner, the teacher, and the task. Charts highlight the facets of affective, psychomotor, and cognitive learning skills, with special attention paid to the purpose, subject, audience, and environment.

Next is learning to learn, which is an overdue concept in most classrooms. Basically how students plan their studies? What plan is there that students can follow and manage simply to carry out the tasks of assignments given to them by you, the instructor? The concept is an old one, but one that has not been developed in a simple, accessible outline so that the student may know in detail how to plan, follow up, and learn how to study. This approach, as outlined in the chapter on "Learning to Learn," is most appropriate, different from others because it is easy to follow and most timely as well.

The "tips" on adult learning in the chapter entitled "Andragogy" are becoming increasingly important in education and training fields. At the present time, the tip of the scale is pressing heavily on the adult group as the major force to contend with in formal education and training. Certainly it must be recognized that a good instructor/teacher will meet the challenge by being knowledgeable about the basic learning characteristics of the adult learner versus the adolescent and/or the child learner.

Next *School Link to the Workforce* confronts the issues posed in a multinational classroom. Often enough there are sufficient numbers of outside factors that hinder the acquisition of knowledge among individuals from the same or similar cultures. Many teachers/instructors find themselves not only teaching people with different language backgrounds, but also with vastly different sociocultural backgrounds. Alert teachers/instructors must be aware of these cross-cultural differences if they are to be successful in meeting the learning objectives. What one culture considers normal, another culture considers bizarre! Learning may be blocked because of unawareness of and sensitivity to the relevant cross-cultural issues of the student.

Overcoming the cultural barrier is possible; becoming a good teacher/instructor in a multicultural environment can be a personally rewarding experience. This has been proven to me in every case in over a dozen countries where I have worked, as well as at the Defense Language Institute, where I enjoyed a long and pleasant association working with students representing some seventy-two countries. I may add that I had similar experiences at the Organization of American States (OAS), in Washington, D.C., as well as at the International Civil Aviation Organization (ICAO), as part of the United Nations, where I also enjoyed some very pleasant and rewarding associations. Overcoming the cultural barrier is easily another fruitful experience that the instructor/teacher can master. It is an entire education, this business of working in a multicultural environment.

The Instructional Systems Development (ISD) concept, applied in a systematic manner, will help in understanding designing, developing, implementing, as well as evaluating course materials. It provides guidance that is difficult to find in any other single-source concept. If properly applied this concept can be used to meet the challenge of designing superior-quality instructional systems. The ISD concept explains the five major activities in planning and implementing an instruction program. These five activities are (1) analyzing systems requirements; (2) defining education or training requirements; (3) developing objectives and tests; (4) planning and developing instruction; (5) conducting and evaluating instruction.

The technique of effective questioning is discussed. The interaction and involvement of students in the classroom is stressed. The exposure of students to the learning process is emphasized.

This text is directed to the education student engaged in the study of secondary and college education—to include the professional study of curriculum planning, curriculum development, and implementation.

Course planning is broken down into practical, definable parts, with special emphasis placed on developing the individual lesson plan.

A variety of teaching methods and techniques are examined, with the objective of assisting instructors/teachers to decide which techniques best suit their needs, circumstances, and students. The use of visual aids remains a mystery to the uninitiated, and frequently instructors/teachers fail to use mechanical support effectively.

Hints are provided for the best use of several of the most common audiovisual devices. Instead of underusing the equipment because of ignorance (how do I thread a movie projector?) or overusing the electronic media (well, I'll show a movie since I don't have lesson plans made for today), the teacher/instructor learns to make rational use of these teaching aids.

We next address the importance of evaluation, testing, and measurement.

Effective and appropriate practices in classroom management, as well as the use of discipline as a positive approach to learning, are included.

A list of vocabulary terms is found in Chapter XVI. A thumbnail sketch of each word or term will give the reader many useful references. Many of the terms are mentioned in the text, but the alphabetical compilation offers the reader a useful and fast guide to terminology.

Finally we see a comprehensive list of selected suggestions for further reading.

Those who find themselves facing a classroom experience can be divided into three categories: novice teachers, experienced teachers, and individuals who, for whatever reason, *become* instructors/teachers as the occasion demands. The latter may be called finger-teachers; someone points a finger at them and says: "You are the instructor," with no second choice. In any event each one of these groups can profit from a careful perusal of this text.

The trained, professional teacher, whether a novice or experienced, will appreciate a new and radical view of the profession. Skills and the "tricks of the trade" are defined in terms of management behaviors. Thus those who have undergone traditional teacher training courses will come away with a new view to what they may have previously considered an ambiguous and undefined set of behaviors and skills. Novices can commence their teaching career more effectively. The trained teacher will be able to drop some of the excess baggage acquired from the old-style courses in favor of practical and useful methods.

Naturally many students went to college and entered professions with no thought of ever serving in an instructional capacity; however, corporate exigencies thrust staff and executive personnel into the classroom. Changing technologies demand that employees keep up to date on the latest research and techniques of doing business, as well as know the language of science and technology. It is not always possible to hire trained teaching personnel; instead those within a company with the technical expertise become instant teachers/instructors! A careful study of *School Link to the Workforce* will arm these personnel with teaching strategies, increase self-confidence, and facilitate the transfer of knowledge so that time in the classroom or workshop turns out to be a mutually profitable experience. Because of its detailed approach to instruction, business executives will find this text most handy.

A final word on the utility of *School Link to the Workforce:* Its focus on the practical aspects and methods of instruction cannot be overemphasized. Upon completion of the text, the reader will have concrete ideas and strategies to implement in the classroom. Finally the overview and review of information offer the teacher/instructor instruction in a nutshell—neatly packaged and ready to be utilized in the field!

Conclusion

Internalization of the tips and suggestions presented in *School Link to the Workforce* is of paramount importance. By doing so you, the teacher/instructor, will become a more effective transmitter of knowledge. Know what you have to say and have an efficient mode of delivery. If you meet these two criteria, then your students can't help but absorb the information you have to impart. Make this material your own; customize it to your needs and personality. In effect add or subtract on an as-needed basis.

After careful study and consideration of the text, you should be able to do the following:

- Specify and review with serious considerations your responsibilities for moral, ethical, and professional quality of education.
- Define the various types of learning behaviors and be able to identify where your instructional material fits into the scheme.
- Be aware of, make use, and suggest students' use of the computer, as applicable.
- Identify the techniques on how to study, so that appropriate counseling of your students will influence their learning.
- Apply the learning characteristics of the adult student in your class presentation.
- Recognize and appreciate cross-cultural differences and know how these differences can have an impact in your instructional effectiveness.
- Recognize and apply the five phases of the Instructional Systems Development concept.
- Inject into your teaching/learning approach effective questioning techniques.

- Identify each method and technique in the preparation of the lesson plan and have an increased awareness of the diversity of methods and techniques available. More important you will define what technique is best suited to your instructional material and circumstances and be able to select the most effective training aids.
- Select and develop test items that are criterion-referenced and that result in student learning.
- Pinpoint specific criteria that will evaluate your performance in the classroom.
- Select appropriate classroom management techniques and use discipline as a positive training vehicle—never as punishment.
- Solidify your background knowledge of instruction by reviewing the list of applicable terms on a continuing basis.
- Select further readings to stimulate your knowledge and practical instructional abilities.

It is the author's hope and wish that you find *School Link to the Workforce* useful as you enter the classroom—whether it is the first time as a novice teacher or one new to the teaching field or for the umpteenth time as a veteran. The ultimate beneficiary is your student, the one who is sitting there, for better or for worse (for better, I suggest), listening as you demonstrate, discuss, lecture, question, and even referee during the learning process.

Good luck in your dynamic instruction.

VICTOR H. BOLADO, Ed.D.

The Student

There are eight rungs of righteousness.
The highest is when you help a man to help himself.

Moses Maimonides
A.D. 1180

The student comes to class because he wants to improve his self-development and personal growth. He is motivated to participate in a training or education experience. This is perhaps the greatest challenge as a teacher/instructor, because you have to discover why the student came to class, what he is seeking, and how you, as his leader, can meet his needs. Unless you are sensitive to these needs, any self-motivation within the student quickly ceases.

You should recognize that many students doubt their ability, fear ridicule, have a low self-esteem, and need a liberal spraying of compliments and help, not criticism. Your primary goal as teachers/instructors is to take students where they are presently, and help them move forward.

Your second goal is to involve your students in the process of learning. Unless the students are allowed to participate verbally, practically, and by first-hand experience, learning is not taking place.

Remember that an effective teacher/instructor possesses the following qualities:

- Knows his subject matter
- Is versatile in setting up different learning experiences for the student
- Has the ability to effectively relate to students
- Involves the students in every class
- Has a sense of humor
- Admits when he does not know
- Maintains enthusiasm in the classroom
- Prepares the student to face the real world by preparing him or her to solve real problems

- Prepares the student to think, not to memorize
- Manages and controls students at all times

How does this philosophy about students stack up with your own thoughts about your students?

THE STUDENT IS*...

the most important person on campus!
Without students there would be no need
for the institution.
NOT a cold enrollment statistic!
A student is a flesh and blood human being
with feelings and emotions like yours and mine.
NOT someone to be tolerated so that we can do
our thing.
STUDENTS are our thing!
NOT dependent on us.
Rather, we are dependent on them.
NOT an interruption of our work, but the
Purpose of our work.
We are not doing them a favor by serving them.
They are doing us a favor by giving us the opportunity
to serve them.

*Anonymous

Chapter II
Prestige, Ethics, and the Educator
What Is "True?"

To say of what is, that it is, or of what
is not, that it is not, is true.
To say of what is not, that it is, or of
what is, that it is not, is false.

Aristotle

Our responsibilities as professionals in the education field are to prepare ourselves to be the best-qualified and the most well-rounded models and teachers. With this thought in mind, this chapter deals with one of the most important areas we must excel in—setting examples, models, for our students and for our community. According to Abraham Maslow, teachers' needs are most important. He emphasizes five needs or motivational factors. At the highest level is self-actualization (competence and achievement); second, physiological needs (basic needs of life—shelter, food, etcetera) third, security of job needs; fourth, social or affiliation needs (feeling they belong and are accepted); and fifth, esteem or prestige (recognition and respect of others).

"Prestige" implies being respected, held in esteem, or possessing influences because of one's position. Men or women may possess prestige because they have characteristics and abilities that distinguish them from contemporaries, or because they are members in a group that, as a whole, commands respect from non-members. As a result merely being a member of that group confers prestige in the eyes of nonmembers. This latter type of prestige is called "group prestige." Members of this group are more or less unconsciously given respect without demanding any personal deservingness of such respect. Some physicians have group prestige. Many fraternity and sorority members similarly benefit from the phenomenon of group prestige.

As "unearned prestige" is gained from membership in this group, however, members' personal characteristics and behavior affect the entire group, which each member represents at all times. Members personally benefit from identification with the group, and the group in turn benefits or suffers from each member's representation. The American teacher corps is one of these prestige groups. This group is highly susceptible to "group judgments" and to judgment of each member based on the member's merits because (1) teachers are more easily identified by group because of their broad acceptance by the family, the community, and the public sector; (2) the education profession is more sharply differentiated from other vocations because of its effect on society's future; and (3) the educator's role affects each and every future head of household; therefore, the participants are identified as a group rather than as individuals.

For better or for worse, the qualities and behavior of individual teachers are as closely identified with school records as with personality. Freedom to live by self-imposed standards must, at times, be sacrificed to a great extent because the prestige of the group is affected by each individual's actions, which can confer unearned prestige.

The desirability of group prestige rests in the esprit de corps deriving from membership, and the inspiration for members to work at their peak effectiveness to meet group standards and to prove their worth to contemporaries. A secondary value rests in the "halo effect" of reputation. When a person or group earns genuine distinction through notable qualities of achievement in one area, there is a strong tendency to accord that person or group confidence, trust, and respect in other areas. On the frivolous side, we have the spectacle of movie stars commenting on use of atomic weapons; on the more constructive side, we have the Red Cross, perhaps a senator, or a congressman. Their integrity, judgment, selflessness, and devotion to responsibility and the public good has won them esteem from society, which allows them to function in an atmosphere of trust and confidence, denies unworthiness of motive in their actions and recommendations, and accords them a measure of influence far beyond their field. The freedom from distrustful scrutiny, jealous curbs, and suspicion of self-seeking efforts earned by these individuals or group increases their effectiveness and benefits the nation.

Such a goal of group prestige is worthy of the efforts of the instructor, teacher, or professor. There is no quick, easy, royal road to achieving prestige. Edison said, "Genius is an infinite capacity for detail." This is true. It is not all of genius, but it is an irreplaceable requisite. Achievement of such enviable prestige will help educators to accomplish their mission of helping to educate society. The professional, rather than political management of education that then becomes possible will mean better-quality education, through personal values, per dollar and per student—all this from teacher prestige.

How can this prestige be achieved? The first element in its achievement is competent, conscientious, efficient performance of all assigned duties, plus. By "plus" I mean that the educator must perform better, and more than simply assigned duties. In the teaching profession nothing can substitute for sound, effective results, economically attained. In American society and by public demand, results are not enough; the end does not justify the means.

The governor of a state may have conducted an efficient and constructive administration during his term of office, but this will seldom save him from defeat at the polls if his personal life and behavior disagree with the mores and conventions of his constituents. Similarly teachers must not only perform their duties and fulfill their responsibilities* in an exemplary-plus manner, they must exemplify the virtues held in public esteem.

Education is supported by public funds. Educators, like the governors of the states, administer or represent those funds. Professional education goals will not be met if public esteem of teachers is corroded by disapproval of their attitudes or behavior, even if these attitudes and behaviors are quite apart from the fulfillment of their responsibilities.** Teachers labor under the same extra-official regulation. It is a price paid by teachers, but not required of farmers, merchants, and manufacturers. The ethical and moral component is a second factor in attaining prestige. It is treated at length in many articles on leadership and management. Its essentials are embodied in legal, religious, and social codes and will not be elaborated here.

The third factor in attaining prestige is public relations—not a flamboyant advertising campaign, such as cigarette companies sponsor, or a medicine-man show. Teachers must be of certain principles because they are looked up to by neighbors, parents, associates, and acquaintances.

The remainder of this chapter covers some principles and techniques recommended as guidelines for educators. Some guidelines require self-discipline, but all should be considered by the teacher because the public judges education largely by what it can observe of the teacher, and much of the observation of teachers is in off-the-official-job situations. Observation of these guidelines, in addition to the usual social amenities, will promote prestige. Give of your thoughts to these guidelines, most of which are plain common sense. The payoff can be much more than the simple efforts expended.

* See Conclusion, page 16.
** See Conclusion, page 16.

Guidelines

Be scrupulously polite and a little formal in all public, business, and social situations. Be socially responsible.* Back-slapping camaraderie and a "just folks" attitude promote a certain sort of popularity. It is doubtful if they promote confidence that citizens need in the men and women on whose nerve, judgment, skill, and discipline rest the chances of the survival of an educated society. It is human nature to afford a larger measure of trust and confidence to the person who appears cooler, more self-contained, more perfectly poised than ourselves. Formality, dignity, and punctilio, over and above that commonly displayed by those whose business is not the profession of education, subtly underline the gravity of the teacher's job. Some judges, physicians, and ministers as groups tend to be reserved. If skillful they do it almost imperceptibly and in a manner that does not offend but still hints of weighty responsibilities, setting the bearer a tiny bit, or more, apart.

This technique is much more effective among persons of middle and upper educational, financial, and social levels than among others, but by the structure of American society, it is with these persons that educators usually associate off duty. Being a prig, a snob, a "wet blanket" is appropriate nowhere. Displaying dignity befitting the seriousness of being a teacher is becoming to the profession. The old British tradition of the royal educational institutions, which required the educator to be in formal dress or uniform from 7:00 each morning until 9:00 each evening, is much too extreme for American attitudes and policies. However in Great Britain, as well as in Spain, in those days, this formality was one factor of identifying a professional individual as a member of a group that, for various reasons, enjoyed prestige and a reputation for selfless, austere, competent devotion to the profession. Heavily "watered down," to avoid offending American sensibilities, dignified behavior identifies educators as calm, thoughtful, cool, dependable, dedicated public servants.

Teachers must relax like everyone else. The tension a teacher has demands a release. Relax in your club, at your home, in the company of fellow colleagues. Maintain your dignity and self-possession. You are the nation's leaders in the preparation of future solid citizens. The influence you have on society is a serious matter. You live with that responsibility* all the time, and it becomes a "normal," "natural" concept by reason of your constant association with education. But to

*See Conclusion, page 16.

the public—when they stop to consider it, and the consideration is constant—that responsibility is an awesome obligation. They expect you, and rightly so, to appreciate the gravity of your responsibility. Show that you do by your demeanor.

Let your conversation as well as your behavior reflect your observance of your responsibility*. The public seldom forgets that it pays your salary. Self-seeking politicians and sensationalistic journalists find it easy to attract attention by citing instances in which the quality of work a school is not "meeting the demands of industry, or the community." Since teachers are considered first-level managers, with school administrators being the middle and upper-level managers, it is normal for the teacher to get blamed in most situations. Simply keeping order and solving local crises does not constitute management. In most cases it is proven that there is nothing wrong with the teacher or the student. How they both are managed or mismanaged is what leads to poor instruction, resulting in poor learning. Unfortunately the teacher becomes the scapegoat.

Educators are, in general, a hardworking group. The public should realize this much. Ostentatious talk of how hard you work as a teacher is poor policy, but an occasional remark, inside and outside the classroom, revealing the extent of your work is an excellent idea.

Emphasize the high, objective standards for teacher retention and promotion held by your school or college. A prerequisite to group prestige is being recognized by the public for the high standards of selection and competence that exist for the group. Be careful in your rating of teachers or instructors under you. Guard jealously the professional education tradition requiring real ability and fine performance to qualify as even an average teacher. No one respects a group whose standards of performance are low. See that your standards, for yourself and your subordinates, are kept high.

Let your conversation with the public sector reflect this attitude and practice. When the opportunity is offered, refer to teachers who suffered career-wise because of an error or not enough ability. Let your acquaintances realize that the mediocre individuals are identified in the teaching profession, and that they have little chance of success in the field of education. Emphasize the keen competition for promotion and the minor infractions that can prevent a teacher from being selected for promotion. Don't brag or be ostentatious about it, but when an opportunity is there, let it be known that competition among teachers is keen and only the competent achieve recognition.

Emphasize the "mission orientation" of yourself, your school, or your college. In your conversations reflect, primarily, concern with the task facing the teaching profession and education in general as well as your interest in seeing that the job is well done.

Never take the position: "What is good for education is good for the community." The proper way to approach the subject is in terms of: "What are the needs of the community and the country?" and "How can this be accomplished?" Answers to these questions, objectively and dispassionately arrived at, will do more to advance the cause of the teaching profession and education than any arguments that might be discounted as selfishly motivated.

All teachers should be missionaries, and accomplishing the mission of education must be their religion. Preach it at every opportunity.

Identify yourself with the community. It is generally undesirable for teachers to be looked on as clannish. National feeling about education is, after all, only the aggregate of feelings prevalent in thousands of communities. Only by mixing with the community can character and abilities be shown. The essence of good public relations, which is a requisite for teacher prestige, is a knowledge by the public of the admirable qualities of the education profession. Mixing with the community is the best way of instilling this knowledge. Know your neighbors. Chat with them frequently, include then in your pattern of social life, and let yourself be included in theirs. Don't be afraid to take the initiative. It is much more to your advantage to sell education and yourself to your neighbor than it is to their advantage to have you as a citizen and neighbor. If married encourage your spouse to attend school activities.

If you can find the time to help in Scout or other youth activities, it will promote goodwill toward your profession as well as become a worthwhile experience for you. Participate as fully as you can in community projects and activities. Be known as one who can be counted on to help in any civic enterprise. Aside from the value to your profession, you will find a rich reward in the recognition and respect you can gain among those who will come to know you. Active work in Sunday school classes is excellent, so is membership and participation in civic clubs.

Learn enough about community affairs and remain current about civic matters to be able to converse intelligently with other citizens.

This identification with the community where you reside will not only increase the prestige of your profession, but it will make your life richer and fuller, as well!

Develop a good knowledge of international affairs and keep up to date on developments. Local and national politics are important topics in any community; international affairs and foreign policy are also important topics. Furthermore, teachers are credited with having a legitimate concern with these subjects. This is not enough. Subscribe to a weekly news magazine and study it carefully. Supplement this basic preparation with a thorough reading of a good local newspaper and, perhaps, a family magazine.

The teacher must be recognized as a professional to be accorded the prestige appropriate to the profession. One of the characteristics of professionals is their knowledge of all subjects related to their specialty. This is in contrast to technicians, whose knowledge of their specialty may be equal or even superior to the knowledge of the professional individual concerned with that area, but whose breadth of knowledge may extend little beyond the specialty.

Be conservative in your actions and public remarks. Spectacular happenings and startling statements make more profound audience impressions than do routine incidents and remarks. Publicly espousing a radical cause, idea, or point of view makes teachers conspicuous if most people disagree with that particular radical position. Teachers tend to be identified in the minds of the community as representatives of the educated group, and can suffer from identifying with extreme or controversial positions. Public remarks on extreme social issues, controversial political problems, and the like should also be noncommittal or conservative. The person you offend by your extreme position is far more likely to portray your position to others in a damaging way than persons who agree with your position are likely to enhance your prestige. Conservatives seldom offend, even if people do not agree with them.

Does all this limit your freedom of thought? Of thought, no. Of speech among the community, no. Of expression, no. You represent not merely yourself, but the professional teacher. You are morally obligated to consider the welfare of your profession as well as your personal desires, and censor yourself accordingly.

Consider the importance of your profession in light of the responsibilities of another profession, the military profession. The strength of America is reflected in our ideas, our ideals, and our values, not simply and only in our highly sophisticated weaponry. No seaman, no soldier, and no airman can be expected to confront death in time of war or crisis when the reasons for his or her sacrifice are not recognized by the citizens for whom he fights.

Conclusion

The dictionary defines *responsibility* as follows:
1. answerable, accountable;
2. ethics, the status of personality considered as capable of responding to the obligation established by moral law or by moral principles and ideals, however derived.

Ethics is more than simply an intellectual exercise. Ethics is an applied discipline—a practical science designed to test logically the rightness or wrongness of human acts. This position places emphasis upon the concept of the "reasonable man," that is, a man whose reasonableness will lead him to act rightly within certain broadly defined limits. The norms of society are understood to be important in determining behavior, but the study of ethics sets out to evaluate these guidelines through the use of methods involving more ultimate tests of reason. Neither the cultural rules of a society nor the teachings of a religious group are to be considered in the determination of ethical conclusions, although religion does influence the individual and is the basis of morality. However, theoretically, ethics is above these temporal influences.

Summary

All of the foregoing admonitions seem to impose rigorous conditions on the teaching profession. They do. To affect the education and values of human beings and to earn the respect that should accompany such command are rigorous tasks. These tasks require men and women of outstanding ability and self-discipline. The public will respect and trust men and women who obviously demand of and maintain for themselves standards of perfection that few others can meet. This respect and trust we call "prestige." It has to be earned, and earning it is a rigorous business; it is limited to the professionals, but it is worth earning. In the long run it means not only a most satisfying experience for you as a teacher, but more than that—what the American family expects, what modern society demands in meeting the high requirements of international competition—and international competition is keen. At one time we were ahead of the competition, then abreast, and now the competition is mounting very fast. It is all up to us now.

A suggestion is made to establish a community "think tank." Whether an educator or a layman heads this group is immaterial. Much can be accomplished if the group includes the business sector, the laymen, and the teacher. The concepts of this chapter and other areas, such as technology, should be discussed, which could be beneficial not only locally but nationally. This concept would funnel new or improved ideas into our school system.

With the "think tank" in mind, in preparation for the twenty-first century, and in anticipation of a much greater world wide economic and social competition, major reforms in our education system are a must.

Every American must be concerned. Parents, leaders of industry, government at all levels, and educators must work together to bring about these important reforms to meet the challenge for world quality standards.

Chapter III
Computer Awareness

Education is the guidance of the individual toward a comprehension of the art of life; and by the art of life I mean the most complete achievement of varied activity expressing the potentialities of that living creature in the face of its actual environment.

Alfred North Whitehead

From coast to coast, thousands of schools are producing computer experts, students who can program the simulation of various educational undertakings. Many computers are designed to help students with special needs. Computers are used in libraries to locate all types of research information. Dynamic challenges, important changes, and most exciting opportunities are in the works for our classrooms and, therefore, for our children to ask questions; to learn about new sources of energy, new ecology discoveries; and, of course, how to draw conclusions to future technological problems. Computer software can generate characters in the study of a variety of languages. On the whole educators believe that the future of education will be even brighter, thanks to the computer. Who knows?—perhaps someday computers will be able to develop a common universal language.

Computers are a valuable asset to any school program. They can help us understand difficult concepts such as those found in math, science, and basic geometry. Some educators predict classes with only the student and the computer, with the teacher simply writing the programs. Students can learn at their own individual speed. Of course many of the revolutionary computer innovations are also improving the home, industry, business, and government operations at all levels.

A computer is a powerful machine that can help you solve complex problems fast. Undoubtedly the most important technological and cultural phenomenon in history, computers cannot only do arithmetic fast, but they can store large amounts of information. However computers cannot think. Thinking remains the responsibility of people. Computers must be given instructions to solve problems or to carry out a variety of programmed tasks, such as playing a video game, solving a problem, computing income taxes, tracking business orders, planning and implementing atmospheric space operations, figuring out orbits for the space shuttles, identifying and tracking down criminals for the police departments, controlling machines, making decisions, diagnosing illnesses, unscrambling the genetic code for scientists, developing new technologies in the manufacture of aircraft, keeping track of your investments, and predicting the weather. These are only a few of the countless, limitless tasks that this versatile machine can accomplish. The great number of tasks the computer can carry out, more effectively and much faster than mankind, seems to be as boundless as space and time. No artificial intelligence can be expected from a computer so far and no comparison with human judgment. However good possibilities exist that in the not-too-distant future, computers will be able to produce just that—artificial intelligence, with great possibilities that the computer will be able to recognize and use every word in the dictionary. So far it makes an excellent comparison as well as an expert on offering second opinions. What one puts into the computer determines what it produces, and the information fed into the system can then be treated and exhibited in a variety of forms.

Battlefield strategies via high-speed computers are programmed and studied at length at the Air War College. The National Aeronautical and Space Administration has a computer system called *TELE-PRESENCE*, which is used to repair orbiting spacecraft and satellites. Each space shuttle contains a minimum of five computers that support the space operations, among other tasks.

A computer is indeed a workhorse. Instructions given to a computer are carried out through what is called a *program*, thus the word *programming* is common in computer language. Just like anyone can learn to drive an automobile, anyone can learn to use a computer.

One simple way to recognize the importance and effectiveness of a computer is to trace the need for the storage of mechanized information. In 1880 it took twelve years to calculate the results of the United States census. In 1890, the first time a machine was used to gather and sort data and perform simple arithmetic, it took two and one-half years to accomplish the identical task. In 1980, using a computer for the first time, it took only eight months to complete the job. In 1990, again with the aid of a computer, results were ready in only a matter of hours. Very few people, if any, could have foreseen the vast technological changes that have taken place over the last several generations.

Today people all over the world, in business, industry, government, medicine, science, agriculture, communication, schools, and homes, use countless computers daily. Computer technology improvements are continually being made, and computer history is being made just as frequently.

Computer programs can be bought according to subject matter. For example you can purchase a program to play a video tick-tack-toe game, or to work out your personal or business income tax. You can also learn to make your own programs by following a few simple instructions. Every day children in the first grade throughout the United States learn to program and use the microcomputer.

Programs, designed according to your own needs, are typed on a *floppy disk* or a *cassette*. Cassettes and floppy disks are permanent records of programs and both can be used over and over again.

Computers are very much a part of the school system today. A computer is a mind extender, which helps us to stretch our brains and enables us to do countless routine tasks quickly, efficiently, and easily. Computers also help us to become more innovative and productive. Calculators help us solve math problems, and dictionaries help us learn new words. Through training and practice, we can learn how to use the computer to help us solve a variety of difficult problems, and also help us understand unknown or difficult concepts.

Chapter IV
The Learning Process—How Students Learn

Teaching no more causes learning
than preaching causes conversion.

Frank Smith, "Insult to Intelligence"

It is a fine thing to have ability
but the ability to discover ability
in others is the true test.

Elbert Hubbard

The Impact of Variable Factors on the Instructional-Learning Process

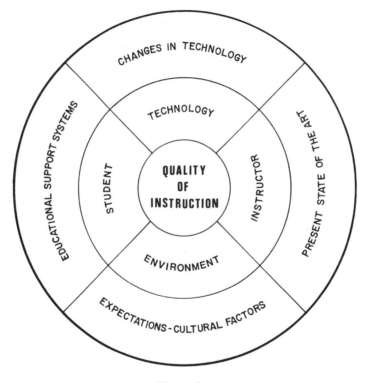

Figure 6

Learning

Definition: Learning is a mental process that involves new knowledge and/or skills and/or attitudes that with the proper stimulus can be recalled and demonstrated in the form of a behavior performance.

Learning is a complex subject, with a number of defining characteristics:

1. *Learning results in a change of behavior.* As a result of learning, students know something or can do something they did not know or could not do before.
2. *Learning comes as a result of practice.* Performing a task once does not mean it is learned. Continued practice is necessary. Unguided practice, without the aid of a planned program and without instructors, may lead students to develop misunderstandings and poor habits. Practice does not make perfect, unless it is well planned and guided by the teacher or instructor.
3. *Learning produces a relatively permanent change.* For example riding a bicycle is a skill that can be remembered with just a few minutes of practice, even after years. It is, therefore, a relatively permanent type of learning.
4. *Learning is not directly observable.* Although learning is not directly observable, we can observe the performance that results from learning.
5. *We learn through the medium of our five senses:*
    seeing
    hearing
    smelling
    touching
    tasting
    We learn through our senses as follows:
    10 percent of what we READ
    20 percent of what we HEAR

30 percent of what we SEE

50 percent of what we HEAR and SEE

70 percent if we SAY IT and REPEAT IT

90 percent if we both REPEAT IT or SAY IT and DO IT

Seeing and hearing are generally the most-used senses, and they are the most useful of the sense channels. However in skill training, touch, smell, and even taste are also important.

In education and training, the maximum use of all sense channels is important. This does not occur automatically. The teacher or instructor must make it occur.

6. *Learning relates to knowledge and experience.* We learn if information is meaningful so that we are able to associate it with or relate it to our existing knowledge and experience.

7. *Learning involves a sequence.* We learn by assimilation of information if presented in:
   - A logical sequence
   - Steps or parts so that between each step or part, a period of mental or practical consolidation can take place

How Students Learn

Learning is acquiring new ways to do things or satisfy desires. It is the modification of behavior through *practice, training,* and *experience.* Notice the functional emphasis in this definition. We do not consider learning as the transmittal of facts from a book to the mind of the reader, or from one person to another. We do not consider that students are learning because facts are being stored in their minds. Students learn to the extent that they can function properly and efficiently in their general work situation and in their lives. They may acquire many facts, but unless they can use them in improving their adjustment to work, they have not "learned" anything.

Learning is an active process that takes place according to a number of well-defined rules and principles. There are six concepts of learning: *the will to learn, action, attention, organization, understanding, and review.* Let us briefly consider each of these concepts.

Will to Learn.

An essential part of education or training is to create interest and motivation. Once this has been done, interest and motivation must be maintained by using techniques such as questions, participation, involvement, and practice. Learning is more effective when students have a will to learn. When interest is already present, it should be applied and developed further. When interest does not exist, it should be built up by the instructor or teacher. The will to learn results from having a definite objective. Students are motivated when they know exactly what they are expected to do and realize why they must do it.

Action.

Learning is an active process, not passive absorption. Education or training in the final analysis depends entirely upon students' participation in the learning situations that confront them. When students are exposed to new ideas, facts, or principles, they are in a "learning situation"; they learn as they react to and participate in that situation. Learning occurs in direct proportion to the amount of the student's reaction to a learning situation.

Attention.

This means focusing the full power of students' minds on the material you wish them to learn. To concentrate effectively on learning, students should be motivated. They should feel some interest or curiosity concerning the material. This is where the instructor/teacher responds. Think of a student—not as a vase to be filled—but, instead, as a fire to be lit. Introduce objectives to help students find their identity and let them establish their own goals, make wise decisions, and practice citizenship. As a teacher keep in mind the learner's needs, abilities, development levels, and interests. Keep in mind the characteristics of child growth development—physical, social, emotional, and mental.

Organization.

Students cannot learn effectively simply by memorizing all the facts about a subject. Before students are able to use material that they have learned, they must understand its organization, that is, how the parts fit together to make a complete picture. If the instructor has talked about the objective, what students will know at the end of the lesson, they can better organize each part to meet the objective. If students know what the objective of the lesson, they can better interpret each detail. This procedure is known as the "whole-to-part" method.

Understanding.

Getting the basic idea that the instructor is trying to get across is the definition of understanding. Students understand by taking notes or by retaining the information in their minds, depending on the amount and level of technical material being presented. The knowledge that a student gets from a lesson can be transferred to a work situation only to the extent that the student comprehends the principle presented by the instructor.

Review.

Few experiences are so vivid that a student can learn them in one trial. Material studied for an hour a day for four days, or even an hour a week for four weeks, will be remembered much better than material studied four hours one day and never reviewed. This is known as the "principle of distributed practice." Although repetition is essential to learning, repetition alone does not guarantee learning. If repetition is to do any good, you must consider the principles of understanding, attention, action, organization, and will to learn. Only if you practice all these principles will repetition produce learning.

Exposure to Learning

1. Students learn faster when your language is simple and meaningful to them. Short words are the best, and short words, when they are old words, are the best of all.
2. Concrete examples help learning, both positive and negative.
3. Students learn faster when the irrelevant parts of an idea or procedure are minimized, while the relevant parts are emphasized.
4. Questions help the learner discover misunderstandings.
5. Build practice into your presentation. Students learn faster when they can use their new knowledge in a real situation.
6. Provide time for the learner to process information. Repeat, pause, ask questions. Get students involved.

Learning Exposure Involvement

- Be adequately prepared to teach your next lesson.
- Have lesson plan completed and reviewed before class time.
- Have tools, training aids, and student handout materials ready.
- Be prepared to demonstrate the tasks covered in lesson plan.
- Be prepared to correctly answer all questions.
- Be in your assigned classroom/shop ten minutes before class bell.
- Leave classroom/shop in proper condition for next instructor.
- Be objective in evaluating the student's performance.
- Protect students' attendance and grade records to prevent tampering.
- Give individual help to your students when needed.
- Review future lessons to see if materials and other items will have to be prepared or ordered. Have them ready prior to class time.
- Be cooperative and helpful in working with others in regard to sharing tools, equipment, and materials.
- Do everything possible to motivate your students toward a complete understanding of the theoretical and practical aspects of the lesson.
- Keep your students active and *involved* during the entire class session.

Learning Theory

For the free man there should be no element
of slavery in learning. Enforced exercise
does not harm the body, but enforced learning
will not stay in the mind. So avoid compulsion,
and let your students' lessons take the form of play.

Plato, The Republic

For a number of years experts have been researching and theorizing concerning the type of activity that takes place within the human brain during the learning process. What are the brain functions that govern the use of effective learning? There is much difference of opinion and little positive agreement concerning this matter. However there is general agreement about three factors of theory that seem pertinent to an understanding of effective learning.

During the learning process the mind acts as a filter. As great numbers of verbal or visual bits are received, the brain works to sort out the important items from the routine descriptive or supportive factors. Therefore learning can probably be further advanced by helping the learner's brain identify the important bits. By repeating and by emphasizing the important bits, learning is taking place.

The brain also tries to organize the learning bits into reasonable arrangements. Verbal bits require considerable effort in this direction. This process might be called "drawing mental pictures."

After the bits have been sorted and arranged, the brain is faced with the problem of storing the bits needed for further use. As is true of any computer, there is probably a limit to the number of items that can be stored in the human memory. Storage efficiency and speed of recalling information are gained, however, whenever it is possible to store a single bit (usually a visual one) instead of multiple bits of description. This increased efficiency is especially noticeable in dealing with concepts, theories, philosophies, and other abstract ideas.

Before the learning channel can be useful, it must be open. Somehow the teacher/instructor must make the student's mind receive the subject matter. Getting and holding student attention are essential in learning. Remember: The instructor/teacher is a salesman of ideas, and many of the world's sales techniques for getting the attention of the client are worth considering. Caution: Get, and continue to get, student attention on the subject, not just on a distracting gimmick.

Learning and Knowledge

"Learning" and "knowledge" cannot exist apart within a person. Identifying "knowledge" is difficult, because teachers'/instructors' own knowledge is different from that of their students'/trainees' or of anyone else's. People's knowledge is a result of their own experiences, and no two people have had identical experiences. Even when observing the same event, two people will react differently; they learn different things from it, according to the manner in which the situation affects their individual needs. Previous experience conditions a person to respond to some things and to ignore others.

The emphasis on "learning by experience" may seem to imply that there are other ways to learn. This is erroneous. All learning is by experience, but it takes place in different forms and in varying degrees of richness and depth. For instance some experiences involve the whole person; others, only his ears and his memory. Therefore instructors are never faced with the question of whether they should provide "experience," or perhaps something else. Rather they are faced with the problem of providing experiences that are meaningful, more varied, and more appropriate. For example by repeated drill, students/trainees can learn to say a list of words, or by rote they can learn to recite the principles of leadership. However they can make principles a part of their lives only if they understand them well enough to apply them correctly in real situations, which they can do if their learning experience has been extensive and meaningful.

Learning a physical skill requires actual experience in performing that skill. Students learn to fly an airplane only if their experiences include flying an airplane. Through practice they perfect their flying skills.

Learning is change in behavior as a result of experience. Learning is purposeful and comes only through experience. It is never single-sided; instead it is multifaced. The learner's full set of learning equipment is always involved. It is an active process.

In planning for teaching, the teaching methods should reflect the nature of what is to be learned. Definite principles are involved in learning skills. Learning concepts and generalizations depends on a broad range of experience and careful guidance.

The laws of learning provide a useful insight into the process of learning. The law of effect is especially significant—it states that learning is strengthened when accompanied by satisfying or pleasurable conditions. (This statement certainly gives a strong hint to the teacher/instructor.)

A knowledge of the laws of learning helps the teacher/instructor to understand and to take advantage of three factors that affect learning: motivation, participation, and individual differences. The student must have a need to know, to understand, to believe, to act, or to acquire a skill. All of these needs, which make up motivation, are inseparable from the personal-social needs of the student. Students learn best when they participate. When learning has a purpose, learning is more permanent. Because of differences in experience, background, intelligence, interests, desire to learn, and psychological (emotional and physical) factors, students learn at different rates. Teachers must recognize these differences and gear their teaching to reach all students—whatever their capabilities and abilities.

The central questions in education and training deal with retention of learning and transfer of learning. Disuse, interference, and repression may account for forgetting. Transfer of learning is involved when students learn one task that affects learning of another, or when students adapt what they learn for use in new situations. The key to both is thorough learning of a relatively few really important concepts and generalizations. This leads to meaningful learning, anchored in the student's experience.

The "Laws" of Learning

One of the pioneers in educational psychology was Professor Edward L. Thorndike, of Teachers College, Columbia University, New York City. Early in this century Professor Thorndike postulated several "laws" of learning. These were rules of principles that seemed generally applicable to the learning process. In the years since, other psychologists have found that learning is a more complex process than some of these "laws" suggest. This does not imply that Professor Thorndike's ideas have been invalidated. While his laws seem to have significant exceptions, they still provide an insight into the learning process and are discussed here for that reason.

The "laws" that follow are not necessarily as Professor Thorndike stated them. During the years they have been restated and supplemented, but in essence they may be attributed to him. The first three are the basic laws, as originally identified by Professor Thorndike. These three "laws" are the law of readiness; the law of exercise; and the most famous and still generally accepted, the law of effect. Other "laws" were added later as a result of experimental studies. Some of these are the law of primacy, the law of intensity, and the law of recency. Let us now examine each of these "laws" and consider how they affect the learning process.

Law of Readiness.

Students learn best when they are ready to learn, and they will not learn much if they see no reason for learning. Getting a student ready to learn is usually the teacher's responsibility. If students have a strong purpose, a clear objective, a well-fixed reason for learning something, they will make more progress than students who lack motivation. Readiness implies a degree of single-mindedness and eagerness. When students are ready to learn, they meet the teacher at least halfway, which simplifies the teacher's job.

Under certain circumstances the teacher can do little, if anything, to inspire students' readiness to learn. If outside responsibilities, interest, or worries weigh too heavily on students' minds; if their schedule is overcrowded; if their personal problems seem insolvable; students may have little interest in learning. Health, finances, or family affairs can overshadow students' desire to learn.

Law of Exercise.

This law states that those things most often repeated are best remembered. It is the basis of practice and drill. The human memory is not infallible. The mind can rarely retain, evaluate, and apply new concepts or practices after a single exposure. Students do not learn touch typing at one sitting. They learn by applying what they have been told, and every time they practice, their learning continues. Teachers/instructors must provide opportunities for students to practice or repeat, and must see that this process is directed toward a goal. Repetition can be of many types, including recall, review, restatement, manual drill, and physical application.

Law of Effect.

This law is based on the emotional reaction of the learner. It states that learning is strengthened when accompanied by a pleasant or satisfying feeling, and that learning is weakened when associated with an unpleasant feeling. An experience that produces feelings of defeat, frustration, anger, confusion, or futility in students is unpleasant for them. If an instructor pilot attempts to teach aerobatic maneuvers to cadets on their first flight, they are likely to feel inferior and to be dissatisfied. As a demonstration that shows students their goal, the aerobatics might motivate students. However as something to be learned immediately, the aerobatics would be frustrating. In terms of the learning objective, this experience would be unpleasant.

Teachers/instructors should be cautious about using negative motivation in class or in the workshop. Showing students that a problem seems impossible to solve can make the teaching task difficult. Usually it is better to show students that a problem is not impossible at all, but is within their capability to understand and solve. Whatever the learning situation, it should contain elements that affect students positively and give them a feeling of satisfaction. Every learning experience does not have to be entirely successful, nor does the student have to master each lesson completely. A student's chance of success, however, will be increased if the learning experience is pleasant.

Law of Primacy.

Primacy, the state of being first, often creates a strong, almost unshakable impression. For teachers/instructors, this means that their learning must be right. "Unteaching" is more difficult than teaching. If new piano pupils learn incorrect finger positions, their teacher will have a difficult task in unteaching the bad habits and reteaching good ones. Every student should be started right. Students' first experience should be positive and functional so that it can prepare them, and lay the foundation for all that is to follow.

Law of Intensity.

A vivid, dramatic, or exciting learning experience teaches more than a routine or boring experience. A student of literature is likely to gain greater understanding and appreciation of the play *Macbeth* from seeing it performed than from merely reading it. Students can learn more about firefighting from watching someone fight a fire than from listening to a lecture on the subject. The law of intensity, then, implies that a student will learn more from the real thing than from a substitute. Since the classroom imposes limitations on the amount of realism that can be brought into teaching, teachers/instructors should use imagination to make the learning situation as realistic as possible. Mock-ups, colored slides, movies, filmstrips, charts, posters, photographs, and other audiovisual aids can add vividness to classroom instruction. Demonstrations, skits, and panels do much to intensify the learning experiences of students.

Law of Recency.

Other things being equal, the things most recently learned are best remembered. Conversely the longer it takes students to apply a new fact or understanding, the more difficulty they have remembering it. For example it is sometimes easy to recall a telephone number dialed a few minutes previously, but it is usually impossible to recall an unfamiliar number dialed a week earlier. Teachers/instructors recognize the law of recency when they carefully plan a summary for a lesson or an effective conclusion for a lecture. They repeat, restate, or reemphasize important matters at the end of a lesson to make sure that the student remembers them instead of inconsequential details. The law of recency can often be applied advantageously in determining the relative positions of lectures within a course of instruction. It is also followed in scheduling discussions immediately after quizzes, tests, or examinations.

All the laws of learning are not apparent in every learning situation. These laws manifest themselves singly or in groups, and for purposes of this discussion, it is not necessary to determine which law operates in what situation. However if teachers understand the laws of learning, they can deal intelligently with motivation, participation, and individual differences—the three major factors affecting learning.

Laws of Learning in Brief

Law of Readiness	Students learn best when they are ready to learn, and they will not learn much if they see no reason for learning.
Law of Exercise	The more often an act is repeated, the more quickly a habit is established.
Law of Effect	People tend to accept and repeat those responses that are pleasant and satisfying and to avoid those that are annoying.
Law of Primacy	First impressions are the most lasting.

Law of Intensity	A vivid, dramatic, or exciting learning experience teaches more than a routine or boring experience.
Law of Recency	Other things being equal, the things most recently learned are best remembered.
Law of Disuse	A skill not practiced or knowledge not used will be quickly lost or forgotten.
Law of Organization	Organized teaching produces organized learning and it is remembered longer.
Law of Success	Nothing succeeds like success. Instructors can help students experience some personal satisfaction from each learning activity and achieve some success in each class presentation.

Types of Learning

There are *three* types of learning:

1. Cognitive deals with knowledge: "What does the student know?"
   Cognitive objective. Intellectually and thought-based. Knowing, learning, recalling facts, words and other symbols, events, principles. Comprehending, interpreting content, extrapolating elements from one to another situation. Applying learned situations. Analyzing, breaking wholes into parts and relating one with the other part. Evaluating, judging, using criteria. Putting parts together. Showing creativity.

2. Psychomotor deals with physical skills: "What can the student perform/do?"
   Psychomotor objective. Making skilled and coordinated movements, e.g., facial movements. Physical movements, manipulating, walking, running, jumping. Perceptual ability of auditory, visual, and coordinative kinds. Communicating nonverbally through facial gestures, creative expression, and posture.

3.   Affective deals with feelings: "How does the student feel about the subject?"
     Affective objective. Responding with feeling of satisfaction. Receiving or showing interest, awareness. Valuing, becoming committed to. Organizing and clarifying values.

Teachers dealing with a skill need to be familiar with the following teaching methods:

1.   *Cognitive* methods include (but are not limited to) the following:
     a.   Reading
     b.   Lecture
     c.   Group discussion

2.   *Psychomotor* methods include (but are not limited to) the following:
     a.   Demonstration
     b.   Return demonstration
     c.   Hands-on training
     d.   Simulation exercises

3.   *Affective* methods include (but are not limited to) the following:
     a.   Modeling
     b.   Role-playing
     c.   Buddy system
     d.   Group discussion/sharing

Figures 6, 7, and 8 describe each of the types of learning in detail.

COGNITIVE LEARNING

	Purpose	Subject	Audience	Environment
READING	Provides good overview of materials, should be first thing trainee-student does.	Any subject, except extremely technical material with difficult vocabulary, is appropriate for reading.	All students, except those with visual handicaps, can read material.	Reading should take place in an environment free of external stimuli with good lighting.
LECTURE	Provides opportunity for review of reading with instructor emphasizing key points, explaining material and answering questions.	Most subjects can be adapted to lecture. Instructor must be careful to break down to basic components and should receive constant feedback from class to be sure they are understanding it.	All students, except those with auditory handicaps, can participate in lecture classes.	Students should be comfortable, lighting and temperature should be adequately controlled. Minimal noise level. Instructor should be visible to all students, as should any audiovisual aids.
GROUP DISCUSSION	Provides clarification of points in peer group setting and exchange of understandings.	Should follow lecture and reading presentation of subject matter. Any subject is appropriate. Group should have a defined task, i.e., develop questions, discuss and report problems, etc.	All students are appropriate. Groups should be no larger than 8 people to provide maximum interaction. Reticent members should be encouraged to speak.	Groups should be at sufficient distance so they don't disturb each other. Should be seated comfortably, and should have good lighting and adequate temperature.

Figure 7

PSYCHOMOTOR LEARNING

	Purpose	Subject	Audience	Environment
DEMONSTRATION	Large group — provides opportunity to see and understand general principles of task. Small group — provides close-up view of task step by step.	Any skill can be demonstrated, but the equipment used by the instructor must be portable, or the group must go to the area where the equipment is available.	Students should know basic fundamentals of task, theory and application before being shown actual performance.	All students must be able to see; lighting and equipment must be adequate.
DEMONSTRATION RETURN	Allows each student to show his understanding of what he has learned.	Any skill can be demonstrated, but the equipment used by the instructor must be portable, or the group must co to the area where the equipment is available.	Students should have seen and stated they understand the task before they are asked to return a demonstration; mistakes should be corrected immediately.	Student must have actual equipment and sufficient time with which to work.
HANDS-ON TRAINING	Allows actual experience in work with equipment, should be repetitive, not just done once.	Any skill can be demonstrated, but the equipment used by the instructor must be portable, or the group must co to the area where the equipment is available.	Students should be allowed to repeat the skill more than once, so that it is reinforced.	Must be as close to actual situation as possible in terms of equipment and speed expected.
EXERCISE SIMULATION	This is "hands-on" with the addition of actual condition play — student is evaluated in his performance of task according to realistic protocol.	Is most productive when a synthesis of several skills is desired, so that the student gets the "feel" of a realistic situation.	Students should be well advanced in training, so that a synthesis of various skills can be demonstrated.	Must be as close to actual situation as possible in terms of equipment, speed, tension and excitement.

Figure 8

AFFECTIVE LEARNING

	Purpose	Subject	Audience	Environment
MODELING	Instructor is <u>always</u> role model for student; they act and react as the instructor does; instructor must be conscious of himself.	In all subjects the instructor's attitude and feelings will be conveyed, frequently at an unconscious level.	All students perceive these instructors.	Modeling occurs whether the learning situation is formal or informal, and also occurs out of class in discussion.
ROLE PLAYING	Especially effective in demonstrating the consequences of attitudes in real life situations.	Attitude training in dealing with others who are perceived negatively is most effectively done with role playing.	The students must be serious, must have developed a minimal inter-relationship, and should be informed about the goals of the training.	Role playing is most effective in an informal learning climate; the instructor should become an observer, and let the play take its course.
BUDDY SYSTEM	Can provide close supervision of student, can inculcate attitudes and values by indirect means. Must be above reproach in both attitude and aptitude.	All tasks can be taught by the buddy system. It is very important that all buddies follow the same procedures and protocols, and that they have consistent evaluation methods.	Students should have a minimal competence in their field. Before being placed in the field they should be supervised closely. Demonstrate their proficiency before actual cases.	The work environment should be clean, safe, and the students should have adequate supplies and equipment to perform their tasks.
GROUP DISCUSSION	Among students, group discussion with more experienced workers can provide insights into successful ways of coping with demands of the job, can reduce fear and anxiety about abilities.	Most subjects lend to discussion, especially the problems and fears which face new students. Discussion should provide guidelines to group.	All students are appropriate; groups should be no larger than 8 for maximum participation. Students should be sufficiently advanced in course to benefit from exchange.	The learning climate should be informal, groups should be at sufficient distance so no disturbance to others is caused, good lighting and adequate temperature is necessary.

Figure 9

38

Motivation as an Influence on Learning

Nothing great has ever been achieved without enthusiasm.
Ralph Waldo Emerson

The factor that has perhaps the greatest influence on learning is motivation, the force that causes a person to move toward a goal. This force is dormant in some people and active in others, but it is always present in some degree. Motivation can be rooted in any or all of the personal-social needs of the student, for example, the need for security, for new experience, for recognition, for self-esteem, for conformity, or the need to help others. Such needs compel people to act, to move, to start working toward an objective, or to achieve a purpose. The teacher's responsibility is first to recognize and identify these needs and then to seek ways of satisfying them through teaching.

To be successful the student must have a need to know, to understand, to believe, to act, or to acquire a skill. The wise teacher realizes that these needs are not separate from the personal-social needs of the student. In fact the most effective motivation comes from this awareness. The teacher must make students want to learn, and in some cases must remove obstacles that students have placed in the paths of their learning. If students cannot find it for themselves, the teacher must find it for them.

A need to learn presupposes goals or objectives. If the motivation is of the right kind, students will know what these goals are and how they can reach them. In the learning situation, the teacher usually establishes the objective for students, making sure that it is clear and specific. Without an objective neither the student nor the teacher can measure progress or evaluate achievements.

Illustrations of weak and strong motivation are around us. For example consider students who attend a required course in communications-electronics without any prospect of using what they study. Since their interest in the course is academic and communications-electronics has nothing to do with their job or future, it is difficult for them to learn much from the course. If, on the other hand, students know that at the end of the course they will be assigned to a job requiring the knowledge of communications-electronics, they will have a goal that goes beyond the mere completion of the course: students can partially satisfy their need for recognition, for security, for self-esteem, and for a new experience by mastering the course material. In this latter instance, even though the need and the desire to know are built in, students need and want to know the objective of the course and to believe that it can be reached.

In meeting the responsibility to motivate learning, teachers/instructors can capitalize on whatever built-in motivation they find in their students. The big challenge is to shape personal-social motivations to make them serve the learning situation. The teacher must first establish learning objectives and then activate forces that will cause the student to work toward them. This is motivation, a most important part of learning.

No matter how well developed the curriculum, how sophisticated the equipment, how well written the textbooks, how much money is spent, or how well prepared the teacher/instructor, without students' internal motivation (forces that develop within students themselves and of their own interest), little or no learning will take place.

Summary

- Students are motivated by sincere recognition of their accomplishments.
- Student performance is increased in an open environment where the teacher and the student can freely discuss, without fear of recrimination, strengths, limitations, successes, and failures.
- You can buy students' time and you can also buy a certain amount of physical activity from them, but you cannot purchase their dedication, commitment, loyalty, respect, or desires. These come only from conditions that allow them to satisfy their higher needs.
- Student needs for doing fulfilling work, doing it well, and receiving recognition are more vital in motivation than those needs that can be satisfied by wages and fringe benefits.
- Factors that cause student dissatisfaction are more concerned with lower human needs, and factors that motivate are more concerned with higher human needs.
- Students have a maximum tolerance level for the amount of criticism they can accept, and when this level is reached, further criticism is counterproductive, resulting in defensiveness and justification.
- The involvement of students in setting their own objectives, even though they must be approved or modified by their teachers/instructors, provides strong motivation toward accomplishment.
- Students will try harder to make a plan or method work if they are involved in the development.

Chapter V
Learning to Learn—How to Study

By nature all men are alike, but by education men become different.

Chinese proverb

This chapter is for students who are interested in learning—how to study for learning. My personal experience in working with students is that they are interested in learning, but that they do not know how to study, how to prepare themselves for learning. By using a simple plan to study, a student will be rewarded with real improvement in study habits and learning abilities.

Learning is not really difficult; however you must follow some fundamental ideas and practices in order to become proficient in learning. Study habits do not develop accidentally. With directed practice, and a little advice and instruction, you can develop good study habits.

If you are willing to follow the study plan described here, you will see a real improvement in your learning abilities.

Learning.

If you relax in an easy chair and read a book on how to play soccer, then go about your business the next few days without thinking again of what you read until you are at the soccer field next month, you will find that your soccer game will improve little, if any. If you merely read this chapter, you will not have learned how to study. Reading alone is not studying or learning: you must practice what you read. This chapter is not intended to be simply informational material. This chapter describes procedures that must be followed and practiced, so that you can learn how to study. Your efficiency will increase if you study this chapter. Follow the principles and procedures outlined, and practice their application.

Efficient study of this chapter requires efficient reading, but few people read as efficiently as they can learn to. First of all, then, let us consider a plan of learning through reading that, if followed, can greatly increase the reader's comprehension and retention. It is a method of covering reading assignments with a maximum of learning and memory, for whatever amount of time is spent. A plan alone is not enough, however. Efficient study also requires some understanding of the psychological factors that promote learning. Let us examine the method first, and then practice it while learning other concepts in effective study.

A Plan.

A plan of study, consisting of three steps, has been designed to take full advantage of the psychological factors in the learning process. In considering each of the steps, we shall ask two basic questions: First how is the step accomplished? Second what benefit will I get from the effective accomplishment of the step?

Reconnoiter-Read-Recall Plan of Study

Reconnoitering is a preliminary survey of a section to determine its general layout and nature, but not to get details. This is precisely the meaning and purpose of the reconnoiter step of the Reconnoiter-Read-Recall plan of study.

Four approaches may be used to accomplish the reconnoiter step. Many writers use topics and subtopics to break their material down into smaller, more easily recognized elements. Some authors use brief descriptive headings at the beginning of these topics to help the reader.

If this aid to reconnoitering is not used, key sentences at the beginning or end of paragraphs may give the gist of the material. A quick survey will reveal whether this study aid is included; if so, it will serve the same purpose as that served by topic headings.

Other authors make a practice of summarizing, at the end of a chapter or article, the substance of the material covered. If this is done, it will prove an effective means for accomplishing the reconnoiter step. Read the summary first, with the idea of getting the general picture of the topic.

One of the first things to be learned in improving study is to use, to the fullest extent, every possible resource offered by the author. This does not always mean following the order of the text. If the author puts something at the end of a chapter that might be more useful to you if you read it first, by all means do so. This is recommended whenever the author includes a summary or study-directing questions.

If none of these study aids is offered, we are forced to depend upon the most difficult, but at the same time the most helpful reconnoitering approach: scanning. Scanning consists of running the eye rapidly down a page, not reading word by word or even looking at every sentence, but picking a sentence here and there to get a general idea of the subject and the author's approach. Developing the ability to scan rapidly and well requires some practice, but once achieved this ability is a valuable aid in effective, intensive study, as well as in quick inspection of material to identify important ideas.

If you perform the reconnoiter step properly, you will see the general picture that the author developed in his article, and the main idea that he tried to present. You will see the organization of the subject, and this will enable you to spot the objective of the article and to work up the will to learn, which is so valuable in learning. It is like looking at the picture of a jigsaw puzzle before putting the pieces together. A view of the whole picture helps you see how each topic fits in with the other topics around it.

Immediately upon reading the title of the article, or as you begin the reconnoiter step, stop a moment and ask yourself: What material should be included under this title? Then throughout the reconnoiter step, formulate questions that you think might logically be answered in a later, detailed reading. For example suppose your reading assignment includes an article entitled "Survival in the Desert." From the title alone you may anticipate information that would answer such questions as these: How can I find food in the desert? How can I keep from dying of thirst? What clothes should I wear? How can I survive?

Under each of these questions you can develop other questions. Under the general subject of how to keep from dying of thirst, for instance, you might ask these detailed questions: What can be used as a substitute for water? Where can I find these substitutes? How can I better my chances of survival if no water is found?

All these questions and many more might be developed from the title alone. More detailed questions may occur to you during the reconnoiter step. Often, too, a list of questions can be found at the end of a chapter or reading assignment. It is a good idea to look for such questions first. Read them over and keep them in mind while you read the material in detail.

What results can you expect from this questioning? We have already mentioned the desirability of having objectives in study. The more specific your objectives are and the more clearly you are directed to the things you are to learn, the more effective your learning will be. These questions provide immediate objectives—not just an overall idea of what you will gain by studying the whole article, but pointers telling you what to look for in each subtopic, sentence by sentence and paragraph by paragraph. They encourage you to look for specific facts rather than generalities. They encourage your undivided attention by giving you something to search for; thus they provide an immediate purpose in your study.

The second step in the Reconnoiter-Read-Recall method of study is to read. Effective reading involves activity. When we begin to read a study assignment, most of us lean back in an easy chair, prop the book in our laps, and read with our eyes. Although our eyes are active—they read every word on the page—all too frequently our minds are relaxed. The result is that we read a paragraph word for word and then find that we have no idea of what we have read. The key to effective reading is action. Your mind is not thirsty soil that absorbs the water of knowledge without conscious effort. Knowledge is more like a football that has been kicked into the air, and must be pursued and caught. The extent to which your mind grapples with each point covered in your reading is the extent to which you learn what you are reading. All learning is an active process, which takes place when learners react energetically and aggressively to the material before them. Read for ideas not words.

The third step in our approach to study is recall. By this we mean rephrasing in your own words what you have read. When you finish reading a paragraph, a topic, or a chapter, lean back, look away from your book, and say in your own words what the author has been saying. In doing this it may help you to look at a topic heading and then mentally recall what was included in that topic. Or if you have underlined the important points, you should reread these and mentally reconstruct the topics as fully as possible. If the book is not your own and underlining is therefore unsuitable, you might construct an outline from memory and then check with the book for accuracy. After completing your outline, it is still a good idea to see if you remember enough of the details to fill in the facts suggested by the outline.

It is important that you recall verbally; that is, actually speak the words aloud or under your breath. Thinking, "Oh, this is what he means...now I remember what he meant...I know all about it," just isn't good enough. We are all guilty of saying to ourselves, "That is a good idea. I know all about it."

When we start to explain that idea to someone else, we find ourselves unable to put it into words. Any idea that is too vague to be explained in concrete, specific words is not likely to be of much value to anyone. You cannot talk intelligently about a subject or successfully use the material if you have only a vague idea of what it is about. After all the only way to know whether a topic is clear enough in your mind to be expressed in words is to try putting it into words. In reconstructing a topic from your outline or from memory, put your ideas into actual words to be sure that you understand them. If you accomplish this step effectively, you are engaging in mental activity, which we have already discussed as an absolute prerequisite to learning. When you outline the author's material and put the substance of his article in your own words, you have achieved another essential concept of learning: organization. You do not know a subject thoroughly if you know every fact about it but still have only a vague idea of the significance of each fact in relation to the other subject matter. Organization of material is the answer. When you are able to outline the subject and reproduce topically the author's discussion, you know the organization that the author has used.

Thorough performance of the recall step does much to guarantee another of the essentials of learning: understanding. If you know the organization that the author follows and can express his ideas in your own words, you have mastered the material sufficiently to put it to use. You will profit from what you learn in proportion to the extent to which you apply it. You may be able to repeat certain facts from memory without understanding their import. For practical purposes such facts are almost valueless. However if you are able to express them in your own words, and in such a manner that they are meaningful to you, you will probably be able to use your knowledge of the subject in appropriate situations.

Practice of the recall step will give you a ready, reliable, and helpful device for evaluating the effectiveness of your study to the present, for determining whether further study on a given topic is necessary, and for indicating areas in which additional study would be most profitable. It is often a waste of time to restudy thoroughly comprehended material or to study new material before assimilating the material you have already covered. If you can re-create a given topic from your outline notes, you know it well enough to proceed to something else. If you cannot proceeding to new material at this point is likely to add to your store of unusable material and to consume much of your time without results. The importance of the recall step can hardly be overemphasized. Actual laboratory experiments have shown that students who study a specified amount of time, whether fifteen minutes or five hours, generally make better test scores if they spend at least half of their total study time in reflective thinking. This means that if you have an hour to study a topic, you will do well to spend about thirty minutes in the reconnoitering and reading steps and at least thirty minutes in the recall step.

Many experimenters recommend spending as much as two-thirds of study time in reflective thinking; hardly any recommend spending less than half. It is easy to slight reflective thinking in your study period, because it is usually harder to think than to read. Furthermore it is much easier to convince yourself that you have thought, when you haven't really thought, than to imagine that you have read when you haven't really read. It is a good idea to use your watch to ensure that you do not slight reflective thinking in your study process. Laboratory tests have proven that if students will spend at least half of their study time in reflective thinking, they will be able to make better scores on tests, taken immediately after study or several weeks later, than if they spend all their time on reading steps. If you are really interested in learning and remembering, give the recall step a fair chance.

Learning Your Three Rs

Every step of the Reconnoiter-Read-Recall method of study has been proven to be an indispensable link in a chain that leads to effective study. However a system can't work miracles. It can't produce learning without expenditure of time and effort on the part of the student. If you are thinking that this system may be good but that it takes more time than you can spend in study and is too complicated to follow, remember three things:

1. Whatever the amount of your study time, if you divide it between reading and reflective thinking, as described here, you will learn and remember more than if you omit the reflective thinking step.
2. Study performed at random intervals and in time fragments does not give as good results as study that is planned and performed systematically.
3. Most people who actually try the Reconnoiter-Read-Recall system of study report that it is much simpler and easier to put into effect than they had thought it would be. Don't assume that it is too difficult and time-consuming for you. Give it a trial.

After a few practice tries, you will find that this method of study works very smoothly and simply, no matter how complex it may seem when you first use it. A little time spent now in developing the skill will pay big dividends later in time saved.

How We Learn

Few people study efficiently. Most think of learning as a process of absorption, an automatic result of reading or listening. They do not know that learning is a science, based on well-defined principles and axioms. Regardless of occupation or ability, the person who uses these principles effectively in study has a tremendous advantage over others who ignore them.

We study for one reason: to learn. Yet most people "study" to cover an assignment, to read a specific number of pages, or to put in a certain amount of time. All these aims are unimportant in themselves. The real aim of study should be to achieve a certain learning outcome, to acquire a new proficiency, skill, or understanding—not to turn a specified number of pages. Let us first ask ourselves these questions:

What is Learning?

What can I expect from Learning?

Learning is acquiring new ways to do things or satisfy desires. It is the modification of behavior through practice, training, and experience. Notice the functional emphasis in this definition. We do not consider learning as the transmittal of facts from a book to the mind of the reader, or from one person to another. We do not consider that students are learning because facts are being stored in their minds. The expression "educated idiot" applies to the person whose mind is filled with isolated facts. The definition of **learning** implies much more than this. Students learn to the extent that they can function properly and efficiently in their general work situation and in their lives. They may acquire a great many facts, but unless they can use them in improving their adjustment to their work, the social order to which they live, and life in general, they have not **"LEARNED"** anything.

Efficient education emphasizes the functional aspect of learning. In the world of work or in society, people are evaluated on the basis of what they can do, not what they know. As far as you are concerned then, learning must enable you to do something more efficiently and effectively. You can seldom learn how to do things better without learning facts. The learning of facts is usually essential to improved performance on the job, but learning a fact does not guarantee such improvement. To be most useful, facts must be learned in relation to something that you may do, and in such a way that you may apply these facts in your work or in your social or cultural life.

Obviously real learning in a professional school is necessary because it results in improved efficiency on the job. The material you study in a professional school has been selected because it can help you do your work better as a member of the profession. If you fail to see how the material included in a particular lesson can help you, the error may be in your analysis of the assignment rather than in the material itself. The mass of material submitted for inclusion in a curriculum is critically examined by some planning agency, which works to eliminate whatever is not really pertinent. Do not lightly discard assigned material on the ground that it does not apply to you; instead consider possible jobs that you may be given later in your career and try to relate this material for your future use.

Factors In Learning

We have said that learning does not take place in some mysterious and inexplicable fashion; neither is it a passive process of absorption that operates automatically when you are exposed to material to be learned. Learning is an active process that takes place according to a number of well-defined rules and principles. In the following paragraphs we shall consider six factors that, if used properly, will assist learning and that, if used improperly, will prevent learning. These are:

1. will to learn
2. action
3. attention
4. organization
5. understanding
6. review

Will to Learn.
The will to learn results from having a definite objective and recognizing the need to achieve that objective. People are motivated to do a job when they know exactly what they are expected to do and realize why they must do it. The importance of a will to learn in effective learning can hardly be overemphasized. Contrast the amount of knowledge that you got from the average high school lecture with the amount that you got from a briefing on an important new job. You learned more from the job briefing, mainly because you were getting something that you were looking for and something that would

affect your future well-being. Here you see the two factors that operate to produce good motivation. To gain the benefit expected from good motivation in your work, you should do two things for each period of instruction: First determine clearly in your own mind what you must get from a period of study. Make your objectives definite. Don't say, "I must get an understanding of so-and-so." Determine exactly what you should bring away from the situation that you didn't have when you went into it. Second answer the question, "How can this material help me in my future work?" Remember: You are not motivated to study unless you can determine how the material will be of help to you. Always relate study material as closely as possible to the work that you may be expected to do in your career, and evaluate it in relation to some position or goal that you may fill.

Action.

We have said that learning is an active process, not passive absorption. If you were like dry soil, you could place yourself in situations where you could simply sit and be educated. But that is not possible. Your education, in the final analysis, depends entirely upon your participation in the learning situations that confront you. When you are faced with new ideas, facts, or principles you are in a "learning situation," and you learn as you react to, and participate in, that situation. Learning is in direct proportion to the amount of your reaction to a learning situation. When you listen to a lecture or read, it is easy to prop your feet on a chair, lean your head back, relax your mind and body, and let the flow of information come from the speaker to your ears, or from the book to your eyes. Unfortunately if only your ears or eyes are active, the information will stop no matter how active you are. Only if you actively seek to catch and use the information will it be transmitted to your brain.

Anything that you can do to generate definite mental action while listening or reading will help you to achieve effective learning. One device is note-taking. If you reword what the speaker or author is saying in order to take notes, you will be mentally reacting to what you hear or see, and you will be learning. Note-taking is one of the best devices for ensuring aggressive mental reaction to what your eyes and ears are taking in. Learning does not take place unless there is mental activity on the part of the listener or reader. You can follow a lecture by comparing the speaker's remarks with his outline, noting his elaboration of different points, and thinking of possible improvements that you could make to his presentation. This keeps you mentally alert, which is the essence of learning. Another technique for ensuring action is to ask yourself at the first of the period, "What should I get from this chapter or this lecture?" Formulate in your own mind several questions that you feel should be answered in the process of the discussion and look for the answers to those questions. This technique gives you something definite to accomplish as a result of your listening and reading, and keeps your mind, as well as your eyes or ears, active in the process of learning.

Attention.

The third factor in learning is attention, which means focusing the full power of your mind on the material that you wish to learn. When working with about 50 percent attention, you "take in" the material you hear or see, but it quickly fades from your mind and is never used. If you attention is between the halfway mark and total attention, you will be able to understand and remember the material you see or hear.

To concentrate effectively on learning, you should be motivated. You can develop a genuine interest or curiosity if you honestly try to relate the material to your present work or future career. Interest usually comes as a result of knowledge. If you can begin to learn something about a subject, you will find your interest will develop as your knowledge of it increases.

Mechanical factors, too, can help or hinder attention. First of all your physical surroundings should not compete with your work for your attention. It's a sure bet which will win when the contest for your attention is between principles of logic and pinups. Study in a room where there are as few distractions as possible. Remove maps showing you the way home, or souvenirs of a vacation, or pictures of friends and family. Take one thing at a time. Study when you are supposed to study; play when you are supposed to play.

Organization.

You cannot learn effectively simply by memorizing all the facts about a subject. Before you are able to use material that you have learned, you must understand its organization, that is, how the parts fit together to make a complete picture. Teachers have in mind a general pattern of information and ideas that they want you to learn. Unless you can recognize the general picture that teachers want to get across to you, you will be lost in details. You know that it is much easier to fit together the pieces of a jigsaw puzzle if you have first seen the whole picture. The same is true in a lecture or in a reading assignment. If you can get the author's central idea and his general "plan of attack," you will be able to follow more intelligently his individual ideas and items of information. If you know the objective of your listening or reading, you can better interpret each detail. This procedure is known as the "whole-to-part" method. First you get the general pattern of what you are to learn; then you get the details in your concentrated study. Studying reference outlines at the beginning of a course is an excellent way to get a general picture of what is to be accomplished in each period. Later we shall consider different ways of obtaining a preview of the author's organization of material and his objectives. You will find it profitable to spend a few moments before the class period scanning the outline that the lecturer has prepared. You can then follow the discussion more easily and understand more clearly the material presented. In short if you get a mental outline of the whole learning situation, you will be ready to learn more effectively the individual details as they come along. Details take on meaning as you see the relationship between them and other details, and between them and the situation as a whole. You must conscientiously try to tie in the details of the article or lecture with your predetermined picture of the subject.

Understanding.

The fifth factor in learning is understanding—getting the idea that the author or lecturer is trying to get across. You can do this by putting, in your own words, the author's or teacher's presentation or statement. When you read or listen to material, you get the organization that the teacher or author considered most logical in dealing with his subject—you get his organization. In order to put the material to best use, you must formulate in your mind the organization that makes most sense to you. This may or may not be the same as that used by the teacher or the author. You have had the experience of working on a problem, of groping blindly in the dark for a solution. Then suddenly like a flash of light, you get an insight into the whole problem. You recognize the governing principle and grasp the essential idea. In looking over your lecture or reading notes, do not stop when you have gone over the material. Keep working on it until you get the governing principle—the basic idea—as well as the individual facts in the situation. Only then will you be able to use it and remember it. The knowledge that you get from a course can be transferred to a work situation only to the extent that you comprehend the principles presented by the author or professor.

Review.

Few experiences are so vivid that we learn them in one trial. Generally speaking we must repeat any operation to make it our own. Material studied for an hour a day for four days, or even an hour a week for four weeks, will be remembered much better than material studied four hours one day and never reviewed. This is known as the "principle of distributed practice." You will find, in your own case, that some review will give you better comprehension and better memory than study concentrated at one time with no review.

Although repetition is essential to learning, repetition alone does not guarantee learning. You may go over material twenty-five times without really learning it. If repetition is to do any good, you must consider the principles; of *understanding, attention, action, organization,* and *will to learn*. Only if you practice all these principles will repetition produce learning. Repetition does not necessarily consist of rereading. Probably the most effective type of review does not include rereading, but mentally working to recall the written material, referring to it only occasionally to check and supplement your memory. Review by recall is real work, but it results in better learning and memory than does rereading. You will not become an efficient learner by reading the principles of learning. Proficiency in their use comes only through comprehension and application.

Remembering

Obviously learning has no value unless it is retained. You have the mental ability to remember as much as is necessary, provided you use that ability effectively. There are three essentials in the effective use of memory. The first is *intention to remember*. Say to yourself, "Here is something I must remember—something that I will keep because it is necessary for me to remember it." That and that alone will enable you to double the efficiency of your memory. Most so-called forgetfulness or absent-mindedness is not because of inability to remember, but simply a lack of effort. It is absurd to suppose that the professor who is a walking encyclopedia of technical knowledge cannot remember where he puts his pencil if he intends to remember that simple action. He fails to remember because he does not pay attention to what he is doing. He does not forget where he puts his pencil; he never really notices where he puts it in the first place. If you will make a conscious effort to file material in your mind for permanent reference, you will find that you can do a much better job of remembering than you thought possible.

The second essential to consider in remembering is *familiarity with material*. To put it simply: The more facts you can relate to a subject, the better you will remember that subject. For example if you know not only the name of a man but the names of the members of his family, his occupation, and his general physical characteristics, you will be more likely to remember that man's name than if you know nothing about him except that his name is Jack Smith. By gathering and organizing a group of facts that support each other and that facilitate recall by association, you will remember them much better than if you try to remember each separately. You will be interested to note that this is another use of the factor of organization.

The third essential in remembering is *review*. You have to be reminded of things occasionally if you are to remember them. After repeated reminders, the memory does not "fade out" as quickly or as completely. Review is simply the repetition of material, spaced at times when you particularly need to remember that material. Repetition is as essential to effective learning as review is to memory.

Study Aids

In the previous chapter we talked about some of the psychological principles to observe in learning. Now let's consider the tools that can help you apply those principles. The objective of this section, then, is to promote the effective use of learning tools.

Underlining.
When you are reading in your own book and want to review the material easily and efficiently, underlining is a convenient device. If you will watch closely for the sentences or phrases carrying the real ideas of the material and underline them, you will not have to plough through detail when you review. Furthermore you are reacting energetically—comprehending the author's organization and ideas—when you identify the key sentences in an article. This is a quick, easy way to focus your attention later in review.

Note-taking.
After you have listened to a class lecture or discussion, the only way to review what was said is to refer to the notes you took during that period. You must take systematic, meaningful, and understandable notes if you are to review effectively, using the factor of repetition which we have discussed previously. In reading you can always go back to the material and

reread it without taking notes. However this requires much time and effort, especially if the material is in a library book or in some other source not immediately at hand. The minutes you spend taking notes as you read will be saved many times over when you review for tests. You are spared the trouble of searching out the original material for review and rereading it, page by page.

Five major rules should be observed in note-taking. First, look for the ideas of the speaker or writer, but express them in your own words. To go back to our principle of understanding, as you listen to a lecture or as you read an article, ask yourself: What is the idea underlying these words? Of course you should note the facts you hear or read, but look a little further to see if the speaker or writer uses these facts to present a principle or idea. When you identify an idea or principle, write it down in your own words. A device that will help you do this in reading is the preview step in our Reconnoiter-Read-Recall system of study. If the material is to be read, scan it to get a general picture of the whole article. Then as you read through it and take notes, you will see how the various parts tie together, and you will understand the organization that is followed. Before listening to an important lecture, look over some library references dealing with the subject. Read them to get some idea of what the lecturer may cover in his discussion. Preparing your ordinary school assignment will often give you this background information. In short get a picture of the material to be covered in the lecture period. If you already know how the parts fit together, you will be able to organize your notes intelligently as you take them during the lecture.

You have learned that note-taking is not a mechanical job of writing down the words you hear. It is a quick, thoughtful analysis of statements. You note their meaning without attempting to record every word. Mastering the art of catching a speaker's or author's important ideas and recording them in your own words is probably the most valuable aid to effective study and efficient learning that can be developed.

The second rule to observe in note-taking is to be brief. A great many people begin with the best of intentions to take notes on a lecture but soon give up in disgust. They say, "By the time I write down one thing he has said, I have missed the next three. There is no way to go back and get them. What's the percentage in that?" The answer is to be discriminating in your note-taking. Don't try to record everything that is said, but listen attentively and take notes on anything that gives promise of being important. Between important points every good speaker allows space, which he fills in with illustrations and discussion. In this way he gives his listeners time to "digest" one important point before he proceeds to another.

Third, record information rather than topics. Some students carefully list topic headings but fail to fill in necessary information about the topics. When listening to a lecture about the Antarctic, for example, it is easy to write under the topic "definition," "characteristics," "temperature," but it contains no information. Be sure your notes are not just a list of headings or topics, without the real meat. Obviously you will not make this mistake if you record the speaker's ideas instead of topical words or phrases.

Fourth, organize your notes. Notes are of little value if they are thrown together helter-skelter, without showing how a major topic is broken down into subtopics or when one topic is dropped and another begun. In reviewing such notes, you see a mass of data without any apparent connection. Follow the speaker's pattern of thought and make clear in your notes the organization of this material. Under each main point, indent to show the various subpoints. Indicate where a topic is changed or where it is broken down into subtopics. To ensure that your notes make sense, reorganize them soon after you take them. You should try to do this in the evening after the class or lecture or after your reading; otherwise after a few days you probably will not be able to make sense of your rough notes. Rework them to make them usable later. This is good review that will save you time in studying for tests.

All your notes on one topic should be kept together. Reserve a section of your notebook for each topic, and keep your notes separated according to topic.

Fifth, take notes constantly. This is not intended to contradict the rule of brevity, but many beginners in note-taking wait for the speaker to say something really inspiring and notable before making a note. This is not a good practice. Some speakers and authors organize their material so that major points are easily recognizable. In many instances, however, it is only in looking back that the audience or reader can identify an important fact or idea. Take notes steadily. Be brief in taking them, that is, use only necessary words, but take notes steadily. Sometimes statements that seem trivial when you hear or read them later assume importance when you consider them together.

Outlining.

Another tool of study is the outline. Notes taken in a lecture or in reading represent a skeleton of the ideas presented by the professor or author. The pattern or organization of these ideas is logical and clear to the professional or author, and with study it becomes logical and clear to you. However this organization is not necessarily the same that you would use with that particular material. Change the organization of your notes, if by doing so you can make it more logical and practical for your purposes. Fill in any abbreviations and gaps that you remember. Systematize your notes and work out the imperfections of organization and expression.

When you have reorganized your notes, you have made your own outline, which presents the material in a form that is most meaningful to you and most valuable for review for future reference. Notes are good for review in spite of these disadvantages: they follow the author's ideas rather than your own, and they are filled with abbreviations and crudities of expression that you use in quick rephrasing of ideas. When you have outlined your notes, these disadvantages are eliminated. Further you gain from having carefully reviewed your material in the process of outlining. You now have a clear, concise picture of the material you listened to or read.

The use of outlines for review has an important place in any student's study program. An outline permits quick self-examination of a subject. A glance at outline topic headings reminds you of a specific area that you have studied. Without referring again to the outline, ask yourself, "What comes under this topic heading?" If you can reconstruct the material that should appear under the heading, you know that area and topic well enough to proceed to another subject. However if you are not sure that you know the topic, the subtopics of your outline will show whether you have omitted anything and will give you additional information.

Notes are valuable in review work because they offer (1) a concise and easily grasped statement of the topic; (2) a method of self-examination to determine your inadequate areas; (3) a checklist to determine whether you covered all areas in your mental recapitulation; and (4) a ready source of additional information when you cannot remember all the necessary facts about the topic heading.

Summarizing.

The fourth learning tool is summarizing. The summary is a brief statement—sometimes a sentence, sometimes a paragraph—that gives the essential elements of the material covered in an article, class presentation, or lecture. Summarizing condenses the ideas of the writer and the facts presented by the teacher. The summary is a valuable learning aid when used with general, nontechnical material that has been fully explained and discussed. In the case of highly complex and technical material, the summary is not adequate; instead notes and outlines are needed. When comparatively few ideas are presented and each idea is discussed at considerable length, you may summarize the article or lecture by briefly stating and explaining the main ideas.

To understand is difficult;
once one understands, action is easy.

Listening, the supreme act of caring.

Listen. When I ask you to listen to me and you start
giving advice, you have not done what I asked.
When I ask you to listen to me and you begin to tell
me why I shouldn't feel that way, you are trampling on my feelings.
When I ask you to listen to me and you have to do something
to solve my problem, you have failed me.
Listen! All I asked was that you not talk, just listen.
Advice is cheap. For fifty cents you can get
both Dear Abby and Bill Graham in the same paper.
And I can do that for myself. I am not helpless. Maybe
discouraged and faltering, but not helpless.
When you do something for me that I can do and need to do
for myself, you contribute to my fear and my weakness.
But when you accept as a simple fact that I do feel what I
feel no matter how irrational, then I can quit trying to
convince you and can get about the business of understanding
what's behind this irrational feeling.
And when that's clear, the answers are obvious and I don't need advice.
Irrational feelings make sense when we understand what's behind them.
So please. Listen and just hear me; and if you want to talk
wait a minute for your turn, and I will listen to you.

Author unknown

57

Listening.

Another learning tool is listening. In school probably more of your learning time is spent in listening than in any other way except reading. All the principles of the learning process, discussed in the previous chapter, also apply to listening. To listen effectively you must have a will to learn. You will not pay close attention to a lecturer's or a professor's points unless you really want to learn about the subject. You must react. You cannot sit relaxed in body and mind and expect the professor's or teacher's points to impress themselves on your brain. You have to be alert to learn. You may relax physically if, at the same time, your mind reacts with total attention to everything the teacher is saying. Listening must be a thoroughly active process to be effective.

The necessity for attention is implied in our discussion of reaction. If you are to listen effectively and understand, you must give your individual attention to the teacher. "Listening with your ears" is a common method of sitting through a class, but you will not learn and retain subject matter unless your whole mind is focused on what you hear. Giving half attention to what is to be learned is a waste of time. Remember this when you are listening: See that your concentration is on the important thing—the idea that the speaker is presenting and its possible use to you. Some listeners are distracted by the speaker's mannerisms or attitude or by other trivia. Of course a good speaker tries not to irritate his audience, but the good listener can ignore such distractions and concentrate on the subject instead.

Organization.

Organization, as a principle of learning, is important in listening. Watch constantly for the speaker's organization of the subject. An understanding of the material studied is essential if it is to be used and retained. You must also listen with the idea of getting the key points presented by the teacher.

Review.

The final principle in listening to learn is review. As noted earlier the only way to review lecture material is to use the reference outline supplemented by your notes. However you should bear in mind that repetition is as necessary here as in any other type of material. Suppose that you observe the principle of learning while you listen to a lecture. By what means can you increase your memory of the material presented? First through intention to remember; second through familiarity with the material involved (which includes grouping of related ideas and building a knowledge of the material connected with the important points); and third through review of notes. Remember: The key to effective listening is reacting aggressively to what you hear, rather than passively accepting it.

Studying at a Definite Time and Place.

Now let's consider some practical suggestions for arranging your study schedule—a time-budgeting plan. First of all each day, set aside a few minutes or an hour, as soon as possible after class, to review the material covered in the class periods. A large portion of what is ultimately lost is forgotten within twenty-four hours after being heard or read for the first time. If you review, at the end of your regular school day (or during any part of the day that is free), that day's material—before it can fade from your mind, your memory of the material will be stepped up tremendously. Obviously it is easier to review and retain familiar material than to relearn material that you have forgotten.

Second, set aside a regular time for your other study, that is, your study in addition to your review. If you can set aside the same time each day and study at that time to minimize the risk of letting the time slip by without having studied. We have all been guilty of intending to do a certain job but failing to get around to it until it is too late. If you establish a routine of studying at a certain time each day and schedule nothing else for that time, it is unlikely that you will miss your study because of poor management of time.

Third, have a definite place for studying. This doesn't mean that you can't study anywhere else. It does mean that whenever you have to study seriously, you should try to study in this particular place. Since the importance of avoiding distractions has already been discussed, we shall review only briefly the characteristics of a good place to study—where conversation, the activities of friends, interesting noises, or reminders of things more pleasant than study do not compete with your work for your attention. Your desk should face a wall and have nothing on it except your work materials. Your chair may have a soft cushion but should not be luxurious enough to encourage you to take a nap or go to sleep.

Habit is a study aid. If you get in the habit of going to a certain place at a certain time to study, you will find that you are beginning to concentrate more easily. You lose time in warming up to your subject because you subconsciously assume the proper frame of mind for study when you enter that particular place at the regular time. When this becomes a habit you have made real progress, because then you go through your study routine with less effort. You will find not only that you get started more easily but also that you study more effectively. You have substituted habit for willpower.

One student, anxious to force himself into a study routine that he knew would be difficult for him, hit on the idea of arranging with his landlady to let him out of his apartment at seven o'clock each morning. Each evening he would lock himself in, shove the key under the door, and work without distractions or interruptions. You will probably not care to follow this heroic example, but the student was able to pull himself out of the academic doldrums. Of course this experiment carried to the ultimate degree the policy of a definite time and place for study!

Reading at a Faster Rate.

A great many people feel that they are handicapped in their study because of their low rate of reading. Some merely bemoan their hard luck in being slow readers, and others try to learn to read faster. Those who try will find that they can step up their reading rate with very little trouble and without sacrificing comprehension.

There are commercial reading courses that report gains of 35 percent to 200 percent in reading speed, in as little as twenty hours of laboratory time distributed over six or eight weeks. Most reading improvement courses enable the average person to read at least a third faster and to remember as much of what he reads as before the course. What is not generally known, however, is that a determined student, willing to make a real effort, can achieve excellent results in improving his reading rate without any outside help at all.

In an attempt to improve reading speed, we should first recognize one important fact: Most of us do not read as fast as we can, or even as fast as we can comprehend. Just as we do not usually walk as fast as we can but choose instead a gait that is easy and restful, in the same way we read at a pace that is easy rather than efficient. Because this is true, the average student can increase his rate of reading from one-fifth to one-third, simply by sitting up alertly, concentrating on the material to be read, and pushing along as fast as he can. We have all read faster many times when we were eager to learn the contents of an important message. The laboratory reading course is designed to make this pattern of reading a habit. Ingenious mechanical devices can encourage you to speed up your reading and to keep it fast, but you can do about as well in your own room if you work at it and exert your willpower. It works!

Choose one of your assignments and time yourself as you read five pages at your usual rate. The next day take another five pages and see how fast you can drive yourself through and still comprehend what you are reading. Force your eyes to take in a big gulp of a line and to move rapidly from one gulp to the next, instead of taking leisurely sips. At the same time, force your mind to dig away at the subject, with the idea of taking in everything that the author is saying. Reading faster requires teamwork between your body and your brain. Your eyes and your whole body posture must be geared to intensive physical reaction. Your mind has to work steadily to catch the material as fast as it is covered, rather than passively absorbing it. Even with the first trial, you will find that you are reading faster than in the past, without sacrificing comprehension and memory.

Record your time for the second day's reading and check your improvement. Next day repeat the process, still timing yourself and note your improvement. About the fourth or fifth day, apply the same method to another of your reading subjects. Check yourself occasionally to see if your mind is taking in what your eyes are covering. You will be surprised at the difference this makes in how much you remember. As a matter of fact, most people find that they remember more after improving their reading rate by 30 percent. This is true because under their old method of study, their minds were loafing even more than their eyes.

The gains that you make in reading speed (and perhaps in comprehension as well) are likely to be both quick and spectacular when you start the time-comparison routine we just described. The important thing, however, is to continue this vigorous approach to reading until it becomes a habit. You can easily pick up reading speed through conscious effort alone, but unless you practice regularly and over a long enough period of time, you will tend to fall back into your old leisurely habits. At this point the reading laboratory has its greatest advantage: The conditions strongly motivate you to read at your fastest possible rate, without having to depend on willpower to force your maximum effort. In the laboratory you keep going at this pace until you become accustomed to it, until it becomes your normal rate of reading. You have then formed the habit of speed reading. Furthermore as you continue to exercise this speed-up approach to reading, your rate will increase and tend to become permanent.

Perhaps you don't want to read any faster; perhaps you prefer a leisurely pace. If you have time to get what you want from your reading without speeding up, you probably have no good reason why you should try to improve your rate. However if you feel that you need to read faster, you can. You can improve your reading rate within a short time if you are willing to force yourself a little to read as fast as you can in most of your reading.

Some people prefer to use novels or other recreational reading to develop their speed, and apply their increased speed to their assignments only after it has become a habit. If you don't want to improve your reading rate while studying, you may still be able to improve in your recreational reading. And if you'd rather spend dollars than willpower to improve your reading speed, look around for a reading laboratory!

A final tip on fast reading: Some types of materials can be read faster than others. Technical, complex material cannot be read as quickly and effectively as simple, recreational material. Efficient reading requires that you vary your speed of reading based on the difficulty of the material and your purpose—amusement, comprehension, general knowledge, and other materials. You can naturally do this. Efficient reading will take care of itself if you force your eyes to go just as fast as you can, but no faster than you can force your brain to take in the material covered.

Proceeding from the Whole to Details.

When you go to work on a topic, get a picture of the whole topic—its general pattern and framework, and the author's objectives and plan of organization. After doing this proceed to work for the individual details.

Reinforcing Memory.

Most forgetting takes place within a short time after you stop studying; then it gradually slows down. Arrange your first review to take place within a few hours after the material is studied; the second, about a week later; and the final review, about three weeks later. You will find that distribution of practice is the most useful review schedule because it ensures retention of the material that you have studied and are reviewing. Perhaps you won't have time to use this system in reviewing all your study material, but if you will carefully select the material that is especially important for you to remember and review it according to this schedule, you will probably retain as much of it as you need.

Chapter VI
Andragogy—The Art and Science of Helping Adults Learn

The great thing about education
is that it should remain unfinished.

Donald Kennedy, President, Stanford University

The Seven Ages of Man

All the world's a stage.
And all the men and women merely players.
They have their exits and their entrances.
And one man in his time plays many parts.
His acts being seven ages. At first, the infant,
Mewing and puking in the nurse's arms.
Then the whining schoolboy, with his satchel
And shining morning face, creeping like a snail
Unwillingly to school. And then the lover,
Sighing like a furnace, with a woeful ballad
Made to his mistress' eyebrow. Then a soldier,

Full of strange oaths and bearded like the pard,
Jealous in honour, sudden and quick in quarrel,
Seeking the bubbly reputation
Even in the cannon's mouth. And then the justice,
In fair round belly with good capon lin'd,
With eyes severe and beard of formal cut,
Full of wise saws and modern instances;
And so he plays his part. The sixth age shifts
Into the lean and slipper'd pantaloon,
With spectacles on nose and pouch on side;
His youthful hose, well sav'd, a world too wide
For his shrunk shank, and his big manly voice,
Turning again toward childish trebel, pipes
And whistles in his sound. Last scene of all,
That ends this strange eventful history,
Is second childishness and mere oblivion,
Sans teeth, sans eyes, sans taste, sans everything.[*]

[*]Shakespeare, *As You Like It*, II, vii

*Treat people as if they were what they ought
to be and you help them to become what they
are capable of being.*

Goethe

No education or training concept can be complete without some comment and discussion of andragogy, that is, adult learning, development, education,[*] and training. First of all there is a distinct difference between the adult's and the traditional student's exposure to learning. The traditional concept, labeled *pedagogy*, does not functionally apply in all its phases to andragogy. Second the growth rate in the number of adults now undergoing educational studies and training continues to increase, to the point where it is becoming the largest group of learners. In experimenting over the years, differences have been noted in organization of learning experiences, selection of methods, styles, and materials, to say nothing of student involvement, that are appropriate for learners in different stages of age development and under different environments and conditions. Training and education must be geared to specific development tasks that people face at different stages of their lives. Normally the new comer in the learning process *gains* information; the adult *uses* information.

Teachers must be aware of the three distinct groups that they may be faced with, depending on where learning is taking place and who is being exposed to learning. Traditionally the major group is categorized as *pedagogy*. Most of us consider pedagogy appropriate for the education and training of children, with some aspects being applicable to adolescents and adults.

The second group, commonly called adolescents, can be categorized as *adolegogy*. This group cannot be realistically compared to a child or an adult for learning purposes. A lot of instruction falls on deaf ears during this stage, and it is an age that is tough on the student and the teacher. It is a difficult stage in life, one with no cure, but a challenging one, nevertheless, to the teacher. Little has been written to cope with the challenge of this development stage. An effective cure may be found in the future.

The third group is now commonly called *andragogy*—without a doubt the fastest-growing development stage of the three groups. Thus this group must be discussed at length.

We have learned through the years that pedagogy is teacher-centered. The teacher is doing most of the preparation, setting up the environment, and getting the attention of the student, which includes rewards and punishment. Andragogy, however, is learner-centered, which must be tailored to the immediate needs and desires of the student, and must include, by selection, the styles of adult learning. In many cases it involves a sensitive confrontation. The interest for learning is

[*]Adult education may be defined as "organized learning to meet the unique needs of persons beyond the compulsory school age who have terminated or interrupted their formal schooling."

already there. In most cases the adult is eager to observe and absorb. The student's experience, desire, and ambition are some of the characteristics common to andragogy.

No theory fully explains how adults learn. Ron Zemke, research editor of *Training*, and consultant, and Susan Zemke, a human resources officer responsible for supervisory and management training, First Bank System, Minneapolis, Minnesota, have done extensive research in adult learning. Ron and Susan have come up with some interesting and very suggestive information about the adult learning process. They have listed thirty points that support reliable knowledge about adult learning. They contend that, historically, societies have equated youth with the ability to acquire information insatiably and age with the ability to use information wisely. In other words wisdom is a separate intellectual function that develops with age. This point can certainly cause curriculum development implications. One single curriculum using one concept certainly cannot serve both functions. Teachers who are used to traditional pedagogical concepts in their teachings must be well aware of some of these implications when faced with an adult or an adult group.

Here, then, are Ron and Susan Zemke's important findings in the process of adult learning.[*] Ron and Susan state that there are thirty points that lend themselves to three basic divisions. First the three divisions, followed by the thirty points.

- Things we know about adult learners and their motivation
- Things we know about designing curriculum for adults
- Things we know about working with adults in the classroom

1. Adults seek learning experiences to cope with specific life-change events. Getting married or divorced, finding a new job, getting a promotion, being fired, retiring, losing a loved one, and moving to a new city are examples.
2. The more life-change events adults encounter, the more likely they are to seek learning opportunities. Just as stress increases as life-change events accumulate, the motivation to cope with change through engagement in a learning experience increases. Since the people who most frequently seek learning opportunities are

[*]Reprinted with permission from the June 1981 issue of *Training*, The Magazine of Human Resources Development. Copyright 1981, Lakewood Publications, Minneapolis.

people who have the most overall years of education, it is reasonable to guess that for many of us learning is a coping response to significant change.

3. The learning experiences adults seek on their own are directly related—at least in their own perception—to the life-change events that triggered the seeking. Therefore if 80 percent of the change being encountered is work-related, then 80 percent of the learning experiences sought should be work-related.

4. Adults are generally willing to engage in learning experiences before, after, or even during the actual life-change event. Once convinced that the change is a certainty, adults will engage in any learning that promises to help them cope with the transition.

5. Although adults have been found to engage in learning for a variety of reasons—job advancement, pleasure, love of learning, and so on—it is equally true that for most adults learning is not its own reward. Adults who are motivated to seek a learning experience do so 80 percent-90 percent of the time because they have a use for the knowledge or skill being sought. Learning is a means to an end, not an end in itself.

6. Increasing or maintaining self-esteem and pleasure are strong secondary motivators for engaging in learning experiences. Having a new skill or extending and enriching current knowledge can do both, depending on the individual's personal perceptions.

    The major contributors to what we know about adult motivation to learn have been Allen Tough, Carol Aslanian, Henry Brickell, Kjell Rubenson, and Harry L. Miller. One implication of their findings for the trainer is that there seem to be "teachable moments" in the lives of adults. These moments affect the planning and scheduling of training. As a recent study by the management development group of one large manufacturer concluded, "Newly promoted supervisors and managers must receive training as nearly concurrent with promotions and changes in responsibilities as possible. The longer such training is delayed, the less impact it appears to have on actual job performance."

7. Adult learners tend to be less interested in survey courses. They tend to prefer single-concept, single-theory courses that focus heavily on the application of the concept to relevant problems. This tendency increases with age.

8. Adults need to be able to integrate new ideas with what they already know if they are going to keep—and use—the new information.

9. Information that conflicts sharply with what is already held to be true, and thus forces a reevaluation of the old material, is integrated more slowly.
10. Information that has little "conceptual overlap" with what is already known is acquired slowly.
11. Fast-paced, complex, or unusual learning tasks interfere with learning the concepts or data that they are intended to teach or illustrate.
12. Adults tend to compensate for being slower in some psychomotor learning tasks by being more accurate and making fewer trial-and-error ventures.
13. Adults tend to take errors personally and are more likely to let them affect self-esteem. Therefore they tend to apply tried-and-true solutions and take fewer risks. Adults even misinterpret feedback and "mistake" errors for positive confirmation.
14. The curriculum designer must know whether the concepts and ideas will be in concert or in conflict with learner and organizational values. As trainers at AT&T have learned, moving from a service to a sales philosophy requires more than a change in words and titles. People need to change their thinking and their values.
15. Programs should be designed to accept viewpoints from people in different life stages and with different value "sets."
16. A concept needs to be "anchored" or explained from more than one value set and appeal to more than one developmental life stage.
17. Adults prefer self-directed and self-designed learning projects 7-to-1 over group-learning experiences led by a professional. Furthermore the adult learner often selects more than one medium for the design. Reading and talking to a qualified peer are frequently cited as good resources. The desire to control pace and start/stop time strongly affect the self-directed preference.
18. Nonhuman media such as books, programmed instruction, and television have become popular in recent years. One piece of research found them to be very influential in the way adults plan self-directed learning projects.
19. Regardless of media straightforward how-to is the preferred content orientation. As many as 80 percent of the adults in one study cited the need for applications and how-to information as the primary motivation

for undertaking a learning project.

20. Self-direction does not mean isolation. In fact studies of self-directed learning show self-directed projects involve an average of ten other people as resources, guides, encouragers, and the like. The incompetence or inadequacy of these same people is often rated as a primary frustration. Even for the self-professed, self-directed learner, lectures and short seminars get positive ratings, especially when these events give the learner face-to-face, one-on-one access to an expert.

21. The learning environment must be physically and psychologically comfortable. Adults report that long lectures, periods of interminable sitting, and the absence of practice opportunities are high on the irritation scale.

22. Adults have something real to lose in a classroom situation. Self-esteem and ego are on the line when they are asked to risk trying a new behavior in front of peers and cohorts. Bad experiences in traditional education, feelings about authority, and the preoccupation with events outside the classroom all effect in-class experience. These and other influential factors are carried into class with the learners, as surely as are their gold Cross pens and lined yellow pads.

23. Adults have expectations, and it is critical to take time to clarify and articulate all expectations before getting into content. Both trainees and the instructor need to state their expectations. When they are at variance, the problem should be acknowledged and a resolution negotiated. In any case instructors can assume responsibility only for their own expectations, not for that of trainees.

24. Adults bring a great deal of life experience into the classroom—an invaluable asset to be acknowledged, tapped, and used. Adults can learn well—and much—from dialogue with respected peers.

25. Instructors who have a tendency to hold forth rather than facilitate can hold that tendency in check—or compensate for it—by concentrating on the use of open-ended questions to elicit relevant trainee knowledge and experience.

26. New knowledge has to be integrated with previous knowledge; that means active learner participation. Since only the learners can tell us how the new fits or fails to fit with the old, we have to ask them. Just as the learner is dependent on us for feedback on skill practice, we are dependent on the learner for feedback about our curriculum and in-class performance.

27. The key to the instructor role is control. The instructor must balance the presentation of new material, debate and discussion, sharing of relevant trainee experiences, and the clock. Ironically we seem best able to establish control when we risk giving it up. When we shelve our egos and stifle the tendency to be threatened by challenge to our plans and methods, we gain the kind of facilitative control we seem to need to effect adult learning.

28. The instructor has to protect minority opinion, keep disagreements civil and unheated, make connections between various opinions and ideas, and keep reminding the group of the variety of potential solutions to the problem. Just as in good problem-solving meeting, the instructor is less advocate than orchestrator.

29. Integration of new knowledge and skill requires transition time and focused effort. Working on applications to specific back-on-the-job problems helps with the transfer. Action plans, accountability strategies, and follow-up after training all increase the likelihood of that transfer. Involving the trainees' supervisors in pre-/post-course activities helps with both in-class focus and transfer.

30. Learning and teaching theories function better as a resource than as a Rosetta stone. The four currently influential theories—humanistic, behavioral, cognitive, and developmental—all offer valuable guidance when matched with an appropriate learning task. A skill-training task can draw much from the behavioral approach, for example, while personal growth-centered subjects seem to draw gainfully from humanistic concepts. The trainer of adults needs to take an eclectic rather than a single theory-based approach to developing strategies and procedures.

Adult Learning Characteristics

- Adults seek and engage in learning when they face a life-change challenge of some sort.
- In adult learning the responsibility for learning is placed on the learner, not on the instructor.
- Only a very small percentage of adult learning is degree or certificate-directed.
- Adults are self-motivated, to a large extent.
- Adults are project-information oriented.

- Adult goals are partially or totally predetermined.
- Adults arrive at a learning situation with ample previous experience and know-how.
- Adults have different tastes and convictions about learning.
- Adults have a great variety of reasons and goals for learning.
- Adults must be assured that what they are learning meets with their own needs.
- All adults have their own style or styles of learning. Select the style or styles that best fit the adult.

Matching Your Teaching or Training Methodology to Styles of Learning

You must be able to recognize or determine your adult students' styles of learning. You must also be prepared to match their styles of learning to your teaching or training designs. This is a must, if you wish to be successful in your teaching or training sessions. Keep in mind that styles of learning differ among adult students.

What are we talking about when we refer to styles of learning? Styles of learning are nothing more than expectations from your adult students as to how instruction best fits their concept of learning—how they feel and sense your instruction in order to perceive your subject matter. Adult students must feel comfortable with your instruction methodology if they are to learn. Adult students think, sense, and react to instruction quite different from students in the young and adolescent stages. The result of this reaction is their reflection on learning.

How can you determine their styles of learning? There are several ways. You may want to consider using a questionnaire. You may want to ask questions of the students. One of the best indicators of your adult students' thoughts in their style or styles of learning is their reaction after your teaching or training session. It will not take the students long to react, and react they will.

Your own plan to select the training methodology to match your adult students' styles of learning will not only set the pace for a comfortable and satisfying learning situation, but you will soon find out that your students will be more receptive if your teaching plan reflects their learning expectations. Adult students tend to be more critical of your instruction. These critiques are normally based on solid, first-hand experiences or already acquired talents. You cannot overlook these critiques because they may well make or break your well-prepared teaching session. For the most part these critiques are seriously presented, and most of them must be considered seriously. Your adult students may prefer one or more of the following styles of learning.

Adult Students' Styles of Learning

THINKING

LOGICAL

SENSING

FEELING

INTUITING

WATCHING

DOING

ENTHUSIASTIC

IMAGINATIVE

PRACTICAL

Chapter VII
Cultural Differences and
Their Impact on Learning

What you do not use yourself
do not give to others, for example, advice.

Winston Churchill

If only we knew what we were
about, perhaps we could get
about it better.

Abraham Lincoln

It will be the purpose of this chapter of material to cover how and in what ways having an international "audience," or a non-English-speaking group can affect the learning process. The effective transfer of knowledge is an art and a skill, and is sufficiently difficult when the teacher's and the students' cultural background is the same. If teachers/instructors are faced with the difficulty of instructing international students at home or indigenous students when abroad, then the issues are compounded. Effective teaching is certainly possible, indeed sometimes even more enjoyable because teachers/instructors, if alert, will be gaining invaluable insights about their students if in tune with them. Instructors/teachers should be prepared to focus on the following challenges:

YOUR EXPECTATIONS—Cultural Pluralism
THEIR EXPECTATIONS—CULTURAL PLURALISM
TEACHING STRATEGIES
PSYCHOLOGICAL AND EMOTIONAL NEEDS
UNIVERSAL SCHOLARLY REQUIREMENTS
OVERSEASMANSHIP
STEREOTYPES
SPEECH—YOURS, NOT THE STUDENTS'
ATTITUDE—YOURS AND THEIRS

Teachers'/instructors' schoolroom experience establishes what they expect from their students. Even new teachers enter the classroom with a particular mind-set, standards, or expectations. The litany might run something like this:

BE ON TIME
TURN IN PROJECTS OR HOMEWORK PROMPTLY
ATTEND CLASS REGULARLY
PARTICIPATE ACTIVELY IN CLASS
INTERACT WITH TEACHER
DO NOT CHEAT
WORK TOGETHER

Expectations—Cultural Pluralism

With international students, working abroad or at home, flexibility is the key to sanity and survival. Teachers do not need to lower academic or training standards, but often must use alternative approaches to the instructional process. Much of our cultural "baggage" involves "time"; other societies simply do not place the same premium on schedules and timetables.

Most anthropologists point to time as a distinct Western preoccupation. The Saudis[*] believe that "time" is life. They have a proverb: "Time is only the air we breathe." My own experience in working with Saudis for a number of years coincides with this proverb. So being on time for a session, following a structured schedule for assignments, or even attending class at all are frequently irrelevant to the international student.

Some societies place a teacher on a pedestal and to question or disagree with a teacher would be the height of rudeness. To us disagreeing with a teacher/instructor is commonplace. Facing a silent class can be unnerving, unless there is a reason for the lack of response. The teacher with international students must not necessarily expect the informal, back and forth type of dialogue common in our classroom. Finally doing one's own work is a must!

Our ethnic fosters independent thinking and action. Societies that run themselves through consensus produce students who are committee workers or quality-circle members. Taking the initiative is certainly a foreign concept. Working together may have religious and/or societal roots. Thus a student who assists his classmate with test answers views the action as helping his brother, as one of his country's basic beliefs. The instructor must not stigmatize the student with the label of "cheater" or view that student as "bad." Instead find an alternative approach to testing.

Teaching Strategies

After becoming aware of the differences between expectations and what occurs in the classroom, teachers/instructors can modify their teaching strategies accordingly. They can introduce their "way" if desired, which is probably not a bad idea if the students intend to further training/education abroad. Teaching strategies should fit the specific class.

The expectations that foreign students have of their learning experience may vary, according to the reasons they are in school or training. Some possibilities include (1) International students may be taking some form of job-related training to enhance on-the-job skills in their own country. (2) International students are taking undergraduate or graduate studies. (3) International students, with degree in hand, are abroad for additional, usually technical, instruction.

After mentally weeding out those students who are in the classroom because they have to be there and are not

[*]Saudi Arabians

especially interested in the curriculum, instructors/teachers should know that international students are often trying to achieve the very highest grade. The teacher's experience will usually be that student expectations do not go hand in hand with student performance; this trait is obviously not the exclusive province of international students!

Frequently on government scholarships, foreign students who find themselves in the classroom abroad feel incredible pressure to perform. In fact doing poorly in a training course or in college can have major ramifications in the students' lives. They may find their job is in jeopardy, their family may lose status in the community, or they may lose financial support in the event of a poor scholastic showing. To do well in the training is essential, and the consequences dire should students turn in a poor performance and not meet their expectations.

Psychological and Emotional Needs

With these thoughts in mind, instructors/teachers need to be alert to the psychological and emotional needs of the international student and to allow for a period of adjustment as the student becomes accustomed to the "new" training environment. The desire to do well in the course is often hindered by language barriers, different cultural expectations, a different writing system, and other cultural experiences. *Psychologically* the student will be on shaky ground, and the teacher can expect intense stress, emotionally and physically. Headaches, high blood pressure, and stomach disorders can result from the emotional stress, and frequently there is a high rate of absenteeism as a consequence. In most cases the trainees are not "goldbricking," but are truly ill. Taking the stress out of this highly charged situation, that is, the classroom experience, is incumbent upon instructors/teachers if they are to achieve the training goal. Flexibility, understanding, and empathy are the keys to success.

Universal Scholarly Requirements

After teachers/instructors find themselves in a training/educational mode with these students, they will immediately recognize that there is no such thing as universality in scholarly requirements or methods. As an example the American emphasis on individual research and experimentation is not a part of "scholarship" in many countries. If instructors/teachers assign a research project, it will probably be necessary to teach techniques of using the library, footnoting, and preparing a bibliography. The majority of countries where I have been posted do not have libraries. Other cultures put a premium on the student being able to repeat, by rote, lectures or text material, so while summaries may present no problem, syntheses and forming independent conclusions based on research data may. Also the tendency to copy word-for-word crops up in student writing—whether on a test, in writing assignments, or in research. Trainees may think they have successfully completed the task by stringing together one lengthy quotation after the other in doing research. Teaching the technique of paraphrasing is essential here. Not only are instructors/teachers responsible for the subject matter to be imparted, but they may find need to instruct students in the strategies to approach the subject and to complete assigned tasks.

Overseasmanship

In my extensive experience living and working with students abroad, some twenty-four years, I have long ago come to the conclusion that what I once considered "cultural imperialism" by the United States is neither that nor propaganda. Instead our efforts abroad are an essential contribution to the task of building an international community of scholars, teachers, and trainers in all nations, regardless of the design or type of "curtain" that may separate any two countries. I have long ago outgrown the concept that only U.S.A. made brands are the best. I have known for many years, however, that the United States possesses the top thinkers, best research laboratories, and best technological know-how, and that many countries are benefiting from this cultural and technological wealth today.

In the past years while living abroad, I have experienced effects of wars, revolutions, and martial law in several countries, including a first-hand revolution in Iran. These events create a frightening intellectual and psychological climate, even though in most cases they pose little or no danger to most Americans. I may also add that these events come under a totally different heading. I call these events "political tragedies."

I bring these events to your attention because in spite of some very far-reaching programs, such as the Fulbright Plan, which has sponsored distinguished researchers and scholars to some 120 countries for years, and countless hundreds of American firms who are training indigenous personnel in thousands of technological and nontechnological fields, you can expect negative repercussions occasionally. I have witnessed these repercussions attacking our professional and intellectual freedoms from time to time. These experiences can be expected and are very much a part of cultural implications.

Back home you take these and all other freedoms for granted. Abroad you may have to struggle alone or as a small group in times of crises. All these experiences are translated into an education after you learn to live with them. Eventually these cross-cultural exchanges may very well bring us, worldwide, closer together and produce more effective citizens of our own country and better citizens of the world.

Nothing so needs reforming as
other peoples' habits.

Mark Twain

Stereotypes

The successful instructor/teacher of international students must forget any preconceived notions and stereotypes of the various nationalities. This is not to suggest that instructors/teachers should be oblivious to cultural differences, but to generalize is dangerous. Approaching each student on an individual basis is the best strategy. Additionally if the learning group is multinational, instructors/teachers must not be influenced by remarks, especially negative ones, made by one nationality about another. Diplomacy is key. Remember what is essential: to instruct or teach or train in a subject matter. To be personally distracted by politics or to allow the classroom to be turned into a forum for "international debate" is to court disaster and to get away from the immediate task. If instructors'/teachers' only previous contact has been through hearsay and not through personal observation or experience, then they must begin the training sessions with a clean slate with regard to the students' personalities—both collective and individual.

Communication

For the transfer of knowledge to occur, teachers must be able to communicate with their students. In practical terms this usually means that the students have learned or are in the process of learning English. Frequently teachers adopt the "poor-me" attitude in their attempts to understand the written and spoken communications in their classes. However communication is a two-way street, and instructors/teachers can do the following to facilitate their students' understanding:

1. Listen to yourself talk and be prepared to explain yourself. Is your speech peppered with slang expressions, idiomatic phrases, or personal mannerisms? Are you guilty of these remarks? "I'm gonna give you a ring..." "They hafta..." and other similar slang expressions? When letters in words are elided (pronounced together), or left out, it is no wonder that foreigners have difficulty in apprehending your speech patterns.
2. Trainers/teachers should know that the problem with accents also goes two ways. It goes without saying, Texans, Georgians, New Yorkers, and Coloradans sound different from one another. Paying particular attention to what is said and how it is said can mean the difference between a successful and unsuccessful classroom experience.
3. In "failures to communicate," instructors/teachers might consider putting the "blame" on themselves. Doing this will put the student at ease and perhaps "save face." Personal pride before peers is most significant in a lot of cultures. Instructors/teachers might use phrases such as, "I'm not making myself clear," "Let me explain this is another way," or "I did not understand what you said." Fear of miscommunication and making mistakes when speaking a foreign language may inhibit classroom exchange. By letting students know that they should express themselves freely no matter the "mistakes," instructors/teachers will promote a healthy exchange of communication and an environment where learning can take place. Getting the class involved in the communication process will also provide feedback on whether or not the student is absorbing the subject matter.

Attitude

Finally instructors/teachers must maintain a positive attitude and persevere with patience. It is a fact of life that teaching international students is different from teaching individuals with the same cultural background as the teacher's. The international student is participating in training in a foreign language, perhaps a task that the instructor/teacher has never attempted. When the student fails to make the expected progress, the instructor/trainer should not label the student "dumb" or "slow." Remember that the student may be dealing with a new language, possibly a new alphabet, a new way of reading—perhaps from right to left instead of left to right, or side to side instead of top to bottom—and new academic conventions. For the speakers of Romanic or Germanic languages, the transition is not as difficult as for speakers of Farzi, Japanese, Arabic, Chinese, and many other languages. Many reference points exist for Europeans that do not exist for Middle Easterners of Orientals. These include the same alphabet, cognate words, comparable sentence structures, and similar grammatical constructions. Whatever the composition of the class, instructors/teachers need to approach adult students on *their* level and not "talk down" to them in a condescending manner. No one likes to be patronized and placed on the defensive, so maintaining a positive and flexible attitude and being aware of cultural differences will ensure that learning takes place.

Instructors/teachers are apt to learn many things from international students by listening, observing, and approaching the task with a positive mental outlook. Applying these suggestions may assist instructors/teachers and make their jobs easier and more pleasant. If instructors/teachers are new to the classroom and the international milieu, they can ground themselves in the technical aspects of what is to be taught, consider some of the cultural and language differences mentioned in this chapter, and then relax in the knowledge that they are prepared to meet the challenge and accept the responsibility for one of the most unique and rewarding of all teaching or training experiences.

Culture—An integrated pattern of human behavior that includes thought, speech, action, and artifacts and depends on man's capacity for learning and transmitting knowledge for succeeding generations.

Webster's New Collegiate Dictionary

Chapter VIII
Instructional Systems Development (ISD)

Tell me...I will forget
Show me...I may remember
But involve me...and I will
understand and remember.

Confucius

Definition: A deliberate and orderly process for planning and developing instructional programs that ensure students learn the knowledge, skills, and attitudes essential for realistic and successful job performance. The system depends on a description and analysis of the tasks necessary for performing the job. Lesson objectives and tests must be clearly stated before instruction begins. Evaluation procedures must determine whether the objectives have been reached, and must specify the methods for revising the process, if necessary, based on empirical data.

Objective

The objective of the Instructional Systems Development (ISD) concept is to *learn to meet requirements*. To achieve this each instructional system must be designed to contain only the education or training appropriate to the individual's needs. Education and training must be based on proficiency, not course length.

Based on this concept, ISD can be applied to develop on-the-job training; a formal course; a correspondence course; a unit, initial, or a continuation training program; as well as special courses, including those relating to new technology.

A single program cannot—and should not attempt to—satisfy all students' needs. Much of the program content will be useful for everyone, but parts will be irrelevant to specific needs. Therefore a plan should be developed and designed for each type of education or training program requirement.

Instructional Systems Development is a deliberate and orderly process for planning and developing instructional programs that ensure personnel (students) are taught the knowledge, skills, and attributes essential for successful job performance, in minimum time and cost.

This widely used training model consists of five phases: *analyze, design, develop, implement,* and *control* or *evaluate.* (See Figures 10 and 11.)

The process requires that all phases interrelate, and each feeds in and from evaluation in a continuing cycle. (See Figure 12.) The concept is research-based and field-tested. It is most comprehensive and an ideal concept for designing and developing instruction.

The system can be used to design standards, forms, and formulas for cost-control in all instructional documents relating to development planning, estimating, budgeting, and record keeping or reporting. As an example a standard formula for calculating level of effort could be:

> Developmental Hours x Instructional (classroom or workshop) Hours =
> manmonths required to complete a plan or project

Deliverables* can be guaranteed throughout every step of the instructional development process. (See Figure 13.) Let us briefly look at each phase.

---

*The tangible output from an instructional project activity, enabling project monitoring, control, and review.

The Five Phases of Instructional Systems Development In Essence

Phase I	ANALYZE—	SELECT TASKS/FUNCTIONS, CONSTRUCT JOB PERFORMANCE MEASURES, ANALYZE EXISTING COURSES, SELECT INSTRUCTIONAL SETTINGS
Phase II	DESIGN—	DEVELOP OBJECTIVES AND TESTS, DESCRIBE ENTRY BEHAVIOR DETERMINE SEQUENCE AND STRUCTURE
Phase III	DEVELOP—	SPECIFY LEARNING EVENTS/ ACTIVITIES, DEVELOP AND VALIDATE INSTRUCTION
Phase IV	IMPLEMENT—	IMPLEMENT AND CONDUCT INSTRUCTION
Phase V	CONTROL/— EVALUATE	CONDUCT INTERNAL AND EXTERNAL EVALUATION, REVISE SYSTEM

Figure 10

The Five Phases of Instructional Systems Development In Detail

PHASE I
ANALYZE

Inputs, processes, and outputs in Phase I are all based on job information. An inventory of job tasks is compiled and divided into two groups: tasks not selected for instruction and tasks selected for instruction. Performance standards for tasks selected for instruction are determined by interview or observation at job sites and verified by subject matter experts. The analysis of existing course documentation is done to determine if all or portions of the analysis phase and other phases have already been done by someone else following the ISD guidelines. As a final step, the list of tasks selected for instruction is analyzed for the most suitable instructional setting for each task.

PHASE II
DESIGN

Beginning with Phase II the ISD model is concerned with designing instruction using the job analysis information from Phase I. The first step is the conversion of each task selected for training into a terminal learning objective. Each terminal learning objective is then analyzed to determine learning objectives and learning steps necessary for mastery of the terminal learning objective. Tests are designed to match the learning objectives. A sample of students is tested to ensure that their entry behaviors match the level of learning analysis. Finally a sequence of instruction is designed for the learning objectives.

PHASE III
DEVELOP

The instructional development phase begins with the classification of learning objectives by learning category so as to identify learning guidelines necessary for optimum learning to take place. Determining how instruction is to be packaged and presented to the student is accomplished through a media selection process which takes into account such factors as learning category and guideline, media characteristics, training setting criteria, and costs. Instructional management plans are developed to allocate and manage all resources for conducting instruction. Instructional materials are selected or developed and tried out. When materials have been validated on the basis of empirical data obtained from groups of typical students, the course is ready for implementation.

PHASE IV IMPLEMENT   Staff training is required for the implementation of the instructional management plan and the instruction. Some key personnel must be trained to be managers in the specified management plan. The instructional staff must be trained to conduct the instruction and collect evaluative data on all of the instructional components. At the completion of each instructional cycle, management staff should be able to use the collected information to improve the instructional system.

PHASE V CONTROL/ EVALUATE   Evaluation and revision of instruction are carried out by personnel who preferably are neither the instructional designers nor the managers of the course under study. The first activity (internal evaluation) is the analysis of learner performance in the course to determine instances of deficient or irrelevant instruction. The evaluation team then suggests solutions for the problems. In the external evaluation, personnel assess job task performance on the job to determine the actual performance of course graduates and other job incumbents. All collected data, internal and external, can be used as quality control on instruction and as input to any phase of the system for revision.

Figure 11

Phase I–Analyze

This phase determines the performance requirements of the job: what must be done and how well it must be done. This process applies to all types of jobs. Skills, knowledge, and attitudes required for successful job performance must be outlined. Steps for Phase I follow. (See Figure 10 and Figure 14.)

a. Establish and formalize need
b. Identify the source of instructional goal
c. Prepare target population survey (describe learners in terms of prior education, interest, aptitude, and learning styles)
d. Prepare job profile
e. Develop task inventory
f. Validate task inventory
g. Develop usual job conditions
h. Develop job task descriptions

Phase II–Design

This phase determines the *changes* needed in skills, knowledge, and attitudes of students so that they can perform a job. These changes are added to the student's entering repertoire of abilities (See Figure 15):

a. Establish enrollment prerequisites
b. Identify constraints
c. Search shelf materials
d. Specify resource requirements
e. Develop training pattern
f. Develop format
g. Develop plan of action and milestones
h. Develop master plan on curriculum development
i. Design preliminary implementation and evaluation plan
j. Conduct project team evaluation workshop

Curriculum Process

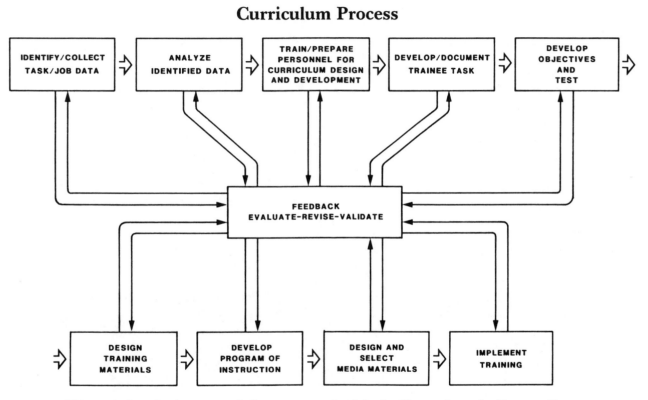

This curriculum development cycle forms a system that is both self-correcting and self-correctable

Figure 12

Requirements and Deliverables

REQUIREMENT	DELIVERABLE

PHASE I—ANALYZE

1. Formalize assignment	1. Work definition checklist
2. Analyze target population	2. Target population analysis
3. Prepare job profile	3. Job profile
4. Develop task inventory	4. Task inventory
5. Screen task inventory	5. Job orientation checklist
6. Develop usual job conditions and standards	6. Job conditions and standards
7. Develop job task description sheets	7. Job task description sheets
8. Assemble job training standards	8. Job training standards assembled

PHASE II—DESIGN

1. Establish prerequisites	1. Prerequisites List
2. Identify constraints	2. Training constraints report
3. Search for shelf material	3. Materials analysis report
4. Specify resource requirements	4. Resource requirements list
5. Develop training pattern	5. Training pattern
6. Develop format	6. Training package
7. Develop plan of action and milestones	7. Plan of action
8. Develop master training plan	8. Master plan
9. Design preliminary implementation and evaluation plan	9. Preliminary implementation and evaluation plan
10. Conduct project team evaluation workshop	10. Workshop summary

REQUIREMENT	DELIVERABLE

PHASE III-DEVELOP

	REQUIREMENT		DELIVERABLE
1.	Organize adapt shelf materials	1.	Shelf materials utilization
2.	Develop objectives	2.	Objectives
3.	Develop tests	3.	Tests
4.	Sequence instruction	4.	Structural course outline
5.	Select methods	5.	Methods design
6.	Select media	6.	Media design work orders
7.	Develop text and supplementary material	7.	Text and supplementary material accomplished
8.	Consolidate plan of instruction	8.	Draft plan of instruction
9.	Validate instruction	9.	Validated plan of instruction
10.	Conduct team evaluation workshop	10.	Workshop summary

PHASE IV—IMPLEMENT

	REQUIREMENT		DELIVERABLE
1.	Orient instructors/management	1.	Progress report
2.	Implement instruction	2.	Progress report
3.	Conduct internal evaluation	3.	Internal evaluation summary
4.	Conduct external evaluation	4.	External evaluation summary
5.	Revise and publish plan of instruction	5.	Revised plan of instruction
6.	Conduct final team review	6.	Team sign-off

PHASE V—CONTROL/EVALUATE

	REQUIREMENT		DELIVERABLE
1.	Design and install final implementation plan	1.	Implementation and evaluation plan
2.	Prepare final report	2.	Final report

Figure 13

SELECT TASKS AND FUNCTIONS

CONSTRUCT JOB PERFORMANCE MEASURES

ANALYZE EXISTING COURSES

SELECT INSTRUCTIONAL SETTINGS

Figure 14

DEVELOP OBJECTIVES AND TESTS

DESCRIBE ENTRY BEHAVIOR

DETERMINE SEQUENCE AND STRUCTURE

Figure 15

Phase III–Develop

There are six necessary steps in this phase (See Figure 16):

a. *Develop objectives.* This is the process of specifying the objectives that the student must meet to satisfy the training/education requirements. Objectives specify precisely what behavior is to be exhibited by the student, the conditions under which the behavior will be accomplished, and the minimum standard or standards of acceptable performance.

b. *Develop criterion-referenced tests.* This is the process of developing and administering tests that directly measure attainment of objectives.

c. *Select media and methods.* This is the process of selecting appropriate media and methods for objectives. Selection is based on the following factors:

    (1) Practical constraints (financial considerations, personnel assigned, and time allotted)

    (2) Instructional nature of the objectives (certain behaviors may be important in education or training but not so on the job)

    (3) Presentation mode implied by the objectives (visual or auditory)

    (4) Type of learning involved (simple visual discrimination, chain or skilled performance, or other methods)

    (5) Best instructional sequence for the objectives

d. *Develop instructional materials.* This is the process of developing and integrating the instructional materials. (See Figure 16.)

e. *Validate and revise instructional materials.* This is a process by which each unit of instruction is tested (validated) as it is developed. This process ensures that objectives are satisfied. First materials are tested on several individuals and revised as necessary. Then they are tested on small groups of students carefully sampled from the potential student population, and final revisions are made.

f. In more detail, you must follow these thirteen actions in the development stage:

    (1) Define and analyze curriculum aim

    (2) Organize and adapt shelf materials

    (3) Develop objectives

SPECIFY INSTRUCTION, PLAN FOR DELIVERY

REVIEW/SELECT EXISTING MATERIALS

DEVELOP INSTRUCTION

VALIDATE INSTRUCTION

Figure 16

(4) Test instructional materials
(5) Validate objectives against curriculum aim
(6) Develop tests
(7) Sequence instruction
(8) Select methods
(9) Print required instructional materials
(10) Develop text and supplementary materials
(11) Consolidate program of instruction
(12) Validate instruction
(13) Conduct project team evaluation workshop

Phase IV–Implement

This is the process of implementing and administering the instructional program (See Figure 17.) It includes training instructors/teachers and scheduling as well as conducting the program of instruction. Seven steps are required in the implementation stage.

These seven steps are:

a. Determine instructional strategies and plan for logistics
b. Orient instructors/teachers and management
c. Implement instruction
d. Conduct internal evaluation
e. Conduct external evaluation
f. Revise and publish program of instruction
g. Conduct final project team review

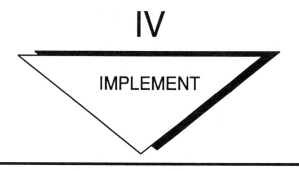

CONDUCT INSTRUCTION

Figure 17

Phase V–Control/Evaluate

(See Figure 18.) This is the process of determining the extent to which graduates of the instructional program satisfy the job performance requirements in the job environment. Detailed records of graduates' performance are kept, and changes to the instructional program are recommended as necessary. Five steps are followed in the final stage, Evaluate:

    a.   Determine whether to improve available materials or develop instructional materials and tests

    b.   Revise format

    c.   Conduct internal evaluation

    d.   Design and install final implementation and evaluation plan

    e.   Prepare final report, obtain approval, and circulate

Constraints

Many constraints exist for each situation. Based on the understanding and knowledge of the Instructional Systems Development process and a consideration of these constraints, procedures and techniques must meet the specific needs. There are, of course, limits on how much of the process can be bypassed. The following are the minimum essentials that should be accomplished to produce an effective instructional program:

1. As best you can, determine the essential job tasks.
2. Determine the skills and knowledge required to perform these tasks.
3. Determine if personnel with the necessary skills and knowledge already exist.
4. Derive objectives that, if met, would assure these skills and knowledge.
5. Develop test items for those objectives that can be used to determine whether the objectives are achieved.
6. Devise the means for the student to achieve these objectives.
7. Determine whether the student has achieved these objectives.
8. Where the objectives were not achieved, revise the system.

V

CONTROL/
EVALUATE

CONDUCT INTERNAL/EXTERNAL EVALUATION

REVISE SYSTEM

Figure 18

Analyzing System Requirements

The impetus for initiating the Instructional Systems Development process is some evidence that there is, or soon will be, job performance that does not meet requirements. First analyze the performance problem to determine whether it is a training/education deficiency. The areas to look at are the job situation, the performer, the behavior required, what happens to the performer as a result of adequate or poor performance, and the adequacy of the feedback to performers about how well they are doing. When such an analysis is made, instruction may *not* be what is needed to resolve the problem. For example you are told, "The safety record in this shop for the past twelve months has been poor. We need to set up a safety training program." The first statement probably is fact, but unless an analysis has been made, the second statement is a guess. You might administer a safety test and find that the people who work in the shop already know all they need to know about safety, but they just are not applying it. More training is not the answer to this problem. Instead you must look for nontraining solutions.

This sort of analysis is critically important, so always check first to be sure that a training/education situation is involved. You may save yourself a great deal of unnecessary effort, and save your business or your company from expending unnecessary time and money.

Developing Job Performance Requirements

One of the most important aspects of the Instructional Systems Development process is the orderly development of information about the job and its components. The information you gather may be massive and in some cases should be stored on a computer for ease of manipulation and retrieval. Whether or not a computer is used, you should know what kinds of data you will need and where the data will be used. Collecting useless data or storing it in a form where it becomes useless is a common problem when the data uses or applications are not understood. The data you collect should be determined by your specific needs and situation.

Identifying Tasks That Make Up a Job—sometimes called "Task Analysis," "Front-end Analysis," or "Needs Assessment"

The first major requirement in the Instructional Systems Development process is to identify all the tasks that make up a job. To identify the tasks and ensure that all of them have been listed, you must identify broader systems data (such as mission and equipment used). To decide correctly if a given task requires instruction, other supporting data, such as the difficulty of learning the task, the seriousness of the consequences of not performing the task correctly, and the probability that performance of the task will occur under emergency conditions, must be obtained. If the particular job you are working on is new to you, or if you are not familiar with the job, you must rely on the help of subject matter specialists. Keep in mind that system data and supporting data are the basic information sources for determining the tasks and determining which tasks require instruction.

The five major techniques for verifying or deriving information from Instructional Systems Development data follow:

1. Interviews
2. Questionnaires
3. Task observation of performance expert
4. Simulation
5. Making assumptions

Interviews and questionnaires are the most common techniques. They are usually directed to the subject-matter specialists. Task observation is useful for verifying the data you have assembled from available sources or subject-matter specialists. In new systems you may need to employ simulation or make assumptions to derive the necessary information. The techniques you apply depend on whether your effort is directed toward a new or an existing system.

Based on the definition of purpose, develop objectives for the questionnaire or your interview(s). Remember: The available sources have much more information about the job than your students need to know. The purpose of the interview and questionnaire is to "pull out" only the relevant information. The objectives of the questions should be to collect specific answers. You may want to limit yourself to the following questions:

1. What are the conditions/equipment "given"?
2. What is the exact performance (action)?
3. What are the standards of performance?
4. What are the "results" of the action?

The next step is to decide what specific information must be collected. Interviews and questionnaires are used in many ways. Specify exactly what you need to know. Develop questions that will get that information for you. You should decide what to ask on the basis of:

1. Your own experience on the job (or similar ones)
2. Available literature on the topic, including professional journals
3. Hypotheses about expected outcomes of the interview or questionnaire
4. Informal discussions with a sample of typical respondents

Your next step is to develop questions. In developing questions the following guidelines are appropriate:

1. Use close-ended questions when you want the respondent to choose answers from a small number of possibilities. This makes tabulation easy, but may not give the range of answers desired.
2. Use open-ended questions when you don't know all the possible answers. The respondent will probably suggest possibilities.
3. Word your questions to the level of your respondents. Make sure your vocabulary and concepts are easy for respondents to understand. For example don't use technical words if respondents are unfamiliar with the technical operation. Also limit the use of jargon with contractors.
4. If the respondents are likely to feel threatened or embarrassed by the topic, phrase questions in a general way, rather than in terms specific to them. For example ask: "Do the operators get bored with the job?" (Not: "Are you bored with the job?")
5. Limit each question to one aspect of a topic (especially for close-ended questions).
6. Decide on a logical order for questions. (Job performance order? General or specific?) Remember each

question increases the respondent's frame of reference and further establishes a "set" for upcoming responses.

7.   Avoid questions that make it easier to answer one way rather than another.
8.   Avoid questions that show bias or expectations, especially during interviews.

Another important factor to consider is motivation. You want respondents to do more than just respond. You want them to respond fully and conscientiously. Telephone or in-person interviews will motivate if:

1.   You are well prepared
2.   You explain the importance of the interview
3.   The opening questions are easy to understand and to answer
4.   You give approval (not hear or acknowledge verbally) for appropriate answers
5.   You rephrase the question or probe more deeply when you get an inappropriate or incomplete answer
6.   You ask the questions in a logical order that respondents can easily see
7.   You complete a discussion of one topic at a time (acknowledge completion of each topic, and don't leap from one topic to another)
8.   You tell respondents how valuable their information is to you

Developing Objectives and Tests

Your next step in the Instructional Systems Development process is the development of objectives and tests. Objectives must be stated in terms of expected behavior: what the student must be able to do at the end of a training/education program. Objectives describe observable student *behavior,* minimum *standards* of performance or *proficiency* expected, and *conditions* under which the behavior is to be exhibited.

An objective is a description of a performance you want students to be able to exhibit before they are considered competent. An objective describes an intended result of instruction, rather than the process of instruction. Consider the following phrases in this light:

Words Open to Many Interpretations	Words Open to Few Interpretations
(Abstractions)	(Performance)
To understand	To recite
To know	To identify
To appreciate	To assemble
To inspect	To solve
To really understand	To list
To prepare	To underline
To operate	To pass a test
To grasp or believe he learned	To learn

An objective always says what a student or trainee is expected to be able to do; always describes the important conditions, if any, under which the performance is to occur; and whenever possible describes the criterion of acceptable performance by describing how well the student must perform. Though it is not necessary to include the second and not always practical to include the third characteristic, the more you say about them, the better your objective will be communicated.

Each objective should be classified so that test items generated from the objective can be shown to be consistent with the objective. The procedure for classification of objectives follows:

1. Determine the task level
   a. Determine whether the student is to *Remember* or *Use* information.
   b. If the student is to *Use* information, determine whether the task level is *Use-Aided* or *Use-Unaided*.
2. Determine the content-type
   a. If the student is to recall or recognize names, parts, locations, functions, dates, or places, then the content type is *Fact.*
   b. If the student is to remember characteristics of similar objects or events, or must sort or classify objects, events, or ideas according to characteristics, then the content type is *Category.*

Why Are Objectives So Important?

1. Provide a basis for selecting materials, content, and methods

2. Evaluate trainee performance

3. Organize teaching plans and student activity

4. Clarify for both the trainee and the teacher what the lesson will specifically cover.

Figure 19

c. If the student is to remember a sequence of steps that apply to a single situation, *or* if the student is to apply the steps to a single piece of equipment or a single situation, then the content type is *Procedure.*

d. If the student is to remember a sequence of steps and decisions that apply in a variety of situations, or if the student is to apply the sequence across a variety of situations or types of equipment, then the content type is *Rule.*

e. If the student is to remember how or why things work the way they do, or cause and effect relationship, *or* the student is to use his knowledge to explain how things work, or predict effects from causes, then the content type is *Principle.*

The classification should be determined according to:

1. What the student is to do (what task he is to perform)
2. Instructional content (the type of information the student is to learn)

The objective should be appropriate for the work to be performed on the job or for later training. The requirements for assuring appropriateness:

1. The *Conditions* should be appropriate for the work to be performed on the job or for later training.
2. The *Standards* should be appropriate for the work to be performed on the job or for later training.
3. The *Task Level* of the *Action* should be appropriate for the work to be performed on the job or for later training.
4. The *Content Type* of the *Action* should be appropriate for the work to be performed on the job or for later training.
5. *Remember*-level objectives should be followed later by *Use* objectives.
6. *Use-Unaided*-level objectives should be preceded by *Remember*-level objectives.
7. *Use-Aided*-level objectives should have adequate aid or should be supported by other objectives.

Objectives must be correctly stated. The *Conditions* under which student performance is expected must be specified. *Conditions* include:

1. Environment
   Physical (weather, location, shop/lab/classroom)
   Social (isolation, individual, team, audience)
   Psychological (fatigue, stress, relaxed)
2. Information
   Given Information (situation, formula, values)
   Cues (signals for starting and stopping)
   Special Instructions (vary)
3. Resources
   Job Aids (drawings, sketches, graphs, checklists)
   Equipment, Tools, Technical Manuals

The *Standards* of student performance must be specified. There are two standards of performance:

1. Performance
   Completeness (how much of the task will be performed)
   Accuracy (how well each task will be performed)
   Time Limit (how much time is allowed for each task)
2. Product
   Completeness (what the finished product will contain)
   Quality (what standard the product will meet)
   Judgment (what objective opinions the product will satisfy)

The *Action* the student performs should be specified with an action verb. Use verbs that are not open to interpretations or opinions. Instead of saying *to understand,* use the verb *to recite.* Instead of saying *to know,* say *to identify.* Be specific when using action verbs so that there is no doubt about the performance that is to be accomplished.

Many terms have been used to describe the various objectives (criterion, terminal, primary, enabling, supporting, secondary, and others). Whatever descriptive terms are used, basically they are all objectives and they should all describe behavior, conditions, and standards.

The important aspect to remember in developing objectives is that each objective contains four elements: the objective must be *specific, measurable, achievable,* and *challenging.* Each of the job tasks must state what the student will be able to do *after* the training or instruction is completed. (To recall these four elements easily, think of SMAC, *S*pecific, *M*easurable, *A*chievable, and *C*hallenging.

The importance of developing effective objectives cannot be overemphasized. Below is a brief summary of the influence that objectives have on outlining teaching plans, selecting materials, evaluating student performance, determining lesson content, and describing student activity in the education or training concept.

What is meant by wanting learners to "know" something? Should they recite, solve, or construct something? Simply telling them to "know" tells them very little—because the word "know" can mean several different things. Until the term "knowing" is defined in terms of what the students ought to be able to do, very little has been said. Thus an objective that communicates best will describe the students' intended performance clearly enough to preclude misinterpretation—by the teacher as well as by the student.

How can that be done? What characteristics might help make an objective communicate and help make it more effective and useful? Several schemes are used in stating objectives, but the format described here is one that is known to work, and one that I have used for several years and consider to be the most effective and easiest to use.

The format includes three characteristics that help make an objective communicate an intent. These characteristics answer three questions: (1) What should the learner be able to "do"? (2) Under what conditions should the learner be able to do it? (3) How well must it be done? The three characteristics follow:

1. *Performance*   An objective always says what a learner is expected to be able to "do."
2. *Conditions*   An objective always describes the important conditions, if any, under which the performance is to occur.
3. *Criterion*   Whenever possible, an objective describes the criterion of acceptable performance by describing how well the learner must perform in order to be considered acceptable performance.

Though it is not always necessary to include the second and not always practical to include the third characteristic, the more you say about them, the better your objective will be communicated. Other characteristics could be included in an objective, such as a description of the students for which the objective is intended or a description of the instructional procedures by which the objective will be accomplished. Though these are important pieces of information in the process of designing an instruction, the objective is not the place for them. But then Why not? you may ask. Because this information clutters up the objective and makes it more difficult to read and interpret. The objective needs to be *useful* and *clear*. If you include unnecessary items, the objective will fail to serve its purpose. Many objectives have been written—but never used.

Objectives should follow some rigid form or format. (I once worked for a school principal who expected teachers to write their objectives on a form printed by the principal. His form had a line printed every three inches down the page, the implication being that every objective should be no more than five inches long and two inches high. Would you be surprised to learn that the teachers were hostile to the principal's concept?) Objectives should not be a particular size and shape; objectives should be *clear*, so that they describe instructional objectives as concisely as possible—no more, no less. So anybody who says that an objective must be no more than two inches high and five inches wide or who says that an objective must or must not contain certain words should be reminded that the function of an objective is to communicate. If it does it is a success. Be happy! If it does not, fix it, and fix it right. An objective should not match someone's idea of "good design" or "good looks"; an objective should communicate instructional objectives. Write as many objectives as needed to describe all instructional objectives that are important to accomplish. The number and size of objectives are unimportant.

Tests.

The goal of instruction is to raise all students' performance to meet the objectives. To make sure a student has reached that level, the test to measure proficiency must be criterion-referenced; that is, test against the criteria for successful performance that was identified in the objectives. Criterion-referenced tests (1) measure the student's achievement against the objectives; (2) provide a standard for judging acceptability, correctness, or success; and (3) assess the adequacy of the total instructional course. They indicate whether the course has been successful in producing students whose proficiency meets the objectives.

Tests are constructed from the objectives. They measure achievement under the conditions and standards specified by the objectives. If a breakdown in instruction occurs, student responses on the test may help you diagnose the cause.

Once a system is in operation, tests measure whether the quality of instruction diminishes over time.

Test Item Consistency with Objectives. (*a*) To make sure that tests are "criterion-referenced," each test item must be "referenced" to a specific objective. A test item is "referenced" to an objective when it is "consistent" with the objective. This means that the conditions and standards in the objective will be maintained in the testing situation. (*b*) The task/content of the test item will match the task/content of the objective. (*c*) The format of the test item will be appropriate for the task/content classification of the objective. (*d*) A test item can be "consistent" and yet be an invalid item. Therefore the test item must be adequately written and related to the job.

Test Item Consistency, Relevance of Test Item to Job, and Test Item Construction. The following is the procedure for checking test item consistency, relevancy to job, and test item construction. If there are several test items for a single objective, they should be evaluated together to determine if:

1. *Conditions* in each item, or *Conditions* under which the items are administered, match the conditions in the objective
2. *Standards* in each item, or *Standards* for scoring each item, match standards in the objective
3. *Actions* in each item match the *Action* of the objective
   a. Determine the *Task Level* and *Content Type* of each test item.
   b. Determine whether these test items match the *Task Level* and *Content Type* of the objective.
4. Each item is typical of the job to be performed after training, or is a necessary qualification for later training
5. *Format* of each item is *Appropriate* for the *Task Level* and *Content Type*
6. Each item is *Clear* (instructions for completing the item must specify what response the trainee is expected to make)
7. Each item is *Confusing* (each item must have only one response that can be interpreted as the best answer)
8. Each item is *Free of Hints* (an item should not give away the answer to itself or to any other item on the test; the wording of multiple-choice and fill-in items should not give hints to answers)
9. Each item is *Well Constructed* (different criteria apply to different item formats)
10. Items present reasonable alternatives for identification of common errors
11. *Use*-level objectives test the objective adequately, and reflect the range of performance required on the job

Three types of tests essential to this program are the *criterion-referenced test*, *diagnostic test*, and *survey test*. Let us discuss briefly the purposes of each of these three tests.

1. *Criterion-referenced Test.* The criterion-referenced test measures acquisition, retention, and transfer of the skills and knowledge specified in the objectives. The test shows how well the total instructional system produces students who can transfer skills and knowledge acquired in training *to* on-the-job situations. The test may be given before instruction as a pretest, and then again afterward to measure how much the student learned from the instruction or in training.

2. *Diagnostic Test.* Diagnostic test items are used to determine attainment of the supporting skills and knowledge that contribute to the ability to perform the objectives. Student failure on these tests identifies weak areas in the instruction. Student answers provide clues to the cause of failure and to the types of revision needed. The diagnostic test can be used during instruction to measure details of performance on the various instructional levels. It can also be used in the validation and evaluation of instruction.

3. *Survey Test.* The survey test determines what students know or can do before receiving instruction. This test contains items from the criterion test and the diagnostic test. It may also include items to indicate reading level, ability to make specific types of calculations that will be involved in the instruction, or any other "prerequisite skills," if you need to be sure of the level of proficiency of the entering students in any of the skills. The test is given to a sample of the population and measures the criterion behaviors. The purpose is to discover which tasks require instruction and how much. When you developed training requirements and objectives, you made some assumptions about what the students already knew. If the survey test reveals that they know more about the content to be learned than you judged, you have underestimated your target population's abilities. You must revise the objectives and training requirements accordingly.

Test items can be either written items or performance items. Performance items are preferred, since they relate directly to job performance. Performance items either test a process (series of steps, such as aligning a circuit, assembling a gearcase), or test development of a product (such as designing a form).

Let us examine the performance (action) part of objectives as a summary, so that we may better recognize the importance of our criterion-referenced tests.

An instructor cannot read students' minds to see how well they understand. Only through some overt activity of students can the extent of their knowledge or skill be measured. Therefore the performance part of objectives should specifically state what the student does. "Develop an understanding of Ohm's law" is an unspecific objective. It can be interpreted too many ways. One person may feel that the student's reciting the law indicates understanding. Another may say that the student should be able to explain the law. A third may contend that the only way the student can satisfy this objective is to use the formula in solving electrical-circuit problems. "Use Ohm's law to determine applied voltage when current and resistance are known," is a more precise objective. An objective stated this way lets everyone—the student, instructor, supervisor, measurement personnel, writers, and course managers—know exactly what the student must learn. It states what behavior the student should exhibit.

Using action verbs reduces ambiguity. Unless you specify student behavior with an action verb, the student will probably end up doing something else. You can think of "good" verbs. You can also think of "poor" verbs that do not accurately communicate a student's actions. The verbs you select should reflect actions that are observable, measurable, verifiable, and reliable. Use the best possible action verbs that satisfy these general criteria, and that are appropriate to the task performance and training requirements. Here are some examples of poor, better, and best verbs:

POOR VERBS	BETTER VERBS	BEST VERBS
appreciate	compare	add
be aware of	compute	adjust
be interested in	construct	identify
enjoy	differentiate	check off
feel	indicate	fill in blank
know	operate	give (an example)
understand	predict	group
	recite	label
	solve	point at
	write	state (a rule)

In developing tests keep in mind a means for diagnosing and correcting problems or weaknesses in the instructional system, during and after the instruction.

Tests that serve these purposes must be valid and reliable. A valid test measures what it's supposed to measure. A reliable test yields consistent results. Several general factors affect the validity and reliability of tests. "Validity" is the relevance of a test to its purpose. There are several specific definitions of validity, depending on the purpose of the testing. For criterion-referenced tests, validity refers to two characteristics of test items: (1) the extent to which test items directly reflect the objectives, and (2) the adequacy with which the test items sample the objectives. One reason for preparing objectives in the first place is that it simplifies construction of criterion-referenced tests. First it describes the condition(s) of performance. Second it describes the performance required of the student after the training has been completed. Third it describes the accuracy and time standard for performance. An objective so described is a prescription for a test that will measure attainment of the objective by the student.

A test is valid if it:

1. Requires trainees to show they can do what the objective states
2. Requires that performance be under the condition(s) stated in the objective
3. Is scored according to the performance standard(s) stated in the objective

"Reliability" is the consistency with which the test measures whatever it measures. If a criterion test is reliable, then students who have achieved the objectives will always pass, and those who have not will always fail. If a test is unreliable, a student may pass or fail for reasons other than ability. The four main factors in criterion-referenced test reliability are:

1. The test itself, including general and specific instructions, and the conditions
   under which the test is administered
2. The student taking the test
3. The scoring procedures
4. The length of the test

Tests provide two kinds of feedback:

1. Whether students retain specifically what they learn during instruction
2. Whether students can transfer what they have learned from the classroom to the job

Tests take two general forms: They are either written measures or performance measures. Each test type has advantages. For example written tests are potentially more reliable, while performance tests are potentially more valid. Written tests are most useful for developing a direct measure of knowledge training requirements. They also provide a more probing measure of knowledge details than is possible with some performance tests. Performance tests are especially suited to evaluating either a process (such as a procedure or chain) or a product (such as an assembled piece of equipment).

Scoring.

Scoring of tests is a major source of inconsistency. You must be careful to keep scoring consistent from student to student. The key principle to observe in scoring is objectivity. Objectivity in scoring is achieved by setting precise standards, and training the scorer to apply them. Develop scoring procedures in which opinion of the scorer is not a factor.

There are two steps in obtaining objectivity:

1. Tell the scorer exactly what he/she should observe while scoring
2. Clearly state the standards of successful performance

Successful performance should be defined so that measurement does not depend on personal judgments. The standards for knowledge training requirements should be specified as a single, correct, written answer. For skill training requirements, the standards should be in terms, such as "did" or "did not do" a particular thing, presence or absence of essential attributes of a product, or measurable numbers.

In some situations measuring instruments of various kinds may be used. See that such instruments are accurate and calibrated.

Scoring procedures can be made consistent by having several scorers score one student. If the scores are not identical, identify the reason for the differences. Make the standards more specific. Repeat the process until scoring is consistent.

If all other factors that influence reliability are under control, you can improve the reliability of a test by making it longer. If several items for the same objective are included, the effects of wording of the instructions and scoring tend to cancel. The overall score becomes more reliable. However if testing time is limited, and there is a choice between adding more items to cover the same objectives, or covering more objectives with new items, the latter course is better.

Retention and Transfer Tests

It is possible that a student might pass a test and still not accomplish the training requirements. This could happen if either the instructional program or the test was inadequate. Here we are concerned with reasons why the test might be inadequate.

The test could be valid, in that it measured how well the student retained the specific course materials. (For example a student who remembered how to solve a specific problem in class would pass the test item requiring solution of the same problem.) Such a test has measured retention. However the student might not be able to solve new problems on the job. The test has not indicated how well the student transfers what he/she learns on the job. Let us examine the difference between a retention test and a transfer test.

Retention tests require students to demonstrate that they have retained knowledge and skills acquired during instruction. The *same* examples and situations experienced in instruction are included on the test. Students must remember what they have encountered during instruction.

Transfer tests require students to demonstrate that they have retained knowledge and skills acquired during instruction *and* can apply them to new situations and examples not encountered during instruction. *Different* examples and situations are included on the test.

You can see that you should maintain strict security on the transfer tests, to prevent students from practicing in advance, or instructors from "teaching the test." However for retention tests, teaching the test is actually desirable. For example some objectives require performance of a task that can only be performed in one way. Thus there may be only one correct way to assemble a weapon, pack a parachute, or identify a specific code. In these cases it's fine to teach the test. In fact it's also desirable to give the students the objectives at the beginning of the course. Remember that retention tests require the student to remember something presented in training.

Planning the Instruction

Systematic specification of instructional conditions, methods, and media is essential to attaining the objectives. Systematic specification means that decisions about the instruction are made according to some set of procedures that are rationally derived and are commonly agreed upon. These procedures must also be reliable. This means that when using the agreed-upon procedures to develop a course of instruction, different people will develop similar instructional systems. Each system would achieve the objectives to the same degree of satisfaction.

    The planning consists of several activities:

1. Sequencing the objectives to maximize the transfer of learning from one objective to another
2. Determining the conditions of learning experiences students will meet as they move through the sequence
3. Selecting methods for carrying out the conditions of learning
4. Selecting the media to express the content of instruction

Developing and Validating Instruction

Feedback is an important part of the development and validation process. Feedback is the information gained as a result of trying out the instruction on a sample of students. The tryout information helps to determine which changes should be made in the instruction. The provision for feedback allows the instructional system to be improved. It also helps to ensure that once the system is put into operation, the objectives will be achieved. Following are the activities in the development and validation phase:

1. Develop instruction
2. Have the instruction reviewed by a specialist for technical accuracy
3. Try out the instruction
4. Administer the tests to assess the tryout
5. Analyze the results of the tryout
6. Analyze the results of the tests
7. Revise accordingly

On the basis of the results, decide whether revision is needed. The scope of the revision may vary. It may be limited to the development and validation phase. In that case you simply recycle through the seven activities listed immediately above. It may include the planning decisions made before the development of instructions. In that case you may have to revive the conditions of instruction, the method of instruction, or the media of instruction. Tryout results may indicate a need to review the objectives and tests. In that case revision would be extensive.

Planning the Sequence of Instruction

Since the learning of skills and knowledge takes a period of time, you must consider the sequence in which the students will encounter the material. In developing instruction your first action is to order the objectives in the sequence to be achieved. Sequence objectives so that transition from one skill to another will be optimal.

The sequence in which a course has been taught in the past is not necessarily the best sequence. The best sequence depends on the relationships among objectives. Objectives may have a dependent relationship, in that they are related in some ways. They may be totally unrelated and independent of each other. Note the contrast between dependent and independent objectives below.

Independent	Dependent
Skills and knowledge in the objectives are unrelated to one another.	Skills and knowledge in the objectives are related to one another.
Learning of one criterion behavior does not make the learning of another easier.	To be able to learn one criterion behavior, it is not necessary to learn one or more other criterion behaviors.
The objectives may be arranged in any arbitrary or random sequence without detriment to learning.	The objectives are arranged in a sequence based on this hierarchy.

When objectives are independent of each other, sequencing is not a problem. However the sequence of dependent objectives depends on three conditions:

1. Are the objectives common-element objectives?
2. Are the objectives prerequisites for other objectives?
3. Are the tasks described in the objectives contingent (require direct input from other tasks)?

Here are some general sequencing guidelines for the various relationships among objectives:

Relationships Among Objectives	Most Efficient Training Sequence	Example
Common-Element Objectives Objectives across tasks share common elements.	Instruction for the elements shared by the criterion behaviors immediately precedes instruction for the unshared elements.	Knowledge of electronics. Common maintenance tasks are taught immediately prior to combining them with specific maintenance tasks.
Objectives and Subobjectives Tasks are contingent on the job: one objective acts as a direct input to the next objective.	Instruction is in the same sequence as actual performance in the work environment.	In the task of developing a course of instruction, the criterion test items are derived directly from the objectives. Thus instruction on how to write objectives precedes how to prepare criterion test items.
Objectives and Subobjectives One objective is a prerequisite for another objective.	Sequence the objectives so that instruction in the prerequisite behavior precedes instruction for the other behavior.	Being able to add is a prerequisite for being able to multiply.
Objectives or Subobjectives No relationship exists.	Sequence in any order.	In performing clerical work, no dependent relationship exists between filing and typing. Either may be taught first.

Generally common-element objectives should be taught early in the course because they represent concepts basic to many tasks. For example in physics the concept of force is basic to learning how simple machines work—levers, pulleys, wheels, inclined planes. So instruction on the concept of force should precede instruction about each type of simple machine. Likewise in statistics the "mean" is used in many statistical tests. Therefore students learn how to compute the "mean" before they learn more complex statistical procedures.

The delay between learning a common element and applying it should be minimal. This is so that what is learned at the onset of training is not forgotten by the time it is encountered in the context of the task objective.

In the Instructional Systems Development approach, test items are derived directly from the objectives. Consequently a student learning to use the Instructional Systems Development approach should learn how to write objectives before learning to construct tests. Similarly some procedural tasks may be part of a larger chain. Some of these include maintenance tasks, troubleshooting procedures, assembly tasks, mathematical or computational procedures. When one task in a chain of tasks cannot be performed until the preceding task has been completed, sequence instruction is the same as the job.

Summary of Sequencing Guidelines

There are four rules for sequencing objectives:
1. First put the common-element objectives, in the order they are required, before the task objectives.
2. Second arrange the subobjectives for each task so that the prerequisite skills and knowledge are covered first.
3. Then arrange the task objectives so that prerequisites are covered first.
4. Finally arrange the contingent task objectives that have not yet been sequenced in the same sequence as their performance on the job.

Developing Homogeneous Blocks of Instruction

Block out large areas within the job that will provide organized, manageable sections of content. Do not assume that your blocks of instruction are unalterable. Subsequent decisions may make you reevaluate what constitutes a block. However blocking out content areas early will help you get a better picture of the scope and nature of instruction. It will also help you assign responsibility to personnel who will develop the instruction.

How many objectives you group into a block of instruction is an arbitrary matter. At this point you are simply identifying objectives that can be grouped in large blocks because of the behaviors involved.

Criteria for Grouping Sets of Tasks

Group together (in a block) sets of objectives that meet these criteria:
1. The objectives are meaningful in relation to each other. Combined they make a self-contained block.
2. When combined the objectives have a natural beginning and an ending point.
3. The objectives are large enough to be further subdivided into smaller related units, yet they are small enough to be manageable, considering personnel available for developing instruction.

Determining General Procedures to Assist Learning

As an instructional system designer, you should use learning principles to plan and develop the most effective and efficient learning environment. There are basic conditions of learning that apply to all types of learning subject-matter content. You can increase the effectiveness of your instruction by providing for them.

The first condition is practice. People learn by doing. So you must devise opportunities for practice of skills and knowledge to be learned during the instruction. The second condition is feedback. While practice is the cornerstone of instruction, it alone is not sufficient for learning. Feedback must be an integral part of practice. Students must have some means of finding out whether their practice is correct, so that they can take corrective action if needed. The third condition is that practice should be guided or prompted, to make it as error-free as possible. When learning new skills and knowledge, most students require assistance. Practice alone does not make perfect. Avoid letting students engage in trial-and-error learning. Do not give them the opportunity to practice their mistakes—once learned they are difficult to unlearn. You can help students avoid errors by prompting and guiding their practice.

While the above conditions improve the effectiveness of the instruction, consider also means of making the course more effective. Strive to get the maximum amount of learning with the minimum amount of instruction. To help you produce effective and efficient learning, guidelines on how to include the above three conditions are presented below.

Do's and Don'ts

1. DO systematically provide *active* practice of the tasks to be learned.
2. DON'T provide conditions that only allow the student to listen to lectures, watch demonstrations, or read something about the task to be learned.
3. Note the contrast in the instructional conditions of *active practice* and *passive* conditions.

Active Practice Conditions
During learning students have the opportunity to produce practice or try their hand at the task to be learned.
Student practice may:
- Be embedded throughout instructional materials
- Occur at wide intervals
- Occur at the end but before tests or on-the-job performance
- Be observable or unobservable

Passive Conditions
Students have no opportunity to perform the task to be learned until after instruction has been completed.
Students merely:
- Listen to instructional materials about the action to be learned
- Read about the actions to be learned
- Watch a demonstration of the materials to be learned

Examples of active practice conditions and passive conditions follow:

Active Practice Conditions
- Solving problems
- Applying principles to examples
- Analyzing data
- Correcting a malfunction

Passive Conditions
- Watching instructor solve problems on board
- Reading about application of principles to examples
- Listening to a lecture about data analysis
- Watching a demonstration of how to repair a malfunction

Providing Students with Feedback

Do's and Don'ts
1. Do tell students if the action they have practiced or the product they have produced is correct. Knowing when they are right will help them to make the correct responses later, and they can focus their efforts on those parts of the task that need refinement.
2. Don't omit feedback. If students are wrong and don't know it, they will learn the wrong response—then they will have to unlearn it. If they take the right action, but don't know why it was right, students probably will not be able to transfer to new situations.
3. Note the comparison between natural and artificial feedback.

Natural Feedback
Arises naturally from the task environment. The results of an action taken is one type of natural feedback. Another type would be the actual product or object produced. This form of feedback is present during learning and on the job. Pushing a button and getting a correct reading on an instrument is one example.

Artificial Feedback
Does not arise out of the task itself. It is provided by additional means, such as instructor critique or mechanical indicator. This form of feedback is present only during learning and must be carefully planned.

Provide cues that will help students to practice the correct responses. Prevent guesswork and see that students are right the first time they respond. Once made a correct answer is likely to recur. Do not allow students to practice incorrect responses. Allowing students to "discover" the correct response by trial-and-error wastes time and creates confusion in students' minds. It is better to prevent an error from occurring at the start, because after an error is made it is likely to recur.

Bringing the Student to Criterion Performance

Provide sufficient practice opportunities to assist the student in bridging the "gap" between entering behavior and the criterion performance. Do not provide the student with too much practice at first. Start with the least amount you judge necessary to do the job and add more practice if needed.

Ideally you should prepare instructional sequences so all students perform all practice requirements relatively error-free. How much practice this will require depends on the nature of the task, the entry level of the students, and the time lapse from instruction to application on the job. A general rule you can follow is that the first version of the instructional materials should be as lean as possible. Provide cues or prompts that are strong enough to ensure correct practice, but no stronger. Fade cues or prompts as quickly as possible, and/or keep the amount of practice as sparse as possible.

Lean programs make for efficient and cost-effective instruction. They are efficient because they provide only the instruction the student needs to achieve proficiency, and no more. They are cost-effective because they provide the appropriate amount of instruction in as few instructional hours as are needed to accomplish the job. The greater the number of hours of instruction taken to reach proficiency, the greater the cost of instruction.

Design a transitional practice situation to bring the student efficiently to criterion performance. At the onset of training, provide students with situations they can handle. Then make practice more difficult until students are capable of handling the most demanding criterion situations.

How Much of a Task to Practice

Decide whether it is more effective to practice a task as a whole, or to practice its various parts separately. Review a number of conditions, such as the size, the difficulty, and the organization of the task. Also consider students' age, intelligence, motivation, and experience.

Selecting Media

Instructional media, whatever the form, serve only one purpose: they are vehicles of transmission for skills and knowledge. Media that will best express these skills and knowledge depend on the most appropriate display of the content, and the practical considerations of cost and availability of resources.

Media may involve the student to varying degrees on an "active/passive continuum." At one end of the continuum is total active involvement, which requires a lot of interaction between student and medium. At the other end is passive involvement. The student merely hears and/or observes the message. Note below the five classes of media, according to their relative position on the active/passive continuum:

MOST STUDENT INVOLVEMENT			*LEAST STUDENT INVOLVEMENT*	
1 **Tutorial Media**	**2** **Environmental Media**	**3** **Print Media**	**4** **Visual Aid Media**	**5** **Transient Media**
Present programmed instructional materials that bear the total burden of instruction	Create an artificial environment and realistically stimulate the learner	Present or play the entire verbal printed discourse with little or no instructor involvement	Support the learning experience	Realistically present or display the entire visual, audio, or audiovisual instructional message with little or no instructor involvement
Accommodate student responding	React to the learner's actions or manipulations	Require support material (adjuncts) to accommodate responding or to keep record of student responses	Call attention to or point out relevant properties to which the student should attend	Stimuli are transient in terms of the duration with which they are presented to the student
Keep a record of student responses	May be designed to record student responses		Require adjuncts to accommodate responding or to keep record of student responses	Require adjuncts to accommodate responding or to keep record of student responses

Next on the continuum are environmental media that react to the student's actions or manipulation. Normally these media do not permit the degree of individualization typical of tutorial media. The word "normally" is used because there is some overlap of the first two classes of media on the continuum. Some environmental media are programmed, which fall into both classes of media.

The third class on the continuum is print media, which require active involvement. The student must engage in active behaviors, such as scanning the text and decoding the print (reading). Reading behavior may be concentrated. The student may process the written text at a very "deep" level, or, the student may merely scan the text.

The fourth class of media is visual aids. These support the instructor's teaching or contain written text and captions that the student must read. As for print media, students must engage in active processing behaviors to get the data in the visual aid. However the amount of information normally contained in a visual aid is generally less than that contained in standard print media. Because they are less capable of carrying the full burden of instruction, the student's involvement will, to a large extent, depend on the nature of instruction the visual aids support.

The fifth class is transient media. This class probably contains the largest number of different media. The stimuli presented to the student are transient in terms of the duration with which they are presented to the student. The message in media such as a film, audio tape, or slide tape presentation moves along at a predetermined rate. If students' attention lags during a film, they may miss an important part of the instruction. Of course if students are watching a film alone, they can put the projector in a reverse mode to review any part of the film, but this is sometimes cumbersome. In the more typical group viewings, students either get the message the first time around or they miss it entirely. Transient media may be "programmed" by including adjunct response booklets, but even here "going back over" the message as one might do in reading a text is very difficult, if not impossible. Typically these media involve the student least because they are generally not programmed. The student merely listens to or watches the message presented by the machine.

An index to the directory of media follows:

TUTORIAL MEDIA

Computer-assisted instruction
Teaching machines
Learning lab
Programmed text

ENVIRONMENTAL MEDIA/AIDS

Simulator
Paper simulations
Games and role-play

PRINT MEDIA

Textbook
Microform

VISUAL AIDS: GRAPHICS

Charts, diagrams, and graphs
Illustrations and drawings
Photographs

VISUAL AIDS: EXHIBITS

Cutaways
Mockups and models

VISUAL AIDS: PROJECTED STILL IMAGES

Opaque projections
Overhead transparencies
Slides

TRANSIENT MEDIA: AUDIO

Radio
Tape recordings
Variable speech tape recordings
Records
Listening lab

TRANSIENT MEDIA: VISUAL

Filmstrip (silent)
Motion picture as repetitive loop (silent)

TRANSIENT MEDIA: AUDIOVISUAL

Slides with sound
Filmstrip with sound
Television
Motion picture
Motion picture as repetitive loop (with sound)

Let us examine the application and qualification for the variety of media available.

MEDIUM: Computer-Assisted Instruction

APPLICATIONS

- To provide individual instruction through intrinsic programming.
- To keep accurate and automatic day-to-day records of students' backgrounds and interests, and to make recommendations for individualized, remedial, or advanced assignment.
- To simulate dangerous or lengthy learning situations.
- To provide instruction when students are widely scattered, or when it is impractical to bring students together at a common place and a common time.

QUALIFICATIONS

- Very few programs having application may be available for off-the-shelf purchase.
- Research has not fully identified all subjects appropriate for computer-assisted instruction courses.
- As only one student at a time can use a terminal, scheduling is a consideration.
- Not feasible for subject matter that will frequently change.

GROUP SIZE	*INSTRUCTOR'S ROLE*	*PRODUCTION COST*	*EQUIPMENT COST*
Individual	Administrator, individual tutor/counselor	Very high (150–300 hours) of development time required per contact hour	Very high initial cost (cost per student hour may be amortized to acceptable level)

MATERIAL/PRODUCTION CONSIDERATIONS

Computer-assisted instruction courses represent an enormous investment in time and money. Individuals needed for in-house development of programs are seldom available. A team of individuals is required since no one person has all the necessary capabilities. A team should consist of an author, an instructional programmer, an audiovisual expert, and a behavioral scientist, among others. The same personnel would be required for any computer-assisted instruction project, but the number and types of individuals may vary depending on the number of courses in computer-assisted instruction being used.

MEDIUM: *Teaching Machines*

Devices that can present information, query learners, and allow overt responses. The information may be presented by audio, visual, or audiovisual means.

APPLICATIONS

- To present programmed materials to a student in a controlled fashion. The rate of presentation is normally controlled by the student, but sequence, knowledge of results, and other areas are controlled by the machine.
- To show the range from simple devices that are manually operated to complex computers.
- To incorporate audio and visual transient media.
- To present linear or branching programmed materials.

QUALIFICATIONS

- Bypassing may be difficult.
- Commercial programs are not standardized and are suitable for use with a specific machine only.
- As students use machine one at a time, scheduling is a consideration.
- Not feasible for subject matter that will frequently change.

GROUP SIZE	INSTRUCTOR'S ROLE	PRODUCTION COST	EQUIPMENT COST
Individual	Administrator, individual tutor/counselor	High	Moderate to high

MATERIAL/PRODUCTION CONSIDERATIONS:

Some programs are available commercially, but they will usually have to be specially prepared. Development of programs requires a substantial investment of time. Personnel should include programmers to write the material and subject-matter specialists to ensure the accuracy of the material. These capabilities are seldom found in one person.

MEDIUM: *Learning Lab*

Carrels, audio tape recorders, microphones for student response and earphones for listening, video tape players and earphones.

APPLICATIONS

Audio tape recorders:
- To present audio material on an individual basis, carrels are provided for each student. Microphones are provided for student response. Responses are monitored by instructors or are recorded on audio tape. Students can compare their answers with correct answers on tape. Tapes may be preserved and evaluated by instructor at a later time. When no microphones are provided, students sometimes write responses in workbooks.
- To use for repeated listening.
- To use with dial-access systems.

Video tape players:
- To present audiovisual material on an individualized basis.

QUALIFICATIONS

- Equipment requires periodic cleaning to maintain sound quality.
- Order of presentation is fixed.
- Not feasible for subject matter that will frequently change.

GROUP SIZE	INSTRUCTOR'S ROLE	PRODUCTION COST	EQUIPMENT COST
Individual (however several carrels may receive same audio or video material at the same time)	Administrator, individual tutor/counselor	Varies from moderate to high	Varies from moderate to high

MATERIAL/PRODUCTION CONSIDERATIONS

Essentially the same as for audio tape. However because the material is programmed, personnel should include programmers to develop the material.

MEDIUM: Programmed Text

APPLICATIONS

- To present programmed materials in a convenient and portable workbook format. Responses are recorded in the workbook or on a separate response sheet.
- To allow students to work through programmed materials at their own convenience—either in class or at home.
- To program by linear, branched, or a combination.

QUALIFICATIONS

- Students may be tempted to simply look at response page and copy responses rather than work through the program.
- In linear programs the rate of learning is controlled by the students, but sequence and knowledge of results is controlled by program. Branching-type programs allow for greater individualization.

GROUP SIZE	INSTRUCTOR'S ROLE	PRODUCTION COST	EQUIPMENT COST
Individual	Administrator, individual tutor/counselor	High	Low per unit, but moderate for groups

MATERIAL/PRODUCTION CONSIDERATIONS

Many programs are available commercially. They are in the commerce and standardized subject-matter areas, skills, and trades. Consequently for specialized training needs, they will normally have to be specially prepared. Development of programs requires a substantial investment of time. Personnel should include programmers to write the materials and subject-matter specialists to ensure the accuracy of the material. These capabilities are seldom found in one person.

MEDIUM: *Simulator*

Sometimes called Part-Task Trainer, Whole-Task Trainer, or Procedures Trainer.

APPLICATIONS

- To allow the student "hands-on" experience with substitute equipment that is safer, less costly, or provides better conditions for instruction than equipment on the job.
- To promote a high degree of transfer because of similarity to the job.
- To provide a realistic representation of the operational setting if properly programmed.
- To represent an entire piece of equipment or a component part of a larger piece of equipment.

QUALIFICATIONS

- Actual equipment may be difficult to obtain.

GROUP SIZE	INSTRUCTOR'S ROLE	PRODUCTION COST	EQUIPMENT COST
Small group or individual	Administrator, individual tutor/counselor	Moderate to high	Moderate to high

MATERIAL/PRODUCTION CONSIDERATIONS

Not normally available. Will have to be specially procured or produced to meet the requirements of the instructional program.

MEDIUM: *Paper Simulations*

Use some means to conceal information or cues needed to solve the problem, such as opaque ink, which can be erased to reveal information; invisible ink, which may be made to appear by stroking the area with a special pen or crayon; punch board; or opaque tape. They leave a permanent record of what information students have "requested" so that their approach to the problem can be evaluated.

APPLICATIONS

- To individualize a teaching strategy in which students must request each piece of information they receive.
- To teach troubleshooting when the concern is learning the system logic rather than the manipulative skills involved.
- To teach troubleshooting when the hardware is not available, or safety or cost considerations discourage the use of the hardware for training.
- To force the student to "think through" a problem.
- For some management games.

QUALIFICATIONS

- The only cues that can be used are static, visual, or verbal.
- Materials cannot be reused.

GROUP SIZE	INSTRUCTOR'S ROLE	PRODUCTION COST	EQUIPMENT COST
Individual	Administrator, individual tutor/counselor	Low to moderate	Low

MATERIAL/PRODUCTION CONSIDERATIONS

Paper simulations require care in preparation and must be carefully pretested. May have to use a commercial contractor to print or put together the final version of what you have developed.

MEDIUM: *Games and Role-Play*

APPLICATIONS

- To represent a social system or interpersonal process in miniature so that students can practice responses to various situations that are similar to those they will encounter on the job.
- To make active participation possible in social situations rather than reading, listening, or seeing how to behave.
- To permit expansion or compression of real time.
- To allow focus on more subtle and less easily defined relationships.
- To use in leadership training, management training, interpersonal skills training, and cross-cultural sensitivity training.

QUALIFICATIONS

- Students may be inhibited about participating.
- Students may become so involved in simulation that they fail to observe processes.
- Evaluation is difficult because some attitudinal behaviors supposedly affected by process are difficult to measure.

GROUP SIZE	INSTRUCTOR'S ROLE	PRODUCTION COST	EQUIPMENT COST
Small group	Administrator, individual tutor/counselor	Varies from very low to high	Low

MATERIAL/PRODUCTION CONSIDERATIONS

Personnel who can develop effective simulation of social interactions are rare. Games are especially complicated, requiring some understanding of game theory and frequent tryout and revision cycles. Games in training have recently come into vogue and as a result more are becoming commercially available.

MEDIUM: *Textbook*

APPLICATIONS

- To present material in printed form, which students learn through reading.
- To furnish students with a highly condensed permanent source of information, which they can study as needed.

QUALIFICATIONS

- May cover too many topics. Difficult to update. Does not accommodate individual differences.
- Sometimes not written in readable form.

GROUP SIZE	*INSTRUCTOR'S ROLE*	*PRODUCTION COST*	*EQUIPMENT COST*
Individual	Administrator, individual tutor/counselor	Moderate to high	Low per unit but moderate for groups

MATERIAL/PRODUCTION CONSIDERATIONS

Require no production considerations. General information concerning textbooks may be obtained from the American Textbook Publishers Institute, 432 Park Avenue, South, New York, New York 10016.

MEDIUM: *Microform*

Microfiche, a sheet of film generally 4" by 6" and containing 98 or 250 pages of book copy, depending on amount of photo reduction, and microfilm (35mm or 16mm film) on which various types of images are photographed and stored.

APPLICATIONS

- To store large masses of printed or visual data in a small space for later readings as projected on reader screen, or as hard (paper) copy printouts.
- To use for independent study or research.
- To allow rapid, low-cost dissemination of printed materials because shipping and packaging costs are greatly reduced.
- To present the equivalent of filmstrip and text by using color microfiche.

QUALIFICATIONS

- Special equipment is needed for viewing, thus hardware problems prevent wholesale application of this medium for day-to-day instruction.
- For many people microforms are harder to read than printed materials. Speed reading of microforms is especially difficult.
- Cross-reference to different parts of a document (that is, text on one page and related diagram several pages away) are awkward to handle on microfiche.

GROUP SIZE	INSTRUCTOR'S ROLE	PRODUCTION COST	EQUIPMENT COST
Individual	Administrator, individual tutor/counselor	Low	Moderate

MATERIAL/PRODUCTION CONSIDERATIONS

Cost of producing microfiche originals and duplicates runs about 10 percent to 15 percent of the cost for equivalent volumes of conventional printed material. May be prepared locally with a minimum staff of two people. Equipment needed is a 16mm microfilm camera; a processor; a duplicator; and miscellaneous cutting, storage, and quality-control equipment. Microfiche can be prepared and in use in a very short time.

MEDIUM: Charts, Diagrams, and Graphs

APPLICATIONS

- To depict visually by means of lines, forms, colors, and various graphic devices, the conceptual structure of a process or the underlying structure of an object.
- To show relationships, chronological changes, distributions, time flow, organizational flow, structure, and components.

QUALIFICATIONS

- Only a small amount of subject content can be displayed. A diagram must be as simple as possible to be effective.
- Reading a chart, diagram, or graph properly may require guidance from the instructor or accompanying verbal captions and text.

GROUP SIZE	*INSTRUCTOR'S ROLE*	*PRODUCTION COST*	*EQUIPMENT COST*
Regular class, small group, or individual	Expository	Very low	Very low

MATERIAL/PRODUCTION CONSIDERATIONS

May be produced locally in a very short time. Can be produced on a chalkboard or other display surface, prepared in advance on slides or overhead transparencies, or reproduced and distributed to individual students. Extensive collections of diagrams, charts, and graphs can be clipped from newspapers, books, magazines, and textbooks. These can be shown using an opaque projector.

MEDIUM: Illustrations and Drawings

APPLICATIONS

- To represent, in still pictures, matter which requires representation in varying degrees of reality from stick figures to detailed illustrations.
- Preferred over photographs when simplification is required for better learning or when exaggeration will call attention to components critical to learning.

QUALIFICATIONS

- Only represent those elements critical to learning. Omit embellishments.
- Use color if it facilitates learning by calling attention to relevant similarities and differences.
- May require accompanying verbal test or instructor explanation for understanding.

GROUP SIZE	*INSTRUCTOR'S ROLE*	*PRODUCTION COST*	*EQUIPMENT COST*
Regular class, small group, or individual	Expository	Low	Very low

MATERIAL/PRODUCTION CONSIDERATIONS

Depends on the nature of the illustration or drawing. If drawings are simple (stick figures) and the quality of the drawing is not critical, drawings can be created locally by nearly anyone. If accurate and realistic representation is critical, the drawings should be created by a person skilled in drawing.

MEDIUM: Photographs

APPLICATIONS

- To represent, in still pictures, a realistic representation of objects, places, or persons. Preferred when visual recognition is critical to learning.
- To represent an object or place from a point of view not normally seen by the student to show important relationship, for example, aerial photographs.

QUALIFICATIONS

- Only represent those elements critical to learning. Omit embellishments.
- Use color only if it facilitates learning by calling attention to relevant similarities and differences.
- May require accompanying verbal text or instructor explanation for understanding.

GROUP SIZE	*INSTRUCTOR'S ROLE*	*PRODUCTION COST*	*EQUIPMENT COST*
Regular class, small group, or individual	Expository	Low	Low

MATERIAL/PRODUCTION CONSIDERATIONS

May be produced locally in a short time. If enlargements or special lighting effects are needed, special equipment will be necessary.

MEDIUM: *Cutaways*

APPLICATIONS

- To show inside of model parts or a process hidden by a covering. They may be life-size or scaled-up or scaled-down version with varying degrees of detail.

QUALIFICATIONS

- Should be used only when three-dimensional representation is essential to learning and the same conditions cannot be represented by two-dimensional form without having a detrimental effect on instruction.
- May require verbal captions or text or instructor explanation for understanding.

GROUP SIZE	INSTRUCTOR'S ROLE	PRODUCTION COST	EQUIPMENT COST
Small group	Expository	Varies from very low to high	Varies from very low to high

MATERIAL/PRODUCTION CONSIDERATIONS

Dependent upon the nature of the representation. Scale cutaways may require skilled cutaway builders and almost always require a substantial amount of time to complete. Simplified cutaways generally require less highly skilled personnel and take a shorter time to complete.

MEDIUM: *Mock-ups and Models*

Three-dimensional representations of objects that differ from the real object in size, material, and/or functional capability.

APPLICATIONS

- To emphasize or highlight certain elements or components by eliminating all nonessential elements of reality not necessary for learning.
- To give some idea of what a functioning prototype would be like.
- To illustrate spatial relationships.
- To teach personnel how to operate the actual machine, apparatus, or system when size, cost, safety, or some other consideration prevents using the actual equipment.

QUALIFICATIONS

- Should be used only when three-dimensional representation is essential to learning and the same conditions cannot be represented by two-dimensional form without having a detrimental effect on instruction.
- May require verbal captions or text or instructor explanation for understanding.

GROUP SIZE	INSTRUCTOR'S ROLE	PRODUCTION COST	EQUIPMENT COST
Small group	Expository	Varies from very low to high	Varies from very low to high

MATERIAL/PRODUCTION CONSIDERATIONS

Dependent upon the nature of the representation. Scale mock-ups or models require skilled builders and almost always require a substantial amount of time to complete. The simpler the mock-up or model, the easier and less expensive it is to produce.

MEDIUM: Opaque Projections
Nontransparent still visuals.

APPLICATIONS

- To project onto a screen, flat, nontransparent objects. Objects of approximately two inches thick or less can be projected.

QUALIFICATIONS

- For large groups room requires considerable darkening, making written response difficult.
- For small groups seated closely around screen and materials of relatively large detail, a lighted room may be used.
- Difficult to accommodate for individual differences among students.
- Bulky for handling and storage.

GROUP SIZE	INSTRUCTOR'S ROLE	PRODUCTION COST	EQUIPMENT COST
Large or small group	Expository	Very low	Low

MATERIAL/PRODUCTION CONSIDERATIONS

Material projected requires no special preparation.

MEDIUM: *Overhead Transparencies*

Transparent still visuals (usually 10" x 10").

APPLICATIONS

- To project still visuals onto a screen. Additional visuals can be overlaid onto the original to show "buildup" of display.
- Transparencies can be marked or written on during presentation to group.
- May be projected in room having normal ambient light.

QUALIFICATIONS

- Difficult to accommodate for individual differences among students.
- Bulky for handling and storage.

GROUP SIZE	INSTRUCTOR'S ROLE	PRODUCTION COST	EQUIPMENT COST
Large or small group	Expository	Very low	Low

MATERIAL/PRODUCTION CONSIDERATIONS

Can be locally produced by minimally skilled persons in a short time. However the cost of reproducing color photography requires special skills and is very expensive. Special equipment for reproducing transparencies is commercially available. Transparencies can be made from original copy by electrostatic or thermal office copying machines. They can also be pasted on acetate.

MEDIUM: Slides

APPLICATIONS

- To project a number of still images onto a screen for group viewing.
- For subsequent presentations slides can easily be removed, updated, or arranged to be shown in a different order.
- Some projections may be operated remotely to allow the instructor to point to critical parts of the image on the screen.
- Student responder devices may be connected to the slide projector so that it does not advance until student(s) has responded.

QUALIFICATIONS

- Verbal explanation must be provided.
- Requires darkened room unless a special daylight screen is used, or rear projection is used.
- Since presentation is normally for group viewing, rate of presentation may be too fast for some and too slow for others.

GROUP SIZE	*INSTRUCTOR'S ROLE*	*PRODUCTION COST*	*EQUIPMENT COST*
Large or small group or individual	Expository; carries burden of instruction (may be recorded)	Low	Low

MATERIAL/PRODUCTION CONSIDERATIONS

May be done locally in a short time. Photographic equipment is frequently available or easily acquired. Slides may be developed commercially or in-house, depending on facilities. Because there is a variety of sizes of slide transparencies and a variety of slide frames, it is important to select size and frame that are compatible with the projection equipment.

MEDIUM: *Radio*

Live presentation, audio tape recordings.

APPLICATIONS

- To present auditory information.
- To present lectures by special subject-matter experts to widely dispersed areas where no specialized instructors are available.
- To present "live" events as they happen.
- Can be prerecorded for presentation at convenient times.
- On a regional basis, can be combined with telephone to allow students to "call in" with questions.

QUALIFICATIONS

- Transitory; dependent on student listening carefully to the materials.
- Difficult to accommodate for individual differences among students.
- Since transmission is typically one-way, student cannot ask questions.
- Practice difficult to integrate into instruction.

GROUP SIZE	INSTRUCTOR'S ROLE	PRODUCTION COST	EQUIPMENT COST
Large groups	Expository or none	Low to moderate	Low

MATERIAL/PRODUCTION CONSIDERATIONS

Special production normally necessary; however, a radio production is about one-third the cost of a television production.

MEDIUM: *Tape Recordings*

1/4" magnetic tape reels, 1/8" magnetic tape cassettes.

APPLICATIONS

- To present sound (spoken, musical, artificial, natural) to groups or individuals.
- To provide auditory information, which students can listen to at their convenience (suitable for repeated listening).
- To record events or broadcasts for replay at a later time.
- To provide narration for slide or filmstrip.
- Used in learning labs, listening labs, and dial-access information retrieval systems.

QUALIFICATIONS

- Backtracking to hear specific portions of the tape may be difficult, especially with cartridges and some less expensive cassette units.
- Equipment requires periodic cleaning to maintain sound quality.
- Order of presentation is fixed.

GROUP SIZE	INSTRUCTOR'S ROLE	PRODUCTION COST	EQUIPMENT COST
Individual, regular class, or small group	Administrator, individual tutor/counselor	Low	Low to moderate

MATERIAL/PRODUCTION CONSIDERATIONS

Easily produced locally in short time. Recordings can be produced easily by unskilled personnel after careful study of the manuals and guides issued by manufacturers of equipment. Tape recordings can be edited to select the portion or portions most useful. Multiple copies of recordings can be reproduced by dubbing, but this requires special equipment.

Audio taped lessons on various topics are distributed by the National Center for Audio Tapes at the University of Northern Colorado, Greeley, Colorado 80639.

MEDIUM: *Variable Speech Tape Recordings*

Special magnetic tape recording device that permits controlled acceleration or expansion of the rate of speech with minimal distortion.

APPLICATIONS

Accelerated Speech (time-compressed)
- To present speech material at faster rate than normal to efficiently utilize the limited time available.
- To expose visually handicapped or people with serious reading problems to audio material at a pace faster than "normal" word rate.

Rate Expanded Speech
- To present lecture material at a slower rate than "normal" word rate, such as may be needed when learning a foreign language or learning to type from dictated materials.

QUALIFICATIONS

- Backtracking to hear specific portions of the tape may be difficult, especially with cartridges and some less expensive cassette units.
- Equipment requires periodic cleaning to maintain sound quality.
- Order of presentation is fixed.

GROUP SIZE	INSTRUCTOR'S ROLE	PRODUCTION COST	EQUIPMENT COST
Individual, regular class, or small group	Administrator, individual tutor/counselor	Low	Moderate

MATERIAL/PRODUCTION CONSIDERATIONS

Make "normal" tape on standard equipment; then use special electronic equipment to convert to variable speech recordings. Standard tape duplicating equipment can be used to make multiple copies.

An alternative would be to contract out the conversion of "normal" tape to a variable speech tape.

MEDIUM: *Records*

33 1/3, 45, or 75 r.p.m. disk recordings and soundsheets (paper thin).

APPLICATIONS

- To present sound (spoken, musical, artificial, or natural).
- Long-playing (33 1/3 r.p.m.) records provide up to 45 minutes of sound.
- Suitable for repeated listening.
- Can be supplemented by graphic material, photographs, or workbooks.
- Records are less likely to be damaged than audio tape.
- Soundsheets are readily mailable.

QUALIFICATIONS

- Practice is difficult to integrate into instruction (student tends only to listen).
- Searching for a specific segment to hear again is inconvenient.
- Order of presentation is fixed.
- Records and soundsheets cannot be revised without replacing.

GROUP SIZE	INSTRUCTOR'S ROLE	PRODUCTION COST	EQUIPMENT COST
Individual or small group	Administrator, individual tutor/counselor	Moderate to high	Low

MATERIAL/PRODUCTION CONSIDERATIONS

Need special recording facilities and trained personnel to produce. However records are usually commercially made. Record players are usually available or easily obtained. For small and medium volume reproduction, tape-based systems are preferred.

MEDIUM: *Listening Lab*

Carrels, audio tape recorders, and earphones for listening.

APPLICATIONS

- To present audio material on an individual basis, carrels are provided.
- Students may use at their convenience. Suitable for repeated listening.
- May be used with dial-access systems.
- Adjunct texts, workbooks, and other printed materials may be used for responding.

QUALIFICATIONS

- Backtracking to hear specific portions of the tape may be difficult, especially with cartridges and some less expensive cassette units.
- Equipment requires periodic cleaning to maintain.
- Order of presentation is fixed.
- Student responses cannot be recorded.
- Feedback is not a built-in feature of the system. Monitoring student responses is difficult; errors may be reinforced.

GROUP SIZE
Individual (however several carrels may receive same audio at the same time)

INSTRUCTOR'S ROLE
Administrator, individual tutor/counselor

PRODUCTION COST
Varies from low to moderate

EQUIPMENT COST
Varies from low to moderate

MATERIAL/PRODUCTION CONSIDERATIONS

Essentially the same as for any audio tape recording. Easily produced locally in a short time. Recordings can be produced by unskilled personnel after careful study of the manuals and guides issued by manufacturers of equipment. Tape recordings can be edited to select the portion or portions most useful. Multiple copies of recordings can be reproduced by dubbing but requires special equipment.

Audio taped lessons on various topics are distributed by the National Center for Audio Tapes at the University of Colorado.

MEDIUM: *Filmstrip (Silent)*

Color or black-and-white 35mm filmstrip, 16mm and Super 8mm filmstrip cartridges, Super 8mm filmstrips.

APPLICATIONS

- To present a number of still visuals in a fixed, highly structured sequence.
- Students determine their own rate of advancement through sequence.
- Suitable for repeated viewing.
- Requires minimum storage space compared to slide trays.
- Rear screen units can be used in lighted room.

QUALIFICATIONS

- Sequence cannot be modified.
- Verbal explanations are limited to captions on slides.
- 16mm and Super 8mm filmstrips are not standardized and availability is limited.
- Front projection requires some room darkening.

GROUP SIZE	INSTRUCTOR'S ROLE	PRODUCTION COST	EQUIPMENT COST
Individual or small group	Administrator, individual tutor/counselor	Low	Low

MATERIAL/PRODUCTION CONSIDERATIONS

May be done locally in short time or may be rented or purchased from the National Audiovisual Center, General Services Administration, Washington, D.C. 20406, or from commercial distributors.

Stand-alone projection systems for 35mm filmstrips have been developed. They are simple to operate, inexpensive, and allow flexible scheduling. In their simple form, they are hand-operated viewers operating on pen light batteries.

For Super 8mm filmstrips, there are very simple handheld viewers that fold flat and can be mailed.

MEDIUM: Motion Picture as Repetitive Loop (Silent)
Color or black-and-white 16mm motion picture film, Super 8mm cartridge loaded projectors.

APPLICATIONS

- To present a single-concept message in which visuals and motion are important.
- Suitable for repeated viewing.
- May be a substitute for a short "live" demonstration, which is difficult to set up.
- May be programmed to provide for active student response or complement a programmed text.
- Super 8mm cartridges and projectors are designed specifically for a single-concept film.
- Prints may be made in large quantities for cost-effective instruction.

QUALIFICATIONS

- Time span for seeing and hearing is fixed.
- To review or see a portion of a Super 8mm continuous loop cartridge film, the entire film must be shown to see the portion of interest. The projector cannot simply be put into a reverse, fast forward, or stop-frame operation.
- Super 8mm cartridges are not standardized.

GROUP SIZE	INSTRUCTOR'S ROLE	PRODUCTION COST	EQUIPMENT COST
Individual small group	Administrator, tutor/counselor	Varies from moderate to high	Low per unit, but moderate for groups

MATERIAL/PRODUCTION CONSIDERATIONS

Films may be made by Aerospace Audio Visual Service, Norton AFB, California 96204, or by commercial contractor. Existing films are available from National Audiovisual Center, Washington, D.C., and from commercial agencies.

MEDIUM: *Slides with Sound*

2" x 2" slide and associated record or audio tape that is synchronized to the slide presentation, sound-on-slide.

APPLICATIONS

- To project a series of still images onto a screen for group viewing.
- To supplement the images with a prerecorded narration.
- Adjunct text or workbooks may be used for self-instructional approach.
- May use several projectors simultaneously for teaching.
- Certain sound-slide projectors can be programmed to stop the presentation to permit some student response/application.
- Student responder devices may be connected to slide projector so that it does not advance unit if student has responded.

QUALIFICATIONS

- Requires darkened room unless a special daylight screen or rear projection is used.
- Tendency to rely too heavily on words, so that images are incidental to instruction.
- Difficult to accommodate for individual differences.
- May lose synchronization between sound and slides. Because of this backing up the program to repeat a segment is difficult.

GROUP SIZE	INSTRUCTOR'S ROLE	PRODUCTION COST	EQUIPMENT COST
Individual, small group, or large group	Administrator	Low	Low

MATERIAL/PRODUCTION CONSIDERATIONS

Easily produced locally in a short time. May require skilled photographers and artists to produce any captions used. The tape recording and synchronization can usually be performed by unskilled personnel after careful study of manuals and guides issued by manufacturers of equipment. Slides and sound are readily revised.

MEDIUM: Filmstrip (with Sound)

APPLICATIONS

- To present a series of still visuals in a fixed sequence.
- To provide more verbal explanation than is possible with captions in silent strip.
- Suitable for repeated viewing and listening.
- Rear screen unit can be used in lighted rooms.
- When used with headphones for listening, concentration is aided.

QUALIFICATIONS

- Loss of flexible pacing which is integral to a silent strip.
- Tendency to rely too heavily on words, so that picture becomes incidental to instruction.
- Sequence cannot be modified.
- Front projection requires some room darkening.

GROUP SIZE	INSTRUCTOR'S ROLE	PRODUCTION COST	EQUIPMENT COST
Individual or small group	Administrator	Low	Low

MATERIAL/PRODUCTION CONSIDERATIONS

May be produced locally in a short time or may be rented or purchased from the National Audiovisual Center, General Services Administration, Washington, D.C. 20406, or from other commercial distributors.

The filmstrip media package contains a phone disk or audio cassette and open-ended filmstrip.

MEDIUM: *Television*

Live presentation, motion picture film, video tape recordings, or video cassettes.

APPLICATIONS

- To present "live" transmission of an event so it is seen as it occurs.
- To present visual and auditory material including many other media (motion pictures, charts, diagrams, filmstrips, photographs).
- Television programming can be recorded on video tape for later showing.
- Students' performance is recorded and then replayed to allow them to analyze their performance.

QUALIFICATIONS

- Time span for seeing and hearing is fixed.
- Active involvement (practice opportunity) is relatively limited.
- Difficult to accommodate individual differences.
- Transitory; dependent upon students' careful attention to the message.

GROUP SIZE	INSTRUCTOR'S ROLE	PRODUCTION COST	EQUIPMENT COST
Individual, small group, or large group	Administrator	Moderate to high	Moderate to high

MATERIAL/PRODUCTION CONSIDERATIONS

Depends on video format; generally production is complex, requiring large and skilled production staff which normally includes a director, a cameraman for each camera, a floorman, an audio man, script writers, a lighting director, and "talent" (somebody who is in front of the camera). However 3/4" VCR systems allow less expensive and less complex productions.

MEDIUM: *Motion Picture*
Color or black-and-white 16mm film or Super 8mm film.

APPLICATIONS

- To present visual and auditory materials including many other media (charts, graphs, still pictures, cartoons).
- Can be previewed and a portion of a large film can be selected for viewing. (The whole film need not be shown.)
- Prints can be made in large quantities so that many groups have uniformity of instruction and are cost-effective.
- May be used as a complement to textbook based on programmed instruction.

QUALIFICATIONS

- Lack immediacy of television.
- The actual event cannot be shown in the process of its occurrence.
- Time span for hearing and seeing is fixed.
- Difficult to accommodate individual differences.
- Transitory dependent upon students' careful attention to the message.
- Picture deterioration may be caused by dust, scratches, and other ways.
- Revision of material is costly and difficult.

GROUP SIZE	INSTRUCTOR'S ROLE	PRODUCTION COST	EQUIPMENT COST
Large or small group	Administrator	High for 16mm; moderate for Super 8mm	Moderate to high

MATERIAL/PRODUCTION CONSIDERATIONS

16mm film production is complex, requiring skilled staff and special equipment. Sound film is costly and may require several months' work. Super 8mm film production can be as complex as 16mm motion pictures, or production can be done with equipment costing considerably less for a complex facility.

MEDIUM: *Motion Picture as Repetitive Loop (with Sound)*
Color or black-and-white 16mm motion picture film, Super 8mm cartridge-loaded projectors.

APPLICATIONS

- To present a single-concept message in which visuals and motions are important.
- Suitable for repeated viewing.
- May be a substitute for a short "live" demonstration, which is difficult to set up.
- May be programmed to provide for active student responding or complement a programmed text.
- Super 8mm cartridge and projectors are designed specifically for a single-concept film.
- Prints may be made in large quantities for cost-effective instruction.

QUALIFICATIONS

- Time span for seeing and hearing is fixed.
- To review or see a portion of a Super 8mm continuous loop cartridge film, the entire film must be shown to see the portion of interest. The projector cannot simply be put into a reverse, fast forward, or stop-frame operation.
- Super 8mm cartridges are not standardized.
- Revisions of materials are costly and difficult.

GROUP SIZE	INSTRUCTOR'S ROLE	PRODUCTION COST	EQUIPMENT COST
Individual	Administrator, individual tutor/instructor	Varies from moderate to high	Low per unit, but moderate for quantities

MATERIAL/PRODUCTION CONSIDERATIONS

Depends on the nature of the production requirement. Simple demonstrations and procedures that do not involve elaborate setups can be easily produced locally in a short time. More complicated productions usually require a skilled staff.

Many 8mm/Super 8mm films can be purchased. Before you have a film made, check to see if what you need already exists.

Instructor Preparation to Implement Program

The importance of the instructor cannot and should not be underestimated. Instructors/teachers are a most vital part of any instructional system and are the key to successful implementation. They must be sure instruction is carried out as designed, and must be certain that students are participating actively in the course of instruction. They must assess student and system performance. This section describes the instructor/teacher role in an Instructional System Development concept and presents some information to support the instructor/teacher responsibilities.

Orientation.

Prepare the instructors/teachers to undertake the functions expected of them in the program. The individualization of instruction offers an approach to education and training that is contrary to many instructors'/teachers' previous experiences. Plan to include the instructor/teacher in the development process to ensure that the course is carried out as designed. See Figures 16, 17, 18, and 19.

Do not assume automatic acceptance of new methods and philosophies. Make sure that instructor/teacher attitudes are positive. Provide them with instruction on the application of new concepts and techniques, as well as the rationale for their use. Show instructors how they will also benefit from new approaches to the instructional system.

The instructor/teacher has two main roles: course administrator and individual tutor/counselor.

Course Administrator.

As course administrator, instructors should make sure that instructional materials, equipment, training aids, and other supplies are readily accessible to the students. They should make certain that the equipment and aids function properly, and that each student is progressing within the preplanned scope of the teaching-learning activities. If deficiencies in student performance keep recurring, instructors assist in gathering data on the segment involved so that it can be analyzed for possible revision. They must administer the various tests to determine the achievement of course objectives. They must gather and tabulate all performance data of the trainee and the system. Instructors must keep track of student progress and coordinate the awarding of reinforcers, and all the details involved in making sure the course works. Where instruction is modular or self-paced, instructors also must schedule students and equipment for effective utilization.

Instructional Systems Development Model Flowchart

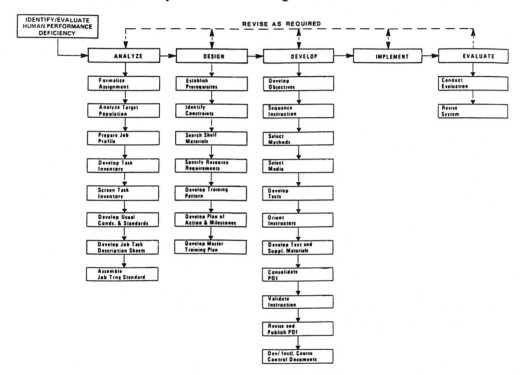

Figure 20

Individual Tutor/Counselor.

From a practical standpoint, it is almost impossible to design an instructional system that anticipates and provides for all students' needs at all times. Some students will always have trouble meeting certain objectives, understanding individual points, and performing certain tasks. The trouble spots will be different for every person. Instructors must be alert for such situations and be prepared to provide assistance where needed. The student's activities may be rechanneled to remedial sequences, or the instructor may provide individual tutoring.

The process of providing counseling to individual students may be new to some instructors/teachers. However in the Instructional Systems Development approach, it is a very important function. Unfavorable attitudes, opinions, or emotions can sharply reduce students' ability to learn. When such attitudes, opinions, and emotions are favorable, a healthy climate for learning is established. Most people are receptive to a good listener. So when interacting individually with students, the alert instructor can often aid the students in overcoming their difficulties before the problem can seriously affect learning. To serve this function effectively, the instructor must understand the instructional material, the objectives, and students' capabilities to know when and what assistance to provide. The overly "helpful" instructor/teacher may blunt the interest and initiative of the students and reduce the effectiveness of the instructional material.

Preparing Instructors/Teachers for Their Role.

Instructors/teachers may not be accustomed to instruction that emphasizes how students perform rather than how instructors/teachers perform. People resist change for many reasons, such as fear of the unknown, lack of confidence in the system, or a lack of personal involvement in developing the change. Instructors/teachers faced with the task of utilizing new teaching techniques sometimes have a natural apprehension concerning new developments.

Instructors/teachers accept innovations more readily when they are given the opportunity to learn about new techniques, provide orientation programs, interact with other instructors/teachers, and go on field trips. Changes are also apt to be seen as more worthwhile if instructors/teachers are encouraged to participate in the planning and development of new or revised instructional techniques.

During the development stage, invite instructors/teachers to take an active part in conferences for an exchange of ideas. Many useful ideas emerge in brainstorming sessions, such as improvement of instructional conditions and resources, methods of presentation, and evaluation of procedures. Problems can be discussed and plans for resolving these problems can be formulated. When allowed to exchange ideas, instructors/teachers will sense that they are expected to contribute to the development of the instructional program. They will know that their suggestions are welcomed and will receive prompt attention.

Many times visits with personnel from other courses at the same school or other schools can be very helpful. Instructors/teachers in other courses may be using techniques similar to those being considered by the visiting group. In this manner the visitors can see the new methods in action and can discuss the advantages and disadvantages of these methods with course personnel.

Summary of Objectives

What do we mean when we say we want learners to know something? Do we mean we want them to recite or to solve or to construct? Simply to tell them to "know" tells them very little—because the word "know" can mean several things. Until you say what you mean by "knowing" in terms of what the students ought to be able to do, you have said very little at all. Thus an objective that communicates best will be one that describes the students' intended performance clearly enough to preclude misinterpretation—by the instructor or the student.

How can we do that? What characteristics might help make an objective communicate and help make it useful? There are several schemes that might be used in stating objectives, but the format described here is one that is known to work, and it is one that I have experienced to be the most effective and easiest to use.

The format includes three characteristics that help make an objective communicate an intent. These characteristics answer three questions: (1) What should the learner be able to do? (2) Under what conditions should the learner be able to do it? (3) How well must it be done? The three characteristics follow:

1. Performance   An objective always says what a learner is expected to be able to do.
2. Conditions   An objective always describes the important conditions, if any, under which the performance is to occur.
3. Criterion   Whenever possible an objective describes the criterion of acceptable performance by describing how well the learner must perform to be considered acceptable.

Though it is not always necessary to include the second and not always practical to include the third characteristic, the more you say about them, the better your objective will be communicated. Other characteristics could be included in an objective as well, such as a description of the students for which the objective is intended or a description of the instructional procedures by which the objective will be accomplished. Though these are important pieces of information in the process of designing instruction, the objective is not the place for them. But then Why not? you may ask. Because this information clutters up the objective and makes it more difficult to read and interpret. The objective needs to be useful as well as clear. If you begin to stuff all sorts of unnecessary items into it, it will fail to serve its purpose. Many such objectives have been written—but never used.

It would also be possible to insist that objectives follow some rigid form or format. (I once worked for a school principal for whom teachers were expected to write their objectives on a form printed by the principal himself. His form had a line printed every three inches down the page. The implication being that every objective was no more than five inches long and two inches high. Would you be surprised to learn that the teachers were hostile to the principal's idea?) We are not looking for objectives that are a particular size and shape. We are looking for objectives that are clear, for objectives that say what we want to say about our instructional intents as concisely as possible. No more, no less. So anybody who says that an objective must be no more than two inches high and five inches wide or who says an objective must or must not contain certain words should be reminded that the function of an objective is to communicate. If it does it is a success. Be happy! If it does not, fix it, and fix it right. You do not work on an objective until it matches someone's idea of "good design" or "good looks"; you work on the objective until it communicates one of your instructional intents—and you write as many objectives as you need to describe all instructional intents you know are important to accomplish. The number of objectives, as is the case with the size of objectives, is unimportant.

Chapter IX
Effective Questioning Techniques

It is easier to be critical
than it is to be correct.

Benjamin Disraeli

Classroom interaction involving student participation is an extremely important part of instruction. The effective use of questioning provides students with more opportunity to express their own ideas and become actively involved in the learning process. The instructor's goals should include developing probing questions, which will make students more active in participating.

Here are some techniques for effective questioning used by many experienced instructors:

1. Use questions to draw information from the students, to provoke and stimulate discussion, and to provide you, the instructor, with "feedback" to help evaluate the effectiveness of your instruction.
2. Use questions to vary the kind of student participation: that is, call on students directly; ask questions of the whole group; then redirect questions to individual students.
3. Pause after asking a question to let the entire class think about an answer; then call on one student to respond.
4. Give students ample time to think about the question before asking for their answer—don't give the answer to them or put words in their mouths. There is nothing wrong with a moment of silence in the classroom.
5. Spread the questions evenly among the class so that each student has an equal opportunity to participate.
6. Avoid using questions as punishment or penalty devices to trap the inattentive or squelch the talkative. Students resent this approach, and you only lose their interest when you use this poor technique.

7. Avoid questions requiring only "yes" or "no" answers; instead ask WHY, HOW, WHEN, WHAT, and WHAT IF.

8. State all your questions in clear and concise terms; reword and restate questions whenever necessary for comprehension.

9. Make students analyze, criticize, and role-play in situations which require more than just a list, review, outline, or summary answer.

10. Ask questions, whenever possible, in which students can relate to their own past experience.

11. Learning is helped by formulating and asking questions that stimulate thinking, imagination, and innovation.

How to Use Questions Effectively

1. Plan your questions in advance.
2. Use one question for one idea.
3. Make the wording definite, clear, and concise.
4. Take individual differences into consideration.
5. Ask the question; then ask for a volunteer or name the learner to answer.
6. Distribute questions fairly among the learners.
7. Ask only one question at a time.
8. Allow ample time for answering.
9. Never use questions as punishment.
10. Be prepared to accept learners' questions at any time. Ask for any questions from time to time. Don't bluff if you don't know the answer. Find it out and tell the learner as soon as possible.
11. Don't deal with questions that will be dealt with later.
12. Acknowledge the answers.

Benefits of Using Questions

1. Stimulate learner's thinking, reasoning, and feeling
2. Generate learner's curiosity, interest, and participation
3. Help learner recall and repeat vital facts and principles
4. Test memory and understanding of knowledge/skill previously learned
5. Keep a check on progress
6. Clear up misunderstanding
7. Direct learners' thinking by bringing them back to the subject or by steering them toward the next topic

Chapter X
Course Planning

Overview

Although teachers/instructors are not directly responsible for certain parts of course planning, such as the curriculum, they need to be familiar with all aspects of course planning that affect their instruction. (See Figures 15, 16, and 17.) Curriculum is, and always will be, of significant concern to the professional teacher/instructor. Keep in mind that the curriculum is a *dynamic* process. (See Figure 12.)

Preparation for Curriculum Development

In order to prepare yourself, and in order to make lasting contributions to significant educational effectiveness, as a curriculist, a practitioner of curriculum development, you must know the needs and requirements that have to be addressed in the preparation, revision, or restructuring of a curriculum. This is most timely because we are in the midst of an era of worldwide presumed school reform. In support of your preparation, an inventory of needs and requirements follows. The inventory is divided into two sections. The first section is labeled knowledge and understanding, or cognitive learning. The second section is labeled skill and competence.

Knowledge and Understanding*

1. To understand children and youth, especially children and youth as learners in school
2. To know the community environment from which youngsters come to school
3. To know the demands that the society at large places in schools
4. To understand the cultures represented by the pupils in our schools
5. To understand psychological principles (e.g., concerning motivation to achieve) that affect pupils' ability and desire to learn
6. To know subject content that is pertinent to teaching and learning in schools
7. To know how subject matter can be taught effectively
8. To be aware of new developments and trends in individual subject.
9. To know how the process of curriculum change and improvement can work
10. To be aware of actions that can be taken to improve, rather than merely change, the curriculum
11. To know how to fit curriculum to learners, as opposed to fitting learners to curriculum
12. To be aware of current and possible systems of school organization and administration
13. To know how to direct enterprises in curriculum planning
14. To know functional methods of instructional supervision
15. To know how to conduct simple educational research
16. To understand the historical foundations of and events in movements toward curriculum improvement
17. To understand possible uses of computers and other machines for curriculum planning

*(Ronald C. Doll, *Curriculum Improvement: Decision-Making and Process,* 8th ed. Needham Heights, Mass.: Allyn & Bacon, 1992.)

18. To know alternative ways of making curriculum plans
19. To understand ways of restructuring schools to achieve educational improvement
20. To be familiar with the ideas of differing schools of educational philosophy
21. To know what curriculum plans to propose for youngsters of differing levels of ability and for youngsters with special handicaps
22. To be able to recognize the presence or absence of sequence, balance, and other features of a suitable curriculum
23. To know one's philosophical beliefs about human potential and schooling
24. To be able to recognize valid research data and conclusions
25. To know where to find help with difficult curriculum problems

Skill and Competence:

1. To be competent in reading and understanding the literature on teaching, learning, and the curriculum
2. To be competent in writing cogently and at length about curriculum matters
3. To be able to state clearly worthy aims, goals, and objectives of schooling
4. To be able to answer the questions of teachers and other people about details of the curriculum
5. To be skilled in working with parents and other community members of different backgrounds, abilities, and cultures
6. To be skilled in conferring with teachers and curriculum specialists about difficult aspects of the curriculum
7. To demonstrate competence in proposing and developing original curriculum designs
8. To exhibit skill in directing and bringing to completion varied planning enterprises
9. To be competent in teaching other professionals and laypeople to plan
10. To be skilled in leading different groups
11. To demonstrate skill in practicing methods of instructional supervision

12. To be able to speak convincingly to the public about curriculum proposals
13. To demonstrate skill in counseling co-workers and assistants
14. To show competence in planning and implementing in-service and staff development programs
15. To show familiarity with available instructional materials
16. To be capable of helping teachers and others devise new and different instructional materials
17. To be competent in creating criterion-referenced tests
18. To be skilled in scheduling and coordinating curriculum-improvement activities
19. To demonstrate skill in reconciling the conflicting viewpoints of fellow planners and in identifying and overcoming barriers to planning
20. To be able to work with officials of state or national educational agencies in the interest of curriculum improvement
21. To demonstrate skill in facilitating regional and state evaluations of the curriculum and of the improvement program
22. To be able to guide curriculum planners to significant sources of evidence
23. To be skilled in representing one's school system at professional conventions and meetings of laypersons
24. To demonstrate skill in working with learners in classrooms to show the worth of new curriculum plans
25. To demonstrate grace and ease at social and professional functions where the reputation of the school counts

Basic Elements of the Curriculum and Instructional Process

	What	*How*	*Where*
Phase I	Establish goals and necessary objectives	Student's background, culture, emotional, and academic needs	Interview student, family; school policy; state policy; community
Phase II	Assess student concerning objectives	Assess prerequisite skills, educational needs, and attitudes that are to be acquired	Interview student, family, community
Phase III	Implement instructional sequence	Prepare instructional design by including learning principles, task analysis, classroom management, and educational alternatives	Chapters VIII, X and XV
Phase IV	Evaluate instruction based on student behavior and student learning outcome	Establish school policies	Chapter XIV

*Ideals are like the stars—we
never reach them, but like the
mariners on the sea, we chart our
course by the stars.*

Carl Schurz

Five Curriculum Metaphors (Anglin and Dugan)

1. The curriculum as a medicine
   for educational ills
2. The curriculum as a greenhouse
   that encourages growth
3. The curriculum as a route
   for traveling to a destination
4. The curriculum as a means of production—
   brainpower production
5. The curriculum as a resource
   for developing and using human abilities

Preparation for Curriculum Development

The first consideration in planning a course of study or a program of instruction is the curriculum. When planning a curriculum, certain factors must be considered:

1. Define the terminal skills (hands-on, decisions, verbal).
2. The literature, language, and vocabulary should reflect the situation.
3. Examine the problems, if any, that are unique to certain groups, such as language, education level, age, and cultural factors.
4. The curriculum should be designed and written in terms that relate to the students and their role.
5. Identify goals of the course to ensure that the student understands intent, and that the teacher/instructor understands the intent of the student.
6. Methods and techniques used by the teacher/instructor should vary, according to lesson objectives, student capabilities and interests, and individual differences among the students.

Instructional Program Components

The representation below shows ranked relationships among the components of a typical instructional program.

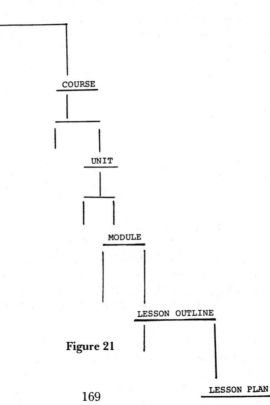

PROGRAM PLANNING

COURSE

UNIT

MODULE

LESSON OUTLINE

Figure 21

LESSON PLAN

Objectives[*]

Objectives must be stated in terms of expected behavior; what the student must be able to do at the end of a training/education program. Objectives describe observable student *behavior,* minimum *standards* of performance or proficiency expected, and *conditions* under which the behavior is to be exhibited.

An objective is a description of a performance you want students to be able to exhibit before they are considered competent. An objective describes an intended result of instruction, rather than the process of instruction. Consider the following phrases in this light:

Words Open to Many Interpretations (*Abstractions*)	*Words Open to Fewer Interpretations* (*Performance*)
To understand	To recite
To know	To identify
To appreciate	To assemble
To inspect	To solve
To really understand	To list
To prepare	To underline
To operate	To pass a test
To grasp, or believe he learned	To learn

An objective always says what a student or trainee is expected to be able to do, always describes the important conditions, if any, under which the performance is to occur; and whenever possible describes the criterion of acceptable performance, by describing how well the student must perform. Though it is not always necessary to include the second and not always practical to include the third characteristic, the more you say about them, the better your objective will be communicated.

[*](Because of their vital importance to instruction, objectives have also been discussed in detail in Chapter VIII.)

Each objective should be classified so that the test items generated from the objective can be shown to be consistent with the objective. The procedure for classification of objectives follows:

1. Determine the task level
   a. Determine whether the student is to *Remember* or *Use* information.
   b. If the student is to *Use* information, determine whether the task level is *Use-Aided* or *Use-Unaided.*

2. Determine the content type
   a. If the student is to recall or recognize names, parts, locations, functions, dates, or places, then the content type is *Fact.*
   b. If the student is to remember characteristics of similar objects or events, or must sort or classify objects, events, or ideas according to characteristics, then the content type is *Category.*
   c. If the student is to remember a sequence of steps that apply to a single situation, *or* if the student is to apply the steps to a single piece of equipment or a single situation, then the content type is *Procedure.*
   d. If the student is to remember a sequence of steps and decisions that apply in a variety of situations, or if the student is to apply the sequence across a variety of situations or types of equipment, then the content type is *Rule.*
   e. If the student is to remember how or why things work the way they do, or cause and effect relationship, *or* the student is to use his knowledge to explain how things work, or predict effects from causes, then the content type is *Principle.*

The classification should be determined according to:

1. What the student is to do (what the task he is to perform)
2. Instructional content (the type of information the student is to learn)

The objective should be appropriate for the work to be performed on the job or for later training. The requirements for assuring appropriateness are:

1. The *Conditions* should be appropriate for the work to be performed on the job or for later training.
2. The *Standards* should be appropriate for the work to be performed on the job or for later training.
3. The *Task Level* of the *Action* should be appropriate for the work to be performed on the job or for later training.
4. The *Content Type* of the *Action* should be appropriate for the work to be performed on the job or for later training.
5. *Remember*-level objectives should be followed later by *Use* objectives.
6. *Use-Unaided*-level objectives should be preceded by *Remember*-level objectives.
7. *Use-Aided*-level objectives should have adequate aid or should be supported by other objectives.

Objectives must be correctly stated. The *Conditions* under which student performance is expected must be specified. *Conditions* include:

1.	Environment	*Physical* (weather, location, shop/lab/classroom)
		Social (isolation, individual, team, audience)
		Psychological (fatigue, stress, relaxed)
2.	Information	*Given Information* (situation, formula, values)
		Cues (signals for starting and stopping)
		Special Instructions (vary)
3.	Resources	*Job Aids* (drawings, sketches, graphs, checklists)
		Equipment, Tools, Technical Manuals

The *Standards* of student performance must be specified. There are two standards of performance:

1. Performance   *Completeness* (how much of the task will be performed)
                                 Accuracy (how well each task will be performed)
                                 Time Limit (how much time is allowed for each task)

2. Product   *Completeness* (what the finished product will contain)
                                 Quality (what standard the product will meet)
                                 Judgment (what objective opinions the product will satisfy)

The *Action* the student performs should be specified with an action verb. Use verbs that are not open to interpretations or opinions. Instead of saying *to understand,* use the verb *to recite.* Instead of saying *to know,* say *to identify.* Be specific when using action verbs so that there is no doubt about the performance that is to be accomplished.

Many terms have been used to describe the various objectives (criterion, terminal, primary, enabling, supporting, secondary, and others). Whatever descriptive terms are used, basically they are all objectives and they should all describe behavior, conditions, and standards.

The important aspect to remember in developing objectives is that each objective contains four elements: the objective must be *specific, measurable, achievable,* and *challenging.* Each of the job tasks must state what the student will be able to do *after* the training or instruction is completed. (To recall these four elements easily, think of SMAC, Specific, Measurable, Achievable, and Challenging.)

The importance of developing effective objectives cannot be overemphasized. Below is a brief summary of the influence that objectives have on outlining teaching plans, selecting materials, evaluating student performance, determining lesson content, and describing student activity in the education or training concept.

What is meant by wanting learners to "know" something? Should they recite, solve, or construct? Simply telling them to "know" tells them very little—because the word "know" can mean several different things. Until the term "knowing" is defined in terms of what the students ought to be able to do, very little has been said. Thus an objective that communicates best will describe the students' intended performance clearly enough to preclude misinterpretation—by the teacher as well as by the student.

How can that be done? What characteristics might help make an objective communicate and help make it more effective and useful? Several schemes are used in stating objectives, but the format described here is one that is known to work, and one that I have used for several years and consider to be the most effective and easiest to use.

The format includes three characteristics that help make an objective communicate an intent. These characteristics answer three questions: (1) What should the learner be able to "do"? (2) Under what conditions should the learner be able to do it? (3) How well must it be done? The three characteristics follow:

1. Performance   An objective always says what a learner is expected to be able to "do."

2. Conditions   An objective always describes the important conditions, if any, under
                    which the performance is to occur.

3. Criterion   Whenever possible an objective describes the criterion of acceptable
                    performance by describing how well the learner must perform.

Though it is not always necessary to include the second and not always practical to include the third characteristic, the more you say about them, the better your objective will be communicated. Other characteristics could be included in an objective, such as a description of the students for which the objective is intended or a description of the instructional procedures by which the objective will be accomplished. Though these are important pieces of information in the process of designing an instruction, the objective is not the place for them. But then Why not? you may ask. Because this information clutters up the objective and makes it more difficult to read and interpret. The objective needs to be *useful* and *clear*. If you include unnecessary items, the objective will fail to serve its purpose. Many objectives have been written—but never used.

Objectives should follow some rigid form or format. (I once worked for a school principal who expected teachers to write their objectives on a form printed by the principal. His form had a line printed every three inches down the page, the implication being that every objective should be no more than five inches long and two inches high. Would you be surprised to learn that the teachers were hostile to the principal's concept?)

Objectives should not be a particular size and shape; objectives should be *clear,* so that they describe instructional objectives as concisely as possible—no more, no less. So anybody who says that an objective must be no more than two inches high and five inches wide or who says that an objective must or must not contain certain words should be reminded that the function of an objective is to communicate. If it communicates it is a success. Be happy! If it does not, fix it, and fix it right. An objective should not match someone's idea of "good design" or "good looks"; an objective should communicate instructional objectives. Write as many objectives as needed to describe all instructional objectives that are important to accomplish. The number and size of objectives are unimportant.

Lesson Plans

A lesson plan is a teaching outline of the important points of a lesson, arranged in the order in which these points are to be presented. It may include objectives, points to be made, questions to ask, reference to materials, and assignments for students. A lesson plan is a step-by-step plan of a presentation.

Each lesson plan must contain an objective or objectives that you expect your students to learn after the presentation is completed. In a training presentation, as opposed to an academic situation, approximately 75 percent of a learning experience should be spent on hands-on learning.

A first step in a lesson is like a first step in a planned journey. At the end of each lesson, you should ask: Did the student arrive at the destination? This means that you must identify your destination before you take your trip. You must begin your lesson by describing *to the students* the desired product. Questions about the course content, the method of instruction, the number of students in class, and many other factors are put aside until the desired learning outcomes have been identified. In the final analysis, your destination should be competence. Here, too, you can expect the product of instruction to be *a changed student.*

A second step in lesson planning is the "means of transportation" for your journey. This is your *subject matter.* Adequate planning of your materials will help you get there. Perhaps your curriculum, textbooks, films, and other supporting materials have been handed to you as an instructor. Now it is up to you to decide what chapters in the textbook must be stressed, if the whole film or a portion is needed, what supporting materials are required, and perhaps some practice exercises of our own making. The proper use of subject matter is an important contribution of a good teacher/instructor. You as an instructor/teacher must remember that a major contributing factor in selecting your class materials depends on your students' background, education, age, and experience. Careful thinking and planning on the teacher's part is a must.

> **A WELL-PREPARED LESSON PLAN**
> **IS A MARK OF A PROFESSIONAL**

There are several ways of organizing plans for a class or a course of study. Some instructors might like to use a daily lesson plan; others feel comfortable using a guide or an outline. In industry training instructors may be expected to complete a lesson plan format prior to presentation of each hour of instruction. Some school officials require only an outline. See the lesson plan format, which may be used in total or as a guide. (Figure 22.)

SAMPLE LESSON PLAN APPROACH

I. Welcome: Meet and greet students before class officially commences to establish rapport and informal, relaxed atmosphere

II. Introductions: To help establish a favorable learning climate
   A. Introduce yourself: work experience, education, family, interests, teaching experiences, hobbies
   B. Introduce class members
   C. Determine, from all students, what their own objectives are, what they intend to learn from your presentation (these comments may surprise you)

III. Introduction to the course: To help explain the purpose and instructional content of the course, and to help students determine how class goals will assist their personal goals and their future assignments in their jobs or positions

A. Course title—sessions planned
B. Objectives of the course—what it is, what it isn't
C. Overview of course content
IV. Introduction to lesson
    A. Overview of current lesson's content and technique
    B. Possible connections with previous experiences, learning
    C. "Why" of the lesson
V. Conduct teaching or learning activities for the lesson, using preplanned methods of instruction
VI. Closing of lesson: To review lesson and evaluate learning
    A. Question-answer period (oral or written)
    B. Have students summarize basic element or lesson orally
    C. Brief wrap-up and review by instructor
    D. Pass out handouts and/or give assignments for next class meeting

---

**A WELL-PRACTICED LESSON PLAN IS
SUCCESSFUL AND REWARDING.**

LESSON PLAN

COURSE TITLE: Teacher Training
REFERENCE NO. 88-4
MAJOR TASK AREA: Class Preparation
PAGE 1 **OF** 2
LESSON TITLE: Lesson Plan
SESSION NO.: 5th day

UPON COMPLETION OF THIS SESSION THE TRAINEES WILL BE ABLE TO:

1. Know the purpose of the Lesson Plan

2. Develop a Lesson Plan

3. Use a Lesson Plan

4.

5.

PRESENTATION: TRAINING TOPICS	TRAINING METHODS	TRAINING AIDS REFERENCE	TIME
1.0 Purpose of a Lesson Plan Lesson plans give teachers confidence while teaching, and also help teachers to: 1.1 Think through a lesson they will teach 1.2 Organize materials and tools required 1.3 Create motivation 1.4 Give right emphasis to important factors 1.5 Use training aids effectively 1.6 Emphasize safety 1.7 Ensure all information is included 1.8 Stay on schedule 1.9 Ask questions at the proper time	Lecture Discussion Question	Teacher's Text pp. 64-84	50 Min.

Figure 22

LESSON PLAN CONTINUATION SHEET			PAGE 2 OF 2 PAGES
PRESENTATION: TRAINING TOPICS	TRAINING METHODS	TRAINING AIDS REFERENCE	TIME
2.0 Developing a Lesson Plan Good training requires careful planning. A well-developed lesson plan has the following elements:			
2.1 Course Title			
2.2 Major Task Area: This identifies the division of the job analysis from which the lesson was taken but is not the specific aim or objective of the lesson.	Demonstration Hand out Lesson outlines		
2.3 Lesson Title: Name of the lesson within the major task area			
2.4 Session No.: The lesson number in the sequence of lessons			
2.5 Reference No.: For filing and recovery purposes, decimal system is recom- mended. Can be correlated with POI (program of in- struction) numbers and tasks			
2.6 Objectives: Specific les- son objectives (what the student will be able to do)			
2.7 Presentation: The act of training, using any combi- nation of methods and aids, including references and approximate time scheduled			
2.8 Summary: The lesson should always be summarized before proceeding to performance phase, or adjourning			

Motivation and the State of the Art

The teacher/instructor should never feel that after developing a lesson plan, it must remain fixed or static. Lesson plans must change for each class, keeping current with what is new, and must reflect changes in the curriculum, new technology, new equipment, changes of concepts, substitution of tools, and new innovations. All these changes require an update of the lesson plans from time to time. However—and this is most important—teachers must be sure they can justify any deviation from their approved lesson plans. Any changes must be well coordinated and approved.

Motivation plays a most important role in each lesson process. If teachers/instructors require their students to do outside class assignments, simply telling them to perform a specific task, to read a text, or to be responsible for some terms in a book, *are not* motivating factors. Instead relate each assignment to a specific part of the class, or a portion of the lesson that is beneficial *to the student,* and explain that to students. Let students know in detail why it is necessary to accomplish each assigned task.

Remain abreast of the latest teaching techniques, but above all keep students motivated with the objective or objectives of the lesson plan.

A teacher/instructor must consider the following points in preparation for a presentation:
- Make sure students understand why the assignment is important *to them.*
- Make sure that students understand what is expected to be done in and out of class.
- The teacher/instructor must always review an assignment at the beginning of the next class meeting to ensure that *all students* understand the material presented and studied.
- To the best of your ability as a teacher/instructor, try to recognize individual differences in the rate of learning. Do not expect exact, equal responses from all students.

It is important to note that there is no single factor that motivates all students all of the time. In my years in the teaching profession, these were the top motivating factors, in the order of importance:

- Feeling of achievement
- Recognition

- Challenge in the classroom
- Responsibility
- Growth and development

Points to Ponder

Check yourself on the following:

1. *See that the student understands the goals of the lesson and the course after you have discussed both after every lesson.*
2. *Your attitude toward, acceptance of, and interest in the student will be recognized immediately by the student.* You never get a second chance to make a good first impression.
3. *Physical discomfort is not conducive to learning.* Try to see that your students are as comfortable as possible. Check the seating, lighting, ventilation in the classroom, and the noise outside the classroom.
4. *Establish an informal, relaxed first meeting with your students, allowing them to feel some responsibility for the success of the course.*
5. *Try to be flexible in your teaching methods.* Whenever and wherever possible, mix your teaching techniques to include lecture, group discussion, guest speaker, demonstration, and audiovisual equipment.
6. Apply the theories of readiness, exercise, and effect, which aid in understanding that the student is actively involved in a learning process—thus satisfying results are attainable. Students learn by doing, and through reinforcement by repetition, they gain confidence.
7. *Be enthusiastic.* GET EXCITED about your instruction.
8. *Be informed, but not a know-it-all.* Stay abreast of new developments in your field, in the teaching profession. Anyone who stops running is old and out of date.

The Instructor's and the Teacher's Profession

As a good instructor or teacher, you should keep in mind and apply these eight fundamental responsibilities of your profession:

1. Instructors and teachers are responsible for dealing justly and impartially with students, regardless of their physical, mental, racial, or experience background.
2. Instructors and teachers should show integrity and loyalty to students and faculty.
3. Teachers and instructors should give wholehearted support to the overall educational curriculum and training program.
4. Supervisors and managers of faculty have a responsibility for providing training and educational update to their subordinates.
5. Instructors and teachers should not give information too far ahead of a learner's present state of knowledge or experience. In most cases this information is wasted and may be confusing. As new information is presented, be assured that learners relate to it. Begin at the level that the person has already attained and proceed from the known to the unknown.
6. Remember, and let the student be aware, that most education and training takes place at the start of a career and should continue throughout a working life. Education and training is a continuous, everyday process.
7. A good education and training concept provides encouragement and guidance so that the student will continue to educate or train himself.
8. It is the instructor's and the teacher's responsibility to use creative intelligence, in an effort to develop the best that is in each of his students. This is done by encouraging and guiding a process of growth by which students educate and train themselves. Aside from the successful completion of this important task, instruction has little meaning or value.

GOOD LUCK IN YOUR INSTRUCTION.

Program Development Process Flow

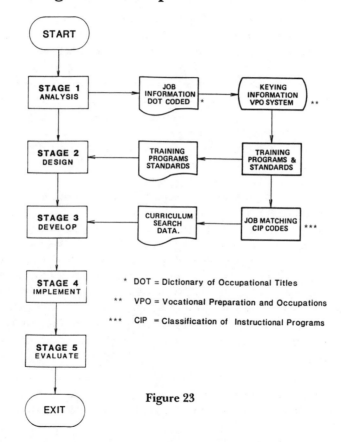

START

STAGE 1
ANALYSIS

JOB
INFORMATION
DOT CODED *

KEYING
INFORMATION
VPO SYSTEM **

STAGE 2
DESIGN

TRAINING
PROGRAMS
STANDARDS

TRAINING
PROGRAMS &
STANDARDS

STAGE 3
DEVELOP

CURRICULUM
SEARCH
DATA.

JOB MATCHING
CIP CODES ***

STAGE 4
IMPLEMENT

STAGE 5
EVALUATE

EXIT

* DOT = Dictionary of Occupational Titles

** VPO = Vocational Preparation and Occupations

*** CIP = Classification of Instructional Programs

Figure 23

183

Summary

The first step in planning a lesson is to define the lesson objective and the desired learning outcomes. The objective should be limited to a feasible outcome, and the objective and outcome should both be stated in terms of student activity. The desired learning outcomes should be stated clearly and concisely, to reflect what the student is to retain from the learning experience.

In planning a lesson, the teacher/instructor needs to do considerable research, the extent of which depends largely on the available time, the teacher's or instructor's experience with the subject matter, and the complexity of the subject.

As the teacher/instructor gathers research material in support of the desired learning outcomes, he organizes it to some extent. The primary emphasis in the final organization of the material should be on the clear and logical arrangement of ideas and procedures. Main points should overshadow subordinate points, and the material should be closely related and arranged so that one idea or procedure leads naturally to the next. This type of organization helps the student remember important points, because each key fact serves as a reminder of related facts.

The final selection of an instructional method may very well be a compromise between the method that is most suitable to the outcome (an ideal approach) and the method that is possible under circumstances (a realistic approach). Many variations, combinations, and adaptations may be made to any method or methods of teaching; in fact the number of possibilities is limited only by the teacher's/instructor's imagination. For this reason the teacher/instructor should recognize the many available opportunities to help his students accomplish desired outcomes.

The primary purpose of having a lesson plan is to ensure that the teacher/instructor considers every factor that might influence the effectiveness of a lesson. Very much like a pilot checklist, the teachers/instructors must have a "list" of factors to follow to ensure that all lesson content and proper sequence is accomplished. This lesson plan also helps the instructor/teacher to keep a constant check on the activities he plans for himself as well as those he plans for the students. This careful preparation helps the teacher/instructor guide his students toward the desired learning outcomes when he presents the lesson he has planned.

A good teacher must consider these points very seriously:

1. Make sure students understand why the assignment is important *to them.*
2. Make sure that students understand what is expected *to be done, in and out of class.*

3. Always *review* an assignment at the beginning of the next class meeting to ensure that *all students* understand the material presented and studied.
4. To the best of your ability, try to recognize individual student differences in the rate of learning. *Do not* expect exact, equal responses from *all* your students.

Chapter XI
Methods of Instruction

Figure 24

Factors to Be Considered

- Scope and the nature of the subject for instruction and the material

- Number of learners

- Time available

- Training aids available

- Economic factors

LECTURE

A lecture is *spoken* by
an instructor to a group

ADVANTAGES:

- Economical

- Covers large quantities of material

- Easy to organize

LIMITATIONS:

- Low or no participation

- Usually one-way communication

- Not for skill training

- Difficult to maintain interest

- No control for learning

- Abstract

Figure 25

188

METHOD OF INSTRUCTION: *Lecture Method*

DEFINITION: A discourse given before a class or an audience for instructional purposes. It may be presented directly (classroom instruction) or indirectly (tape recorder, film, or television).

APPLICATIONS

- Early stage of learning.
- Use if time is short and many ideas must be presented.
- Use if number of instructors is limited and an instructor is responsible for a large number of students.
- Use when subject matter changes frequently.

QUALIFICATIONS

- Limits student participation. The lecture becomes a "telling session" for the instructor.
- Checking student learning before testing is difficult.
- Student attention and interest may wander.

GUIDELINES FOR LECTURE METHOD

- Prepare an outline or plan in advance.
- Organize the material into meaningful topics to promote understanding.
- Use visual aids to express abstract concepts or to show relationships.
- Allow time for a question-and-answer period to clarify points of confusion.
- For indirect presentation a short speech may help to hold student attention.

DEMONSTRATION

(Models, displays, samples)
A demonstration shows how
something works or how to
work something, to a group
or an individual

ADVANTAGES:

- Makes explanations "real"

- Appeals to several senses

- Saves learning time

- Creates dramatic appeal

- Strengthens learning by arousing curiosity
  in "how does it work?"

LIMITATIONS:

- Size of group is limited

- Blocking of equipment

Figure 26

190

METHOD OF INSTRUCTION: *Demonstration Method*

DEFINITION: An accurate portrayal of the precise action necessary to perform skills
or processes. It may be presented directly (classroom instruction) or indirectly
(film, television, slides and audio tape, or tape recorder, if oral only).

APPLICATIONS

- Early stage of learning.
- Most useful in teaching motor skills, simple manual skills or processes, and foreign languages, or other verbal chains.
- To set the standard of performance.
- To focus attention on basic procedures.
- To provide overviews or set goals of instruction.

QUALIFICATIONS

- The demonstrator must be a skilled performer who is able to verbally explain each step being demonstrated. This may require many hours of practice.
- Since the student does not perform during a demonstration, you cannot evaluate student learning except through questioning.
- The number of students observing a demonstration may be limited by the nature of what is to be demonstrated.

GUIDELINES FOR USE

- Have an expert make demonstration using actual equipment or apparatuses the student will use on the job.
- Simultaneously provide simple explanation of the ongoing procedure as it is being performed. Tell the "why" as well as what is being performed. Point out critical aspects of the procedure.
- Provide repetition of complex operations.
- Immediately follow by supervised practice. If immediate practice is not feasible, ask student to verbally describe the performance or process.

ON THE JOB

To tell, show, observe, and correct
an individual in an actual job situation

ADVANTAGES:

- Application for a great variety of situations

- Close contact between learner and instructor

- Close observation and evaluation of progress

- Learner gets constant feedback

- More informal

LIMITATION:

- Time-consuming

Figure 27

192

INVESTIGATION AND REPORT

Learner's investigation of and reporting on specific assigned topics and issues related to a central problem or subject

ADVANTAGES:

- Gives excellent training in data collection/information gathering and presentation

- Gives opportunity to evaluate learner's progress

- Provides basis for group/individual discussions

LIMITATIONS:

- Not for skill training

- Time-consuming

- Limited participation

Figure 28

193

ROLE-PLAYING

Acting with a practical purpose

ADVANTAGES:

- Individual efforts
- High level of interest

LIMITATIONS:

- Shy individuals perform below standards
- Always unnatural
- May create too much laughter
- Wastes time if not treated seriously

Figure 29

WORKSHOP/SEMINAR

Exchange of knowledge and skills between people in mutual functional areas or a group of persons meeting together for the purpose of studying a common subject under guidance of an instructor/expert

ADVANTAGES:

- High level of participation

- Allows opportunity to study in depth

- Sharing/exchanging of experience/knowledge/skills

- Encourages learner to work

- Theory and practice are treated concurrently

- Improves individual proficiency

LIMITATION:

- Not for few people

Figure 30

An exchange of ideas and intelligence is a discussion,
but an exchange of ignorance is an argument.

                                                    Confucius

GROUP DISCUSSION

Purposeful conversation and exchange of ideas between the instructor and the learners and between learners

ADVANTAGES:

- High level of participation

- Creates new ideas

- Solves specific problems

- Gives all views of subject

- Learners also learn from each other

- Instructor gets to know learners better

LIMITATION:

- Not for large groups

- Only a few may talk

- Unrelated subjects may creep in

- Sometimes difficult to reach definite conclusions

Figure 31

METHOD OF INSTRUCTION: *Group Discussion Method*

DEFINITION: An instructor-controlled, interactive process of sharing information and experience related to achieving an educational or training objective.

APPLICATIONS

- Intermediate and final stages of learning.
- Use in formal course or in training.
- Use as an extension of existing knowledge or to clarify and amplify familiar material.
- Use when students must learn to identify and solve problems, and to frame their own decisions.
- Use when students need to be exposed to a variety of approaches, interpretations, and personalities.
- Use when teamwork is needed.

QUALIFICATIONS

- Time-consuming and limited by class size.
- Requires that participants have sufficient background so that they can talk about subject.
- Avoid using group discussions in early stages of learning when new material is being introduced. At this stage students are new and inexperienced in the topic area.

GUIDELINES FOR USE

- Know the subject matter to be discussed.
- Verbally outline the specific problem or issue, or provide a case study of the situation to be read before the discussion.
- Call upon individuals to clarify, analyze, and summarize.
- Guide the discussion; do not lecture.
- Be patient with group's slow progress to understanding.
- Be alert to group's tendency to wander.
- Be alert to tendency of one or two students to dominate the discussion to the virtual exclusion of the others.

METHOD OF INSTRUCTION: *Self-Directed Instruction Method*

DEFINITION: Readings on document research that students undertake on their own without special guidance or instruction.

APPLICATIONS

- Final stage of learning.
- Use as an adjunct to other methods of instruction.
- To improve an individual's present job performance.
- To prepare an individual for promotion.
- To allow a student to pursue a special interest not shared by other students.

QUALIFICATION

- Student must be motivated and have initiative.

GUIDELINES FOR USE

- Provide students with a reading list tailored to their special needs.
- Provide students with a statement of objectives that specify what they will be expected to accomplish.
- Devise means of evaluating learning, for example, written or oral tests, performance tests.

METHOD OF INSTRUCTION: *Questioning Method*

DEFINITION: A discourse by students before an instructor in which the students relate
                          what they have learned through previous study. The discourse is in
                          response to questions from the instructor.

APPLICATIONS

- Use in formal course, field training detachment, or correspondence course.
- Useful for assessment of learning by the instructor.
- Useful for providing feedback to students about what they have attained by learning.
- Most useful for verbal content and concepts.
- Having to explain or paraphrase information to others, students are forced to analyze the material at a deeper level than if they were not compelled.

QUALIFICATIONS

- Learning for recitation may be rote.
- Participation of other students not reciting is limited, and their attention and interest may wander.
- In correspondence courses, recitation may take the form of written discourse, which the student mails to an instructor.

GUIDELINES FOR USE

- Tell the students well in advance that they will be assessed by a written or oral recitation. If students are not prepared to recite, the method has little value.
- Before recitation be sure that instruction and assignments are at the proper level for the students. There must be some assurance that all members of the class can learn the material before recitation.
- Provide for question-and-answer session. This allows an opportunity for students to get feedback on their performance and allows an opportunity to further assess students' learning.

METHOD OF INSTRUCTION: *Performance Method*

DEFINITION: Student interactions with things, data, or persons, as is necessary
to attain training objectives. Includes all forms of simulation and
interaction with actual equipment or job materials. Performance may
be supervised by classroom instructor, tutor, coach, or peer to
provide needed feedback.

APPLICATIONS

- Intermediate and final stages of learning.
- To permit the student to apply learning to actual situations.
- To allow practice with job and similar conditions, under supervision and guidance.
- For verbal learning, problem-solving, or rule using. Performance may be recitation or take the form of a written report.

QUALIFICATIONS

- Time-consuming because students must be given the opportunity to practice until they reach proficiency.
- May require special facilities and equipment, which may be expensive and difficult to obtain. Once obtained equipment must be constantly maintained.
- Usually requires a higher student/instructor ratio than other methods of instruction.

GUIDELINES FOR USE

- Plan student skill development from the simple to the complex.
- Provide explicit instructions for students to follow when they are practicing.
- Provide safety precautions for the protection of the student and equipment.
- Set up realistic work problems.

PROGRAMMED INSTRUCTION

A self-teaching method

ADVANTAGES:

- Learner can study when convenient

- Mistakes are seen privately

- Learners learn at their own pace

LIMITATIONS:

- No human contact

- A program cannot easily be altered to show changes in content

- Motivation is built into the wording

Figure 32

METHOD OF INSTRUCTION: *Programmed Instruction Method*

DEFINITION: Instructional materials are prepared specifically to employ techniques of programming. Classical programmed instruction variables include small steps carefully sequenced and cued to reduce errors. Immediate feedback, and freedom on the part of students to vary their own rate of learning.

APPLICATIONS

- All stages of learning.
- Useful in accommodating individual differences in rate of learning, in background, and in experience.
- Useful if scheduling is a problem, as students may work through materials when convenient.
- To provide uniformity of instruction, as all students may progress through same material. May be the sole source of instruction or may supplement other methods of instruction.

QUALIFICATIONS

- Development cost is comparatively high.
- Development time and revision time are comparatively long because of the requirement that these materials be validated.
- Some students using programmed instruction object to lack of social interaction.

GUIDELINES FOR USE

- Be sure the student has all the material, equipment, or devices to complete the program.
- Be sure that students understand that the program is not a test. Responses made during the program are to help them and not to provide a basis for grading.
- Establish student accountability through (written) agreement with the student that sets up a schedule for completion of the segment of the program, or require completion of the program as a prerequisite for something the student is known to want. Periodically check on the student's progress.
- Provide some means for the student to get assistance if it really is needed.

Summary

Lecture Method   A method of instruction in which the instructor has complete responsibility for presenting facts, principles, and ideas orally.

The lecture approach can be used as an effective means to cover material or a message quickly. It *does not*, however, stimulate critical thinking, develop problem-solving skills, or teach skills.

The instructor should have a *specific reason* for using the lecture method of instruction. Be sure to keep to your subject, and to the best of your ability, try to put any new vocabulary that is foreign to your students in layperson's terms. Highly technical subjects cannot be effectively absorbed by the student by using the lecture method of instruction. Use examples in your lecture, either personal or hypothetical, to facilitate comprehension. Keep your lecture as brief as possible; shift to other methods of instruction. You will be more effective.

Tips:
1. Pause at intervals during the lecture to conduct question-and-answer sessions.
2. Follow the lecture with group discussion about student experiences related to the subject of the lecture.
3. Include, if possible, instructional aids as part of the lecture to arouse and maintain interest.
4. Remember: Creativity equals experimentation and growth. The eclectic instructor can expand, modify ideas, pull from many new sources, and discard old sources and methods.

Demonstration Method   A method of instruction in which the instructor explains and shows the student the precise action necessary to perform skills or processes.

Discussion Method   A method of instruction in which the instructor uses questions to cause students to participate actively in a learning situation by exchanging ideas, opinions, and experiences to reach conclusions that will support learning objectives.

Group Discussion
Techniques

1.   Field trips

2.   Field observations

3.   Field interviews

4.   Guest speakers

5.   Committee projects

6.   Bulletin board

7.   Role-playing

8.   Buzz groups

9.   Brainstorming

10. Panel discussion

11. Debate

Individual Instruction	Normally individualized instruction, on a one-on-one basis.
Questioning Techniques	Use thought-provoking questions to involve the student. Ask questions that require *more* than yes or no for an answer. (See Chapter IX, "Effective Questioning Techniques.")

Chapter XII
Using Instructional Aids

Advantages of Instructional Aids

- Appeal to variety of senses

- Simplify explanations, especially when material is complex and difficult to explain

- Create more vivid and lasting impressions

- Add realism

- Provide additional activity and interest

- Create a change of pace

- Improve quality of instruction

- Give participants an idea of their levels of knowledge/skills

Things to Watch For

- Audible aids must be audible

- Visual aids must be visible

- Aids are no substitute for instruction

- Careful selection is necessary

- Aids should be simple, understandable, and relevant. Their design and function must be decided by matching them to the learning difficulty which they are intended to overcome.

- Aids are the product of imagination and effort as much as of cost. A skilled instructor using paper, string, glue, and other easily obtainable materials can produce highly original and effective aids of his own.

MODELS

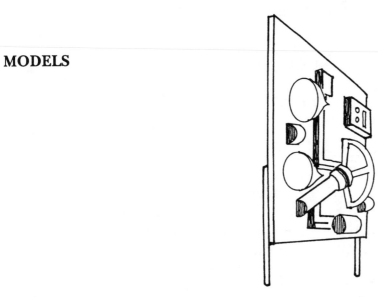

- Learners must be given an opportunity to feel and examine the model at close range

- Don't prolong class period because of particular interest of one or two students

Figure 33

OVERHEAD PROJECTOR

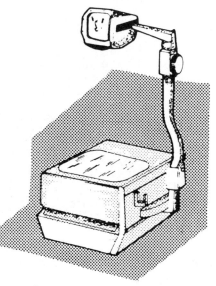

- Avoid leaving the light on when you have no transparency on the stage

- Remember not to allow head or shoulder to get in the way of projector

- Don't move the projector while "on"

Figure 34

SLIDE PROJECTOR

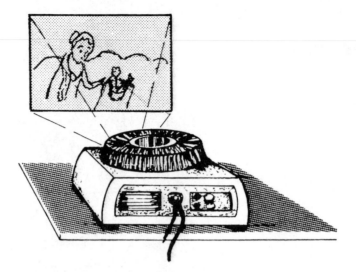

- Projector must be pre-focused and tested, and lens must be cleaned before class period

- Projector must be firmly and securely in position, with electric cords protected

- The projected image should fill the screen

- Darken the room—only as required

Figure 35

OPAQUE PROJECTOR

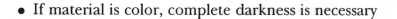

- If material is color, complete darkness is necessary

- Don't project for lengthy periods due to heat and heat damage

- Don't use flammable objects

Figure 36

AUDIO/VIDEO TAPE RECORDER

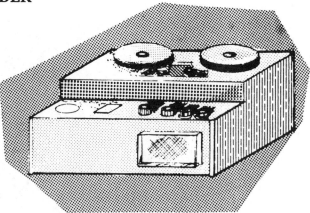

- An effective aid for self-development, demonstrations, case study, and role-playing

- Before you start to record your presentation, practice to get to "know" the recorder

- Run tests before your recording and playback to determine proper settings of controls for volume and tone

Figure 37

SOUND FILM PROJECTOR

- Pre-focusing and adjusting of equipment is a must

- Be sure projector is firmly positioned and electric wires are protected

- Thread the film prior to class

- Make proper introduction before you start

- Don't show an unfamiliar film

- A spare bulb is a must

Figure 38

FLIP CHART

- Turn pages carefully

- Be sure color and size of writing or printing can be seen by class

- Stand to the side

- Don't lean against the stand

- You should know the contents of your flip chart presentation so you know what comes next

- Don't leave chart on display after it has been used

Figure 39

CHALKBOARD

- Plan the material, considering:
  —The surface size of the board
  —The distance between the board and the last row

- Do your chalkboard presentation on a piece of paper prior to class

- Print legibly, neatly, and large enough

- Use the eraser not your fingers when correcting your writing

- Clean the whole board

- Don't talk when writing

Figure 40

MAGNETIC BOARD

- Be sure objects are not too heavy for the magnet

- Plan your presentation, piece by piece

- Have board tilted back at a slight angle

- Don't talk to the board

Figure 41

Summary

Instructional aids are devices that present supporting or supplementary materials to improve the teaching-learning process. The use of aids is based on widely accepted theories about mental processes. These theories suggest that the mind works as a filter in sorting out the important items of the verbal or visual information which is present. Then it tries to organize these items into reasonable patterns. Finally the brain finds it more efficient to store single visual bits of information, instead of large numbers of verbal bits.

There are many reasons for using instructional aids. Among the reasons most significant to teachers are opening and keeping open the communication channels; increasing the retention of learned material; ensuring that teacher and student have a common mental picture of meanings; understanding relationships; and teaching more in less time by the elimination of long verbal descriptions.

Aids come in a variety of types, such as chalkboards, projected materials, models, charts, and maps. Sensible guidelines should be used in planning and using any instructional aid. These guidelines include planning each aid to support a specific idea; keeping instructional aids as simple and uncluttered as compatible with the learning outcomes; ensuring visibility as to size and location; properly sequencing aids; and planning aids in rough draft form.

An effective instructor should always be aware of new ideas in the field of instructional aids. Recent years have seen an explosion of new materials and techniques in the field of instructional aids. They present many new opportunities for the instructor, but they may also confuse the instructor by their very abundance and variety. While instructors must keep in mind the teaching goals to be achieved, they must also be selectively receptive to new possibilities.

Instructors must keep abreast of new materials and the potential uses for them. They should read extensively about these new materials in professional journals. Above all they should develop creative imaginations. There is always a better way to accomplish a learning outcome. An active imagination will reveal unlimited possibilities. The only ultimate control is that the instructional aids must support the ideas being developed for better learning.

Chapter XIII
Testing

A grade is an inadequate report of an inaccurate judgment by a biased and variable teacher of the extent to which a student has attained an undefined level of mastery of an unknown proportion of indefinite materials.

Paul Dressel

DEFINITION: A *test* is an evaluation tool in which facts, situations, problems, and questions are presented in a standard way and are designed to stimulate responses that can be reviewed and evaluated objectively.

A test can be utilized:
1.   Before (pretest),
2.   During,
3.   After the instruction, to (A) assess the learner's level of knowledge and skills prior to instruction, (B) compare learning during and at the end of instruction, and (C) receive feedback on the effectiveness of instruction.

Why Test?

It is important to measure students' progress in their studies to determine the effectiveness of instruction, and to determine the results of the instructional objectives. Testing serves a variety of functions: it tells whether students are learning; it helps to determine specifically the areas where instruction may be weak; it can highlight important points that the student should be getting from the instruction; and it also promotes progress for the student. Testing is an important part of instruction, which cannot be overemphasized.

A primary reason for testing is to improve instruction and increase learning. In addition repeated testing makes students more confident in taking tests. When used as a review instrument, examinations are teaching devices. The results of testing and review may be used to identify teaching strengths and areas for improvement. End-of-course examinations help to determine the final standing of students and provide excellent insight for teaching improvement.

When examinations are being constructed, objectives for desired changes in learning behavior should be the most important consideration. For purposes of subsequent measurements, these changes in behavior may be defined in terms of the subject-matter content and the level of learning or skill that a successful student should be able to demonstrate.

Only observable behavior may be measured. Identifying, reciting, or listing are the most common observable behaviors associated with learning at the knowledge level. The behavioral abilities that result from learning include comparing, differentiating, contrasting, generalizing, explaining, and perhaps solving. At the application level of learning, observable behavior demonstrated by successful students includes solving complex problems, interpreting situations, determining related causes and effects, performing an integrated sequence of related actions, constructing, adjusting, and repairing.

A valid test measures achievement in one subject-matter area and excludes test items from other areas. Conversely a test that measures the achievement of overall course objectives must include test items from all subject-matter areas. A test-item worksheet will help ensure comprehensiveness and validity.

Two broad categories of test items are selection and supply. The selection category includes true-false, multiple-choice, and matching items, all of which provide alternatives for the student to choose. The supply category includes completion, short-answer, and essay items, all of which require the student to supply whatever information is requested. Selection items enjoy the advantages of high objectivity in scoring; the capability of measuring students' knowledge of facts, ideas, or principles in a relatively short time; and ease in arriving at statistical analysis. When properly constructed they can measure learning at any level. Supply items have a distinct advantage over selection items when recall of information, ability to express ideas, or original thinking are to be measured. The preparation for supply tests requires thorough study, which, in turn, is also an aid to learning and retention. When properly constructed supply items can measure learning at any level.

Supply or selection test items can measure learning at the highest level. These tests can aid in differentiating between students of high achievement and estimating the degree of transfer of learning achieved by students.

Writing test items is one of the instructor's most difficult tasks. It is perhaps less important that an instructor be able to recall any specific principle of item-writing than understanding the basic concepts involved.

Characteristics of Performance and Written Tests

There are major differences between performance and written tests. Performance tests require trainees or students to do something. Written tests require students to verbalize or write about something. A performance test requires individuals to accomplish a job-like task under controlled conditions. It emphasizes nonverbal aspects, and may require individuals to look up, read, and use certain technical materials. The test items represent skills that trainees must perform, or the decisions they must make on the job. These test items are dependent on a sequence in which they are presented. Errors early in the sequence may affect final outcome of the task. Written test items, however, require the individual to demonstrate knowledge by responding to various types of written questions. The written test emphasizes verbal or symbolic aspects. It may require individuals to look up, read, and use certain technical reference materials. Test items on written tests are independent questions, not dependent on sequence. Errors on one item will not affect performance on another item.

Criterion-Referenced Test

A criterion-referenced test is a type of achievement test because it measures what a student has already learned. Criterion-referenced tests are not called standardized tests because they are not always given to everyone according to the same, or "standardized," procedures, and they do not compare a student's performance to the norm. Criterion-referenced tests are designed to measure specific skills within a subject area. Test results indicate skills a student has or has not learned.

Results of criterion-referenced tests can give the following information:

1. Skills or knowledge that a student is expected to learn from a course or instructional program
2. Topics or skills that a student has already learned
3. Skills or knowledge that was taught in the course or instructional program

Criterion-referenced tests determine if behavior, as reflected in learning objectives, has been altered. This type of test may involve multiple-choice items, fill-in items, essays, or performance of a task. If the test is given immediately after learning sequences, it is a test of acquisition; if the test is given considerably later, it is a retention test; and if the test requires performance not learned during the instruction, it is called a transfer test.

The purpose of criterion-referenced tests is to evaluate attainment of the objectives and to measure the effectiveness of the instructional system. This type of test is developed from both common-element objectives and subobjectives.

Survey Test

A survey test may be administered while the instructional system is being developed to determine what the target population already knows or can do before receiving instruction. This survey test is developed from common-element objectives and from subobjectives.

Effective Tests

An Effective Test Should:

1. Be related to instructional objective(s) in terms of performance, constraints, and criteria
2. Be clear, concise, and usable
3. Be consistent and valid (it should cover the instruction accurately and in a balanced way; it should measure what is necessary to measure in not too easy or too difficult way)
4. Guide the instructor in identifying:
    a. What he has to instruct
    b. What and how well he has instructed
    c. What areas of instruction need to be improved

5. Guide the learner in identifying:
   a. How much he already knows and how well he is progressing
   b. What areas he needs to study/practice more

Suggested Procedures for Valid Testing

Recommend to students that the best preparation for any test is systematic study and achievement during the school year. Important features of daily instruction that relate to testing competence follow:

1. Preparation for the Testing Situation
   - Encourage long-range planning, starting with the beginning of the school year to organize instruction that will cover subject areas in the curriculum or course of study.
   - Teach the skills or subjects, not the test. Teach subject emphasizing its practical use. Avoid teaching a subject or skill only in the format tested.
   - Use formal text exercises periodically throughout the course of study through meaningful informal testing and the use of management system testing components.

2. Planning for the Test
   - Coordinate the test schedule with other staff members. Notify the special teachers/instructors if your students cannot attend their program due to the test session schedule.
   - Whenever possible schedule the test for the morning. The length of the test session should follow the limits specified in the test manual, if one is provided. Allow time for distribution and collection of testing materials and for checking the students' grading of the answer documents.
   - Inform students well in advance of the test time and dates.
   - Stress to students the importance of:
     —Being present for the test
     —Getting a good night's sleep
     —Eating a proper breakfast

- Reduce homework assignments during the test week.
- Review the test manual or test document to be sure that you understand the directions and can anticipate trainees' questions.
- Plan seat work for students who finish the test early.
- Avoid routine, pencil-and-paper testing activity, and do not use a negative tone.

3. Administration of the Test
    - Post the "Testing—Please Do Not Disturb" sign outside the classroom or workshop during the testing session.
    - Arrange seating so that students are separated and can work on their own effectively.
    - Be sure that lighting and ventilation are good. During the test session, stay alert and check on the ventilation conditions.
    - Be sure there is a sufficient supply of sharpened pencils. When responding to students' questions during the test, be aware not to answer the questions for them.
    - Follow the test times exactly as printed in the manual or on your own testing plan. Write the beginning and ending time on the chalkboard as a reminder to yourself and the students.
    - Walk around the room or workshop during the test session.
    - Do not allow students to move about the test area when they are finished with the test.
    - During the test maintain a serious, but positive attitude toward students.

Chapter XIV

Evaluation

*The toughest thing about success
is that you have to keep on being
a SUCCESS. Talent is only a
starting point.*

Irving Berlin

*Beware of little expenses;
a small leak will sink a great ship.*

Benjamin Franklin

Definition: The assessment of learning activities within a specific instructional area for the purpose of determining the validity of objectives, relevancy and sequence of content, and achievement of specified goals; leads to decisions associated with planning, programming, implementing, and recycling program activities.

Background

Evaluation has many meanings. To some people it means giving grades to students. To many students it means a series of hurdles to overcome during a course of study. To many instructors it means hours of work drafting questions to puzzle the students. To people in industry, it means a refinement of work to pass a rigid inspection. If instructors find results that confirm what they already know about the students, the written examination or rating becomes an unnecessary chore required by the administration. If evaluation meant all of these things and nothing more, it would be well to stop thinking about evaluation and think only about ways to increase the learning process. As soon as one thinks seriously about the increase of student learning, however, one is forced to think about evaluation—for evaluation is an integral part of the learning process.

Although evaluation appears at the tail end in most textbooks, evaluation is continuity. It must be frequent and recurrent. Evaluation is needed at all stages of curriculum development, and at all stages of instruction. It is a most skillful characteristic of evaluation that it must be accomplished with validity and reliability.

Whenever any significant learning takes place, the result generally will be a definable, observable, and measurable change in the learner. It is precisely the defining, observing, and measuring or judging of this specific new change with which educational and training evaluation is vitally concerned.

True evaluation is a continuous process that neither starts nor stops with the students. After instruction begins instructors cannot blindly assume that their students are learning. Some sort of evaluation is essential to determine what and how well the students are learning. Only with this information can an intelligent plan be used to improve instruction. To achieve a purpose in education, there is nothing more critical than evaluation.

The Meaning and Nature of Evaluation

Evaluation in education and training can be defined as the process of making a meaningful estimate of value for some useful purpose. Anything that can be seen, heard, or otherwise sensed can serve as the basis for educational and training evaluation. Such observations are made of only a sample of the individual's change; reliable and effective evaluation is possible only if the sample represents the individual's total change in the area measured.

Differences can be expected in the observations made by instructors because of their own individual differences in intelligence, learning ability, aptitude, job knowledge, and ability to verbalize their thoughts. Since these differences exist, they must be recognized in establishing any evaluation procedure. Failure to do so can only result in unfair and inaccurate measuring of student achievement.

The evaluation process must be systematic and continuous. Often students' progress in meeting course objectives can be observed in class discussions, interviews, term papers, laboratory exercises, special projects, and tests. Weighing all observations to establish their real value is an important part of evaluation. Informal day-to-day evaluations made by instructors are highly influenced by their own hopes and wishes. Instructors are more prone to remember students' actions that indicate they are learning, not those actions that indicate they are not. Thus a more systematic approach is needed.

The Evaluation Cycle

In its largest sense, evaluation is the means of determining how well the instructor and the student are progressing toward certain goals or objectives. Goals are common to any educational or training activity, although they are called by many names and are stated in a variety of ways. Regardless of form each objective specifies what is to be accomplished (i.e., the subject matter to be learned or skill to be acquired) and why it is to be accomplished (i.e., the purpose). These objectives serve as the starting point for any effective evaluation process. (See Figure 42.)

The Student Evaluation Cycle

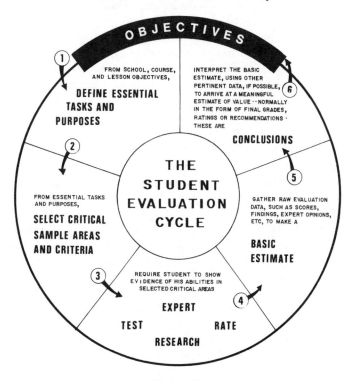

OBJECTIVES

1. FROM SCHOOL, COURSE, AND LESSON OBJECTIVES, **DEFINE ESSENTIAL TASKS AND PURPOSES**

2. FROM ESSENTIAL TASKS AND PURPOSES, **SELECT CRITICAL SAMPLE AREAS AND CRITERIA**

3. REQUIRE STUDENT TO SHOW EVIDENCE OF HIS ABILITIES IN SELECTED CRITICAL AREAS

EXPERT

TEST　　**RATE**

RESEARCH

4. GATHER RAW EVALUATION DATA, SUCH AS SCORES, FINDINGS, EXPERT OPINIONS, ETC, TO MAKE A **BASIC ESTIMATE**

5. *(arrow to CONCLUSIONS)*

6. INTERPRET THE BASIC ESTIMATE, USING OTHER PERTINENT DATA, IF POSSIBLE, TO ARRIVE AT A MEANINGFUL ESTIMATE OF VALUE -- NORMALLY IN THE FORM OF FINAL GRADES, RATINGS OR RECOMMENDATIONS - THESE ARE **CONCLUSIONS**

THE STUDENT EVALUATION CYCLE

Figure 42

Basic criteria or standards are necessary for a meaningful measurement or judgment. These criteria define what may be considered successful and what is unsuccessful or failing. They are, then, the "yardstick" for educational and training evaluation.

From the stated objectives (i.e., the specified tasks to be accomplished), samples that are related to the criteria must be selected. As previously suggested it is impractical to measure all changes in the learner that could result from a learning activity. The samples selected, regardless of how they might be stated, represent abilities or traits that successful students should possess as a result of their learning activity. To be useful in the evaluation process, these traits must be observable, definable, and measurable. In addition the combination of samples must be sufficient to cover essential elements of the original objective.

Next the samples must be weighed against the criteria using a suitable means. What means would be most effective depends in large part on the instructor's circumstances. The instructor might select such means as testing, rating, research, or even expert opinion. *Ideally every student should be evaluated on the job for which his learning is designed to prepare him.* Thus his successes and failures would be a basis for judging his success in the course. As a practical matter, this is not always possible, but every effort must be made to make it so. Therefore the evaluation instrument should simulate the job as closely as possible. The closer the simulation, the better the chances for a true evaluation.

Frequently, instructors use written tests for formal evaluation. These are convenient vehicles to estimate how well students meet the criteria for each sample—especially in subject areas involving basic theory; principles; or abstract facts, ideas, and concepts. Performance ratings provide a second means of evaluation. Such ratings, because they are based on performance of students, are likely to provide the truest possible judgment about students—assuming that the subject matter is such that observable performance is one of the teaching goals. Expert opinion and research (e.g., follow-up studies, questionnaires, course critiques) might also be considered a practical means of evaluation. These would primarily be aimed at improving instruction rather than measuring individual learning. Since testing and performance rating are the means most closely related to the instructor and his individual students, notes on testing follow.

All of these means tend to overlap in their actual application, but every means is used for the purpose of bringing the sample and the criteria into some reasonable and informative relationship. Whatever the means it should possess the five characteristics of evaluation described later in this chapter.

Weighing samples against criteria results in some basic estimate—often in terms of findings, raw scores, ratings, or reports. Even in the simplest situation, evaluation does not end here. At the very least, the meaning of the basic estimate must be interpreted in relation to course objectives.

The final step in the evaluation cycle (so far as an individual student is concerned) is the formulation of conclusions about the student, based upon refined estimates of his achievement. The instructor must always bear in mind that evaluation is a process of estimating value for some purpose. The conclusions reached, therefore, must be in a form that has meaning in terms of that purpose. In addition these conclusions must be in a form that has meaning to the school, the instructor, and the student; all must be able to effectively interpret grades and ratings. Unless these conclusions can be used as a means of communicating to those who need and can use them, much of the value of the entire evaluation process will be lost.

Characteristics of Evaluation

If any evaluation instrument is to provide an effective estimate of achievement, it must be reliable, valid, objective, comprehensive, and differentiating. Whenever the instructor's judgment must be used in the evaluation process, he must consider these characteristics as a basic guideline. Actually each of these characteristics is interrelated. For example there is no such thing as a completely valid or invalid, reliable or unreliable, instrument.

After considering the meaning of the five characteristics, the instructor can easily understand how evaluation instruments may vary in quality, but it is extremely difficult to think of these characteristics independently. Indeed the effects of these characteristics are so interrelated that it is perhaps less important to show their differences than their interrelationships. Comprehensiveness, for example, can materially affect validity. To be valid an evaluation must be comprehensive; that is, it must be inclusive enough to do what it is supposed to do. Lengthening a test usually increases its reliability also. Comprehensiveness is frequently achieved by the use of multiple-choice, true-false, and other selection-type test items, because they generally take less time per item and more of the subject can be covered. Also such tests may be scored objectively. Increased objectivity, in turn, usually makes test results more reliable. When efforts to differentiate are carried to an extreme, however, reliability is decreased. The most efficient evaluation instrument achieves a satisfactory balances among all five characteristics.

Reliability.

A reliable measuring instrument yields consistent results. If identical measurements are obtained every time a certain instrument is applied to a certain dimension, the instrument may be considered reliable. An unreliable instrument cannot be depended upon to yield consistent results. An altimeter that has play in its moving parts, a steel tape that expands and contracts with temperature changes, or cloth tapes that are affected by humidity cannot be expected to yield reliable measurements.

No instrument is perfectly reliable. The finest balance used in chemistry laboratories do not provide perfect reliability. Obviously some instruments are more reliable than others; for example, laboratory balances are far more reliable than those used in grocery stores.

The reliability of an instrument can be estimated by taking many measures of the same item. For example a rough measure of the reliability of a thermometer can be obtained by taking several readings of a fluid held at a constant temperature. Except for the errors made by the person taking the readings, the amount of scatter in the readings may be considered as the degree of unreliability in the thermometer.

Reliability has the same meaning whether applied to educational tests and ratings or to balances, thermometers, and altimeters. The term refers only to the consistency of the results obtained from the instrument. To measure the reliability of a rating scale or examination is a much more complex problem than to measure the reliability of a mechanical device. If the same calipers are used at different times to measure the bore of the same cylinder, the results should be nearly identical each time, because the size of the cylinder does not change between measurements. This is not the case with educational evaluation. Knowledge, understanding, abilities, or skills measured by an educational instrument do not remain constant. For example in educational testing, the student can be expected to change from one application of the test to another because he learns some things and remembers some of the solutions.

Validity.

An evaluation instrument is valid when it measures what it is supposed to measure and nothing else.

The fact that a measuring instrument is highly reliable does not necessarily mean that it is valid. The instrument that has maximum consistency (high reliability) may not be measuring what it is intended to measure. That is to say, an instrument may have very high reliability and low validity at the same time. For example the butcher who hides a lump of solder under the pan of his scales might get reliable measurements but invalid results (at least from the customer's point of view).

If a mechanic wants to measure the diameter of a bearing with a micrometer, he must be sure that the contact surfaces of the bearing and the micrometer are free from grease and dirt. Otherwise he may be measuring the diameter of the bearing plus some extraneous matter. His measurements would then be invalid.

A test used in educational evaluation follows the same principles of validity. If an examination is intended to measure the ability of students to apply knowledge, it must measure application, not the ability to recall and write down facts. If an examination is intended to measure ability to visualize blueprints in three dimension, a student's score should not be affected by his ability to describe his visualization in writing. If an examination is designed to measure the student's understanding of the operation of a four-cycle internal combustion engine, his ability to read printed matter should not be a factor in his score.

The validity of an evaluation instrument is always determined by comparing it with some criterion or standing that is relevant to the test, test items, or rated trait. For example when the purpose of the test is to identify or measure a special aptitude, the student's subsequent performance in that area is the most relevant criterion for test validity. If a written test was designed to measure aptitude for piloting an airplane, the validity of the test should be determined by a comparison of the test results with the demonstrated ability to fly an airplane. If students who score high on the pilot selection test later prove to be excellent pilots and if those who score low on that test are unsatisfactory pilots, the test is highly valid.

The degree of relevance of the test, test items, or rated trait will determine the acceptability of the validity attained. Relevance may be logical or empirical. Logical relevance is estimated by using criteria such as on-the-job performance, behavior on the job, course of study objectives, pooled judgments, or curriculum and text analysis. These criteria are listed in the order of their acceptability for determining validity. Empirical relevance is estimated by using statistical analysis of the test results, item to be validated, or data gathered from previously validated evaluations. These evaluations may be the results of other tests, grades, or ratings attained in equivalent or similar materials.

The validity of educational evaluation may sometimes be determined by comparing results with later performance on the job. The real objectives of instruction are concerned with improving job performance. If the objectives are relevant to the job, then job performance should be the criterion for determining the validity of evaluation instruments used during the course.

It is frequently impossible or impractical to compare evaluation results directly with job performance. The comparison is difficult principally because of these considerations: (1) follow-up contacts with students must be maintained, sometimes for long periods; (2) genuine job ability and quality of performance are difficult to measure; (3) the factors that contribute to job performance are interrelated, and many of them do not begin before the evaluation has been performed; and (4) much time usually elapses between the administration of the test and an adequate opportunity for students to demonstrate their ability to perform.

Sometimes the curriculum is not designed to improve performance in a specific job, but rather to raise the student's overall level of ability. Most advanced courses of study in educational systems are of this type. Most of the educational achievement evaluation instruments used in these curricula are designed to measure overall achievement that cannot be related to specific job performance. In such situations it is difficult to identify a relevant criterion for determining ability.

When job performance cannot be used as the criterion of validity, the validity of an evaluation instrument is best gauged in terms of the overall objectives of the curriculum. Evaluations used in the classroom are valid only to the extent that they measure achievement of the instruction stated in terms of specific abilities. The evaluation instrument measuring achievements should require students to demonstrate these abilities. When the objectives of instruction are stated in terms of understandings, applications, and factual knowledge, instruments should be designed to measure achievement of these objectives.

A rough estimate of the validity of a classroom test may be obtained from the judgment of several competent instructors. To estimate validity they read the test critically and consider its content in relation to the stated objectives of the instruction. Items that do not pertain directly to the objectives of the course should be modified or eliminated.

Because it is related to purpose, validity is the most important feature of any evaluation instrument. The instructor must carefully consider whether the test or rating scale measures what it is designed to measure. Much effort should be directed at improving validity. Efforts directed solely at improving the reliability of an instrument do not necessarily improve its validity. They may, on the contrary, progressively decrease its validity.

Objectivity.

The personal bias of the rater or test scorer should not affect the score. For example an engineer is responsible for selecting three men to complete an emergency construction job. He calls in six available men for a conference and evaluation. He compares their weight, height, age, and general physique—all physical characteristics to be considered. The engineer can make the comparisons objectively, but these facts are not enough; he must estimate how each of the men would react under stress. He reviews what he knows about the emotional stability of each man, his attitude toward his work, his loyalty, and the degree of his skill. In making these evaluations, the engineer tries to be objective, but his personal bias will undoubtedly influence the results of his evaluation. Thus part of his evaluation lacks objectivity.

The opposite of objective is subjective. In the preceding illustration, the engineer's judgment of personal qualities is subjective. In classroom evaluation essay tests tend to be subjective, since the grade given any answer may be influenced by the scorer's opinion of the student's manner of expression, handwriting, personal qualities, or by other extraneous factors. The grades that one scorer gives on an essay test may vary from day to day, or grades may vary between scorers. In either case personal bias tends to affect the scores.

If an examination is completely objective, different persons scoring any one test paper or one person scoring the same test paper at different times will arrive at the same score. Such a high degree of objectivity may be achieved at the expense of more desirable qualities. However if tests and rating scales are carefully constructed and if the most likely responses are anticipated, classroom evaluation can be much more objective.

Comprehensiveness.

An evaluation instrument must sample liberally whatever is being measured. Suppose, for example, the owner of a grain elevator wants to evaluate a carload of wheat. If he analyzes a bushel of wheat from the top of the carload, he would still have a poor test—one that is not sufficiently comprehensive. A judgment based on this evaluation could not be safely applied to the entire carload—the wheat at the bottom of the car might be infested with insects. However if the owner takes fifty test tubes of the wheat from scattered positions in the carload, he might analyze less than a bushel of wheat, but he would have a much more comprehensive evaluation of the contents of the car.

In classroom evaluation a test or rating must sample liberally the objectives of instruction. At best, however, any evaluation is only a sample of the entire course. Just as the owner of the wheat elevator has to select samples of wheat from scattered positions in the car, the instructor has to make certain that evaluation includes a comprehensive sample of the course objectives. In both instances the evaluators must deliberately take comprehensive samples; neither should depend on chance.

Differentiation.

The evaluation instrument must be constructed to detect small differences. Suppose, for example, that a machinist wants to measure six bearings that are slightly graduated. If he uses a ruler to measure the diameters of the bearings, he finds little or no difference between the smallest bearing and the second-smallest one. If he compares the third bearing with the first bearing, he might detect a slight difference in size, but he could not depend upon the ruler to assort the six bearings. If he measures with a micrometer, which can measure very fine gradations, he can easily differentiate between the diameters of the first and second bearing, the second and third bearing, and so on up the scale.

In classroom evaluation a test or rating must be able to measure small differences in achievement in relation to the course objectives. When a test or rating scale is constructed to measure differences in achievement, it has these three features: (1) there is a wide range of scores, (2) all levels of difficulty are included, and (3) each item distinguishes between the students who are low and those who are high in achievement of the objectives.

Determining the Means of Evaluation.

Having now developed an understanding of the evaluation process and the five characteristics of evaluation, the instructor must choose the evaluation instrument. This choice is determined by the means that will best meet the requirements of the five essential characteristics. This, in turn, depends upon the circumstances surrounding the school, the instructor, and the student.

The instructor must consider at least the following factors when arriving at a decision regarding the best means to evaluate his students:

The Reasons for Evaluation.

If evaluation is solely for the purpose of assigning grades, simplicity would probably be an overriding factor in deciding whether to test or rate. If, as should be the case, evaluation is to improve instruction, pinpoint student deficiencies, identify specific degrees of skill achievement, or predict success on a future job, then each means by which these purposes can be accomplished must be analyzed.

The Nature of the Required Behavior.

Does the life of some person or expensive piece of equipment depend on the student's correct performance the first time he attempts it on the job? In some cases (e.g., in medical or maintenance fields), it would seem essential that at least the critical elements of the acquired skill be performed by the student for the purpose of evaluation. Less important or less critical skills might be represented as effectively on a pencil-and-paper test. The instructor and his supervisors, as qualified experts, are the best judges of this factor.

The Time and Facilities Available.

Are the students required to perform the skill during the learning process? If so evaluation might be an extension of this same activity; if not actual performance may be less critical. In either case the facilities available for evaluation are an essential factor in making the choice. Time may also influence the decisions (e.g., how much time must be set aside for evaluation by each means, and is that time available?).

The Availability of Qualified Faculty.

When choosing the best means to evaluate, the teacher/instructor must consider the availability of qualified faculty to judge (1) performance of students in terms of rating, and (2) responses of students in terms of grading specific instruments, such as essay and other selection-type tests.

Only when these factors have been considered and weighed can the teacher choose the means for evaluating students. Most likely he will realize that no one means will accomplish all purposes. Under such circumstances the teacher must either use a variety of evaluation instruments or compromise by accepting the achievement of his purpose to a lesser degree than desired.

Observation of Instruction

Instructor_____ Location_____

Activity_____ Date_____

CHECKPOINTS FOR OBSERVATION	3	2	1	0	na	NOTES
STEP 1. PREPARATION						
Put the group at ease						
Gained attention of the group						
Had a lesson plan prepared						
Had a clear, specific title						
Explained objectives to trainees						
Had necessary tools and material						
STEP 2. PRESENTATION						
Followed lesson plan						
Lesson was based on objectives						
Established good group relations						
Used a good motivational approach						
Used training aids effectively						
Used chalkboard effectively						
Used good questioning techniques						
Gained trainee participation						
Stressed safety when applicable						
Spoke distinctly and effectively						
Used various instructional media						
Demonstrated self-confidence						
Kept control of the group						

Figure 43

CHECKPOINTS FOR OBSERVATION	3	2	1	0	na	NOTES
STEP 3. APPLICATION						
Had each trainee perform operations						
Corrected errors immediately						
Gave individual attention						
Made certain lesson was learned						
STEP 4. TEST						
Based test items on lesson content						
Made assignment clear to trainees						
Established a relaxed atmosphere						
Used objective test items						
Used an objective rating system						
Ensured attainment of objectives						
GENERAL						
Presented a professional appearance						
Maintained group enthusiasm						
Had a tool control plan						
Kept tools and equipment in place						
Had a materials control program						
Had a housekeeping plan						
Maintained a clean environment						
Subtotal						
Total						

Comments_____

Signature_____

Review

1. How does evaluation fit into the teaching-learning process?
2. What is the difference between evaluation and testing?
3. A chemist takes great pains to clean a crucible before weighing it.
   Which characteristics of good measurements does he attain by this action?
4. A test on instrument flight rules was so long that only a fifth of the class completed it.
   a. Why is the validity of this test questionable?
   b. What factor might explain the high reliability of the test scores obtained?

Summary

Educational and training evaluation is a process to estimate the value for a useful purpose. It is concerned with the estimation of learning effectiveness and is, therefore, inseparable from the learning process. The process begins with a clear definition of objectives, in which specific criteria (standards) and samples (test items or traits) are defined to serve as vehicles for estimating the effectiveness of essential elements of the subject area being evaluated. These criteria and samples are the tools for constructing whatever means of evaluation most valid—a test, rating scale, research, or expert opinion. In practice either testing or performance ratings are means used to estimate how well students meet the criteria for each sample.

To be most effective, the evaluation process must be systematic and continuous—occasional or disorganized observations usually lack comprehensiveness, validity, and reliability. To be usable the conclusions reached must be presented in a form that can be properly interpreted by the school, the teacher, and the student. Whatever means is used, it should possess—to the maximum possible degree—the five characteristics of evaluation: reliability, to yield consistent results; validity, to measure what it is supposed to measure and nothing else; objectivity, to be sure the personal bias of the scorer does not affect the score achieved; comprehensiveness, to provide a liberal sample of all course material being measured; and differentiation, to detect small differences between the level of achievement of students.

How well each of the various means of evaluation will meet the requirements of the five stated characteristics is the test for choosing one means rather than another. To evaluate students correctly, a variety of means should be used. In choosing between any two equally valid means of evaluation, simplicity should be the deciding factor.

Chapter XV
Classroom Management

The instructor has some important responsibilities that go hand in hand with instruction. Some reminders follow:

1. Adequate preparation cannot be overemphasized. As an example a good instructor has his lesson plan well prepared and practiced long before presentation time.
2. Materials that support instruction should be on hand.
3. An instructor must never be late for class.
4. An instructor should have an excellent attitude and make a good impression at all times.
5. A copy of the lesson plan, including dates and name of instructor, should be posted in a conspicuous place in the classroom.
6. Class attendance is mandatory. The class attendance form must be filled in daily.
7. A blackboard, when not in use, should always be clean.
8. There should be no distraction in the classroom.
9. A well-organized instructor practices good classroom management by controlling students at all times.

Discipline is a sensitive area and one that many instructors prefer not to discuss. Discipline can be constructive in most cases. When understood and carried out appropriately, discipline can be productive. Remember that discipline has two meanings: discipline can be punishment, which has a negative taste and normally a bad effect, or it can be training, which has a positive and inviting attitude. Take the positive approach: be effective. Enlighten your student when discipline is necessary. Go the training route when feasible.

Note that I said "when discipline is necessary." There are at least four reasons why a student may need to be disciplined. None of these may require punishment. The student may have a poor attitude, you may not be communicating with the student, he may simply lack the talent to be in your class, or, he may lack motivation. Let's discuss these four typical problem areas to avoid possible confusion.

Attitude.

Poor attitude is a problem, but there are solutions. The first step is to find out if the student is aware of what is expected of him or her. There is a good possibility that the student sees things one way and you see them some other way. Has the student been informed of his or her responsibilities? By discussing the problem with the student in private, you may be able to rectify the problem. Listen attentively to what the student has to say. He may very well give you the solution to the problem.

Communication.

Lack of communication could be the problem. Think back for a moment. Have all policies regarding what is expected of the student been made clear to the student? Are there written policies on the matter? If so perhaps the student did not get a copy. Is he or she aware of all your standards? If the student did get a copy of the policies and he or she has ignored the policies, the next step is to consider discipline. (See "Approaches to Discipline.")

Talent.

On the subject of talent, the problem is not as acute. Additional education or training may be the answer. A possibility exists that the student can be helped by getting additional extracurricular assistance. He may be tested or interviewed to determine his aptitude and needs. A private discussion with the student may provide the necessary information.

Motivation.

The best solution to good motivation in the classroom or in the training workshop is an effective environment. The instructor must establish and maintain a good learning climate to motivate students. Keep in mind that motivation is next to impossible to impart. Motivation mostly comes from within the student. However without an effective classroom environment, motivation can be expected to be next to nil.

Approaches to Discipline.

The first step on your part is to be certain of the facts. Do not accept hearsay evidence to discipline anyone. This is a serious step, which must be accomplished effectively. When you know all the facts, you are ready to set up a private discussion with the student. In preparation for your discussion, find out what the student has accomplished. Find out his or her good points. Begin your conversation with a positive statement, a compliment, if you may. You may want to begin with: "I see you have volunteered for this class," or "I noticed on your records that you are an 'A' student." Set up a receptive climate before you discuss the problem. Approach your discussion, not from a punishment point of view, instead use the other meaning for discipline: training. You are now ready to help the student.

Next ask your student if he or she is aware of the violation or situation. If the answer is yes, invite a solution from the student. If his or her solution is not acceptable to you, continue with your discussion. Reword the problem until you agree and he or she accepts the solution and the action to be taken.

At the end of the discussion, come back to your original complimentary statement. Compliment the student again. Let the student leave with a positive attitude concerning your discussion.

Make it a point to set up a follow-up meeting on your calendar. If the problem has been solved at this next meeting, be sure to compliment and thank the student for his attitude and contribution. Recognize the student's efforts and improvement.

In dealing with some discipline problems, you will find that many students confuse working hard with producing good results. A student's experience often allows him or her to produce good results that are even better than working as hard. An effective discussion in this area will clarify things for the student.

The key to many training or educational classroom problems is, in most cases, the approach to an effective and constructive discussion with your student. Determine first what the problem area is, then discuss it in private.

Chapter XVI
Terminology

*The difference between the right word and almost the
right word is the difference between lightning and lightning bug.*

Mark Twain

Achievement Test —A test for measuring an individual's progress in the mastery of a subject to be learned. Its validity is usually determined on the basis of content or concurrent validity. (See Criterion-referenced Test.)

Action —Any activity that is induced by a stimulus. In instruction it designates a variety of behaviors that may involve a single word, selection among alternatives (multiple choice), the solution of a complex problem, the manipulation of punch buttons or keys. (See Response.)

Adaptability Test —Designed to predict job success of applicant for skilled, unskilled, office, data processing, secretarial, and supervisory jobs. This test distinguishes between persons who learn tasks quickly, adapt to situations easily, follow instructions accurately, and those who perform better in routine or repetitive jobs.

Adaptive Technique —Any of several techniques used in programming to accommodate individual differences. It may permit students to bypass material they already know or may provide them with additional instruction as needed. Also called adjustive devices.

Adjunct Programming —A programming method in which the instructional program supplements a handbook, technical order, regulation, or other source of information. The program is intended to instruct the student in the use of the supplemental material or to expand upon the content. (See Intrinsic Programming.)

Adolegogy —A stage of human development that individuals generally go through during their teenage years. This period includes growth toward sexual maturity, independence, and an orientation of identification focused on peers. It is also the time in life when probably the greatest conflict exists between the drive for individuality and the desire for conformity. Adolegogy is a time of obvious physical changes as well as emotional upheavals.

Advance Organizer —An introductory statement that describes the general concepts and materials to be covered during instruction.

Affective Learning —Dealing with changes in interest, attitudes, and values, and the development of appreciations and adequate adjustments.

Algorithm —An orderly procedure or exact prescription for solving a problem. In an algorithm the physical layout of the presentation shows the relationship between input data, rules, and outcomes. Algorithms replace continuous prose as an instrument for communicating complex rules and regulations.

Andragogy —The science of developing in adults the attitudes, habits, knowledge, and experience necessary for their continuing personal, social, and occupational growth. It perceives adults as knowledgeable and experienced learners who need and are able to benefit from direct experience; utilizes their past experiences to determine the relevancy of training needs; and provides for interpersonal learning situations in which they can continually evaluate their progress, independently or under minimum guidance.

Aptitude Test —A test or battery of tests designed to show a person's capacity for a particular type of behavior in a single field or in several related fields.

At-risk Students —Students who misbehave, don't do their homework, come from dysfunctional families.

Attitudes	—Attitudes are predispositions or tendencies to react specifically toward objects, situations, or values; usually accompanied by feelings and emotions. Attitudes cannot be directly observed, but must be inferred from overt verbal and nonverbal behavior.
Audioinstructional Device	—A book or other device, such as a teaching machine, designed to present a program of instruction without the aid of a live instructor. (See Teaching Machine.)
Audiovisual Media	—Teaching materials that communicate information through sight or sound sensors. The following are the most commonly used AV equipment:

1. Film Projector	—A film projector enables one to view films taken by 8mm, 16mm, or 35mm moving picture cameras. Films may be projected on a screen, and they may or may not be accompanied by sound.
2. Filmstrip Viewer	—A training device equipped with a built-in viewing glass or rear projection screen for viewing filmstrips. It may have cassette, cartridge, record, or tape capability for audiovisual presentations.
3. Personal Computer	—The personal computer is a relatively new audiovisual teaching device. Students/trainees who have access to a personal computer and the appropriate software are able to engage in individual instruction. The display affords students/trainees immediate feedback as they progress through the training module.
4. Opaque Projector	—A training device used for enlarging and projecting opaque materials, such as pictures, books, charts, and illustrations, onto a screen.
5. Overhead Projector	—The overhead projector is a training device that allows the instructor to project transparent materials (plastic transparencies) onto a screen. Also the instructor may write directly on the glass face of the overhead projector to enlarge and project materials.
6. Slide Projector	— A training device designed to project slides or transparencies

mounted in small frames. It may be silent, or cassettes, cartridges, records, or tapes may be used for audiovisual presentations.

7. Slide Viewer —A training device equipped with a built-in glass or a rear projection screen for viewing slides. It may be silent, or cassettes, cartridges, records, or tapes may be used for audiovisual presentations.

8. Sound-Slide Program —An audiovisual instructional program that uses 35mm slides and recorded sound. Sometimes this program is referred to as slide/tape, and in the case when the recording is a part of the slide frame, as sound-on-slide.

9. Videocassette Recorder —The VCR unit is another teaching device. The VCR employs a cassette recording of the instructional material that, when played back, is displayed on a standard television monitor.

Basic —An acronym used as it applies to computers, specifically to programming: *Beginners All*-purpose *Symbolic Instruction Code*; a programming language available for personal computers; a computer language designed by two Dartmouth College Professors, John Kemeny and Thomas Kurtz.

Behavior —Any activity, overt or covert, capable of being measured. The action of an organism, that is, anything that an organism does, including overt, physical action; internal physiological and emotional processes; and implicit mental activity.

Behavioral Objective —A statement that specifies precisely what behavior is to be exhibited, the conditions under which behavior will be accomplished, and the minimum standard of acceptable performance.

Brainstorming —(1) A method of small-group discussion with about six to ten members under the leadership of a chairman, which aims at the creative solution of organizational problems through the use of open-ended questions. Generally it proves successful, since the members are usually *a* selected on the basis of education and/or experience of a wide range; *b* placed in a permissive and status-free environment that not only encourages and stimulates, but also depends on quick, spontaneous, and imaginative participation; and *c* not criticized or otherwise limited in their expression or contributions. Often referred to as "green light session." (2) A popular nontechnical term for certain techniques for the stimulation of creative thinking in the development of new ideas. Consists of individual or, more generally, small-group activity in which a deliberate attempt is made to think uncritically, but creatively about all possible approaches and solutions to a given problem. The group participates in spontaneous and unrestrained discussion which usually involves evaluative feedback.

Branch —In programmed instruction a point of choice at which students are sent to alternative items depending on their responses to the particular item. (See Intrinsic Programming; Bypassing.)

Buddy System —A type of training whereby a new employee is assigned a "buddy" to help him to become oriented to his/her job and fellow employees.

Business Education —The preparation, in colleges, of specialists in a variety of core business courses supplemented by the required studies in liberal arts. Initiated in the United States in the late eighteenth century as a response to needs created by the Industrial Revolution. It began with proprietary secretarial and vocational secondary schools. After World War I colleges began to offer, typically, the principles of economic theory to business problems. After World War II a broad curriculum reform was initiated in business education. Specialization was discouraged and all business course disciplines were stressed. By 1978, more than 200 colleges had been accredited.

Buzz Group (Session) —A small, informal group of about four to ten persons, usually selected from a large group, to consider and discuss what they have heard at a lecture or forum, informally, and usually with total participation. The discussion, which should ideally develop a group point of view, lasts for about twenty to thirty minutes. After the discussion a chosen representative presents those ideas or questions that the group decided to ask the speaker(s) during the general discussion period. (See Brainstorming.)

Bypassing —In programmed instruction this is a technique that permits students to skip certain portions of the materials because they have prior knowledge. A criterion item may be inserted in a linear program, and if students pass, they are sent forward several items (bypassing); if they fail the criterion item, they do an intervening sequence of review or remedial items.

Byte —A character. The eighth EBCDIC (Extended Binary Coded Decimal Interchange Code). Acronym is pronounced "ebb-see-dic." Data on byte can be recorded at different densities of bytes per inch, depending on the type of computer and magnetic tape being used.

Career —(1) An occupation that an individual chooses, develops himself in, and usually pursues throughout most of the productive years of his/her life; (2) a profession; (3) an enterprise.

Career Counseling (Guidance) —An interpersonal relationship in which a counselor or other qualified professional attempts to help an individual select and prepare for a career that is suitable for his aptitude, needs, or interests. (See Counseling; Guidance.)

Carrel —(1) A small cubicle or study desk set aside, usually in the library stacks, for the use of faculty members and students for individual study; (2) a student study station with unitized desk, table, or both designed to facilitate effective study by the student (described as *wet* when it includes electronic devices and *dry* when it lacks such devices); usually established in connection with a system that makes available packaged sets or kits of learning material for self-managed instruction; (3) a separately identified location, although generally considered part of the room into which it opens and which it serves, for example, a study hall, regular classroom, or laboratory.

Case Study —(1) A method of investigation and analysis of individual or organizational decision-making, problems, or related factors over a period of time; (2) the written record of such investigation and analysis, which is often used as a method and process for studying, evaluating, discussing, role-playing, or otherwise participating in decision-making over problems involving historical, quantitative, normative, strategic, in-depth, or complex topics. Also referred to as "case analysis" or "case history method." An analysis of the origin of individual and family problems and of the methods used in counseling; generic term for individualized counseling methods that utilize cumulative records or other collection of all available evidence—social, psychological, physiological, biographical, environmental, vocational—that promises to help explain a single individual or a single social unit such as a family.

Central Processing Unit (CPU) —The brains of the computer operation. Two major components of CPU are the control unit, which can read and understand the *program*, and the *arithmetic logic unit*, which can be considered a fancy calculator. The two-step operation is, first, the use of the memory data, and, second, the interpretation of the data to produce the results of problems, data, equations, or other information required. The CPU operates at great speeds. Cycles are estimated to be in the millionths of a second.

Chaining —The linking together of a series of discriminable responses in a particular order. The completion of each response provides the stimulus for the next response. May involve chains of verbal responses, such as reciting a list of numbers, or chains of motor responses following a procedure.

Chip —A small sliver of silicon in the shape of a square or rectangle and as thin as a human hair. The surface of the chip is covered with a network of thousands of tiny tunnels and canals that act as pathways for electricity. Some chips act as a computer memory; other chips serve as electrical charges and act as a computer processor or brain. They can remember and store information, and they can shuffle information and produce solutions. Computer chips, as masterminds, can solve a million problems and/or can remember a hundred thousand birthdays in one second.

Cognitive Learning —This deals with the recall or recognition of knowledge and the development of intellectual abilities and skills.

Communication —(1) The arousal of common meanings, with their resulting reactions, between communicator and interpreter through the use of language or other signs and symbols; a social act involving two or more persons in a field situation; face-to-face the roles of the communicator and interpreter are constantly shifting, in other situations there is less possibility for this interaction; (2) the establishment of a social unit among human beings by the use of language signs and by the sharing of common sets of rules for various goal-seeking activities; (3) (philos.) the process whereby a human society continues to exist by transmitting its values, concepts, attitudes, habits, and skills (nonmaterial cultural components) so that the young may participate in the common life.

Compiler   —The part of the computer that processes the answer or compiles the data.

Comprehensiveness   —Examinations covering the entire field of a major study, given in the final undergraduate or graduate year of college.

Computer   —An electronic processor that can store, retrieve, and process data. A machine that handles information and can duplicate any human activity in which information is processed by logical steps. Computers are machines that can perform such tasks many millions of times faster than any human being.

Computer-assisted Instruction   —An instructional method whereby students interact (usually) individually to instruction presented through a variety of media, usually computer controlled or monitored. Students can respond to the stimuli in a variety of ways, such as with a keyset or pointing device. Students are immediately informed as to the accuracy of their responses to determine the probable reason for any errors and to present additional instruction in accordance with the diagnosis.

Computer-directed Training System   —A training system that involves dependent subsystems (functional software and courseware) and related documentation. Functional software enables the course designer to code course material and the student to interact with courseware. Courseware is the subject matter and instructional data in whatever media required by students to complete their course through the use of the computer terminal.

Computer-managed Instruction   —In computer-managed instruction, students do not necessarily interact directly with the equipment, as with computer-assisted instruction, though they may be "on-line" for testing, diagnosis, and prescription. The role of the computer in computer-managed instruction is to aid the instructor in managing the instructional program.

Conference   —A rather informal training device in organization whereby a small group of managers or employees meet to consider, discuss, and/or decide upon an idea, issue, or a course of action.

(See Group Discussion.)

Constraint —Limiting or restraining conditions or factors, such as policy considerations, time limitations, environmental factors, and budgetary and other resource limitations. In PERT a condition in which an event in a network may not begin until the event preceding it has already been completed. In systems design and management, a term referring to any limitation or restriction inherent in or imposed upon human, organizational, or environmental resources or conditions.

Constructed Response —An answer requiring recall or completion as opposed to recognition; for example, drawing a diagram; filling in a form; labeling the parts of a piece of equipment; writing a sentence, paragraph, or essay.

Consultant —An expert in a specialized field who serves in an advising capacity to an officer or instrumentality of a business organization as distinguished from one who serves as an officer or employee in the performance of duties and responsibilities of that agency or organization. (See Expert.) (1) An expert in a specialized field, without administrative authority, whose advice is sought in improving an educational program, the facilities offered, or methods of cooperation; (2) a professionally trained person on call to offer guidance and help in promoting and improving the educational program.

Cost-Effectiveness —A comparative evaluation derived from analysis of alternatives (actions, methods, approaches, equipment, weapon systems, support systems, force combinations) in terms of the interrelated influences of cost and effectiveness in accomplishing a specific mission or objective.

Counseling —(1) A relationship in which one or more persons with a problem or concern desire to discuss and work toward solving it with another person or persons attempting to help them reach their goals; (2) individualized assistance through (*a*) personal interviews in which the student is aided in the making of his own decisions and choices, such as the vocation he will follow, and (*b*) referral to personnel specialists for professional and personal assistance with problems and adjustments; (3) the personal-treatment phase of assistance, with or without diagnosis of causes of the student's problems; one of the basic services in the body of services constituting guidance; (4) a systematic, private, and face-to-face communication process between a counselor (or supervisor or teacher) and a student. It is used to (*a*) gain understanding into the causes and nature of any problem or dissatisfaction involving the student and/or organization; (*b*) provide help to release feelings; and (*c*) give psychological support to help the student to do something about his problems.

Courseware —The technical data, textual materials, and audiotapes, slides, movies, videocassettes, and other audiovisual instructional materials.

CPU —(central processing unit). The brains of the computer operation. Two major components of CPU are the control unit, which can read and understand the *program,* and the *arithmetic logic unit,* which can be considered a fancy calculator. The two-step operation is, first, the use of the memory data, and, second, the interpretation of the data to produce the results of problems, data, equations, or other information required. The CPU operates at great speeds. Cycles are estimated to be in the millionths of a second.

Criterion Frame —In programmed instruction item(s) at the end of instruction that contain no prompts. Intended to give evidence that the criterion behavior has been acquired.

Criterion-referenced Test —Test to determine if behavior as reflected in objectives has been acquired. May involve multiple-choice items, fill-in items, essays, or actual performance of a task. If given immediately after learning sequences, it is a test of acquisition; if given considerably later, it is a retention test; if it requires performance not specifically learned during instruction, it is a transfer test.

Critique —(1) Criticism or critical examination; (2) (literature) scholarly analysis of an essay, article, or other literary work; (3) (philos.) careful and thorough investigation into the grounds of the claims of a belief or position, as opposed to dogmatic assertion or settlement of a claim (Kant); (4) a critical estimate of an activity designed primarily for the purpose of improving one's future performance therein; (5) review of work with a student teacher to point out his strong and weak points in practice teaching and offer suggestions for improvement.

Cross-cultural Interface	—In any society there are sets of commonly known givens, customs, if you will, upon which education in any form may be based. Individuals with similar cultural backgrounds will have little difficulty in communicating with or learning from others of the same cultural milieu. However when individuals from widely disparate cultures come together with the purpose of communicating, learning, doing business, and so on, cultural gaps exist, which may make communication difficult, if not impossible. Cross-cultural interface seeks to bridge that gap and facilitates learning or doing business. To interface across cultures, the teacher must be aware of and sensitive to the cultural differences of students and have some notion of how these differences will have an impact on the learner. Teaching strategies may then be modified and adjusted so that the student will not be hindered by another culture's "baggage." *Example:* In a history class, an instructor teaching American history to Americans will be reasonably sure that students will know who the "Founding Fathers" are when he/she refers to them. An international student with little knowledge of American history would be at a loss to identify the Founding Fathers, unless their names were specifically mentioned.
Cross-Training	—A planned program of exposing an employee to job experiences that one would not normally receive in a current job assignment in order to gain valuable job knowledge and experience, and a change in attitude toward one's job, co-workers, and, generally, the entire organization.
Cue	—The event, situation, condition, signal, or stimulus to which a response must be made.
Culture	—(1) The aggregate of the social, ethical, intellectual, artistic, governmental, and industrial attainments characteristic of a group, state, or nation and by which it can be distinguished from or compared with other groups, states, or nations; includes ideas, concepts, usages, institutions, associations, and material objects; (2) (psych.) the level attained by the individual or social group in the accumulation of knowledge and the integration of social behavior patterns; (3) good taste in personal conduct; knowledge of the intellectual heritage of the race; appreciation of art and letters and of beauty in nature, and a reasonable, consistent, personal philosophy of life; (4) a complex entity of all explicit and implicit ideas, values, customs,

institutions, beliefs, attitudes, habits, or related behavior patterns that are learned from and practiced by means of communication and social contact between people in a certain area or period; (5) the environment of ideas, experiences, beliefs, traditions, customs, institutions, sciences, arts, technologies, humanities, and common sense of doing things that are part of the shared life of a society.

Culture Shock —Excessive stress, confusion, disorientation, and other related psychological imbalance that individuals may experience upon entering a new culture, society, or way of life.

Culture Shock Test —A test that is designed to acquaint those who expect to work outside their own culture with some of the things that may get them into trouble. Topics include Western ethnocentrism, cross-cultural experience, cognitive and behavioral flex, specific and general cultural knowledge, customs acceptance, and interpersonal sensitivity.

Curriculum —A dynamic (ever-changing) plan for achieving intended learning outcomes concerned with the results of instruction. The curriculum is a motion picture, rather than a still picture—an on-going work of art rather than a completed one. Curriculum is composed of selection, structure, and learning outcomes. *Selection* includes books, other materials, ideas, travel, people, and modern communication media that result in cultural content, and expose interest and motivation. *Structure* identifies sequence and order. *Learning outcomes* is the knowledge, the skills, and the attitude. *Knowledge* includes information, facts, principles and generalizations that produce a "whole" person as a citizen, and in civility, using different modes of inquiry, and principles of logic. *Attitudes* are beliefs, values, feelings, creative thinking, appreciation, self-esteem, and other aspects of growth skills as specialties in the techniques, processes, and abilities that enhance the individual versatility to use knowledge and physical resources effectively to enlarge the horizons of his or her world.

Debate —A formal, open, and democratic exchange of opposing thoughts and opinions by persons or groups who must reach a decision on some problems in a relatively short time.

Decision Logic Chart/Table	—Guide to assist in the decision-making process. Represents the inputs or set of inputs likely to occur for a given situation, and recommends a course of action or, if appropriate, alternative actions.
Developed/Designed Training	—Training provided to meet unique training requirements of a division, department, or other units of a private or public sector organization. It may be available under contract with outside experts, such as educators or educational institutions, consultants or consulting organizations, training specialists or training organizations, or professional leadership societies and associations.
Diagnostic Test	—(1) Any testing device that is primarily designed to identify and specify the nature and source of an individual's health problems or other physical, psychological, developmental, or emotional problems; (2) personality tests given by school counselors or psychologists are referred to as diagnostic tests.
Differential	—(1) Widely used test that may be administered individually or in groups, and is designed to predict future success in career fields; (2) test given, generally, when a student or students are changing career fields.
Direct Training Cost	—The dollar amount assigned to cover such items as tuition; laboratory or library fees; books; and other related materials, equipment, or supplies.
Discriminating	—Making different responses to the different stimuli. A discrimination requires a person to determine the differences among inputs and to respond differently to each.
Distributed Practice	—During learning the process of spacing numerous, relatively short practice sessions throughout the learning period.
Dogmatic	—(1) (of persons) Given to highly authoritative pronouncements; (2) (of statements) without critical scrutiny and challenge as to grounds and evidence; (3) (of systems) based on assumptions that cannot be scrutinized; (4) (of teaching) characterized by authoritative statements on the part of the teacher intended for acceptance by the pupils without question; to be contrasted with teaching that guides pupils in thinking their own way through problems.
Education	—(1) The aggregate of all the processes by means of which a person develops abilities, attitudes,

and other forms of behavior of positive value in the society in which he lives; (2) the social process by which people are subjected to the influence of a selected and controlled environment (especially that of the school) so that they may attain social competence and optimum individual development; (3) ordinarily a general term for the technical or professional courses offered in higher institutions for the preparation of teachers and relating directly to educational psychology, philosophy and history of education, curriculum, special and general methods, instruction, administration, supervision, etc.; broadly the total pattern of preparation, formal and informal, that results in the professional growth of teachers; (4) the art of making available to each generation the organized knowledge of the past.

Educational Administrative-style Diagnostic Test —Designed as a training tool, this test gives scores on many styles of leadership such as deserter, missionary, autocrat, compromiser, bureaucrat, developer, benevolent autocrat, task orientation, relationships orientation, and effectiveness.

Educational Leadership Appraisal —A performance-based procedure for the observation and assessment of leadership behavior. It focuses on potential to exercise leadership in an administrative position within a school system, appraising the administrative along twenty-three leadership dimensions grouped into the broader categories of management, organization, communication, problem-solving, task orientation, and interpersonal qualities that ideally represent the aptitudes, abilities, competencies, and qualities generally demanded by the school administrator's job. It involves a series of individual and group judgment and creativity exercises, simulations, role-playing, tasks, decision-making, problem analyses, interviews, and leaderless group discussions.

Educational Media —The equipment and materials used for communication in instruction. It includes motion pictures, television, printed materials, computer-based instruction, graphic and photographic materials, sound recordings, and three-dimensional objects.

Educational Objective —One that ordinarily is attained upon the completion of a program consisting of any curriculum or combination of unit courses or subjects offered by an educational institution that normally leads to an earned college degree.

Educational Resources Management Systems —The system of researching, documenting, analyzing, or otherwise handling information pertaining to various long-range plans, objectives, programs, and resources for purposes of selecting the most appropriate ones for decision-making about present educational objectives and needs within the framework of optimum cost-effectiveness standards and conditions.

Educational Television —Television programs presented as a part of an instructional or training program.

Educational Training Technology —Theories and practices of implementing or substituting conventional teacher-learner processes and environments with modern mechanical or electronic devices and methods. (See Computer-assisted Instruction.)

Education Test —Any test that is aimed at establishing the extent to which an applicant for employment has mastered the academic, professional, or technical skills and knowledge required in his field of endeavor.

Ego —The entire person. In psychoanalysis a hypothetical construct referring to the conscious, self-directing, and controlling aspect of the psyche that mediates between the basic, unconscious impulses and their corresponding tensions, conflicts, and the demands of social living.

Ego Involvement —A psychological process or condition whereby an individual becomes identified with an idea, person, or event that he regards vital to his needs.

Employment Tests —Usually a standardized system of tests designed to aid in the choosing of applicants by estimating the extent of their future success as employees.

Encapsulation —A strategy of regulating interpersonal and group conflict through rules and principles mutually agreed by all participants in the conflict.

Endowment —(1) A permanent financial provision for any purpose or object (such as funds provided for the use of a school, church, or research agency), the principal of which must be kept intact and prudently invested, while the income may be expended for the purpose for which the provision was made; may be general, as for all the purposes of a college, or special, as for the support of a chair in American history; (2) natural capacity for physical or mental development as determined by the heredity of the individual.

Enrichment —Supplementary material that aids the student in progressing through the course but is not considered crucial to learning.

Enrichment, Curriculum —(1) The process of selectively modifying a curriculum by adding educational content to that which already exists; intended to supply the means to meet the individual educational needs and interest of learners enrolled in a class; curriculum enrichment may be either horizontal or vertical; (2) a program for the gifted within the framework of the regular classes; consists of deliberate differentiation of curriculum content and activities for the superior pupils in a heterogeneous class.

Entering Behavior —The skills and knowledge students have when they enter a course of instruction. Includes information about school performance, school completion, type of training received, instruction patterns, and test scores. Sometimes includes other information which may be relevant to development plans, such as social or economic status, ethnic or racial background, and physical or psychological deviations. Also called Incoming Repertoire. (See Knowledge; Skills; Survey Test.)

Evaluation —(1) The process of ascertaining or judging the value or amount of something by use of a standard of appraisal; includes judgments in terms of internal evidence and external criteria; (2) (psych.) the process of determining the relative significance of phenomena of the same sort in terms of some standard; (3) the consideration of evidence in the light of value standards and in terms of the particular situation and the goals that the group or individual is striving to attain; (4) a judgment of merit, sometimes based solely on measurements, such as those provided by test scores, but more frequently involving the synthesis of various measurements, critical incidents, subjective impressions, and other kinds of evidence weighed in the process of carefully appraising the effects of an educational experience; (5) procedure to determine the effectiveness of the performance of an instructional product or process in order to ascertain specific causes for the effectiveness (see also Chapter XIV); (6) the process of ascertaining or judging the value or amount of an action or an outcome by careful appraisal of previously specified data in light of the particular situation and the goals and objectives previously established.

Evaluation, Curriculum —The assessment of learning activities within a specific instructional area for the purpose of determining the validity of objectives, relevancy and sequence of content, and achievement of specified goals; leads to decisions associated with planning, programming, implementing, and recycling program activities.

Examination —Any process for testing the ability or achievement of students in any area; in ordinary speech the terms "examination" and "test" are frequently used as synonyms. If a distinction is to be made, an examination should be regarded as more comprehensive and complex than a test.

Exchange Program, Fulbright —A program initiated by an act of the Seventy-Ninth Congress, it provides for the exchange of students, teachers, lecturers, research scholars, and specialists between the United States and designated countries. Financial implementation of the act is effected by the use of funds derived from the sale of surplus properties left in designated countries at the close of World War II. The purpose of the act is to further international goodwill and understanding. All forms of study and research are included. The program is supervised by a Board of Foreign Scholarship composed of ten prominent American educators and educational administrators, which is responsible to the Department of State. The cooperating agency, known as the Conference Board of Associated Research Councils, supervises exchange projects on the university-lecture and postdoctoral research level.

Experience —(1) The acquisition of knowledge, attitudes, or skills through one's own perception and participation, or knowledge, attitudes, or skills so acquired; (2) (philos.) (*a*) the context of the life process as distinct from the order of things in themselves or the realm of essences or reality; (*b*) the process of interaction between a human being and his physical and cultural environment. In nonempirical or rationalistic philosophies, experience, as opposed to true knowledge, involves sense perception, habit, impulse, and emotion—hence although it may tell us something about our practical affairs, it is not a reliable source of knowledge of universal principles or essences; in empirical philosophies the inclusive matrix of human action and thought; experience, as the basis or context of all knowledge, involves the process of seeing relationships between what one does or plans to do and the consequence of doing it so that these connections may be used in guiding subsequent experiences.

Experiment —(1) The trial of a planned procedure accompanied by control of conditions and/or controlled variation of conditions, together with observation of results for the purpose of discovering relationships and evaluating the reasonableness of a given hypothesis; (2) an integral part of any learning process, usually with less conscious attention to the elements listed under (1) and containing more of the trial-and-error elements; (3) the administration, under controlled conditions, of treatments to a group or groups that have been specifically constituted for the purpose and the analysis of the effects produced or induced in the subjects or units as a result.

Experiment, Laboratory —(1) An experiment under the more strictly controlled conditions of the educational or psychological laboratory or clinic, as contrasted with an experiment under the practical limiting conditions existing in regularly established classrooms; frequently performed on one person or on a very small number of persons; (2) (sci. ed.) an experiment performed with an apparatus and materials manipulated by an individual student or a small group to find either.

Extrovert —A socially expressive, usually easy-going type of person, who is oriented toward and is dependent upon the presence of, or frequent interaction with, other people.

Eysensk Personality Inventory Test —Consisting of fifty-seven items, this test is designed to evaluate dimensions of personality in terms of (1) extroversion vs. introversion, outgoing vs. retiring; (2) neuroticism vs. stability, emotionally stable vs. labile; and (3) lying vs. telling the truth.

Face-to-Face Group —A sociological term referring to a group of two or more persons that is usually characterized by intimate, direct communication and interaction, and a relatively shared way of perceiving and reacting to environmental stimuli.

Facilitator —The leader, moderator, or resource person in encounter or sensitivity-training groups.

Factor Analysis   —A technique for studying the intercorrelations among a set of variables, such as test scores, in order to (1) find the factors or dimensions that account for certain results, and (2) determine the extent to which each variable relates to or is associated with each of the hypothetical factors.

Faculty   —(1) The body of persons responsible for instruction and administration in a school, college, or university; (2) the teachers of an educational institution; (3) a branch of learning or instruction in a university, as the faculty of arts and sciences or the faculty of law.

Fading   —In programmed instruction the progressive diminishing of prompts within a teaching sequence so that all prompting is absent from the criterion frame. (See Prompt; Criterion Frame.)

Feedback   —Information that results from or is contingent upon an action. The feedback does not necessarily indicate the rightness or wrongness of an action, rather it relates the results of the action from which inferences about correctness can be drawn. Feedback may be immediate, as when a fuse blows because a lamp was incorrectly wired, or delayed, as when an instructor provides a discussion pertaining to an exam taken the previous week. (See Knowledge.) The flow of information back into the control system so that actual performance can be compared with planned performance. (1) Error-correcting information returned to the control center of a servomechanism (or to the nervous system and brain of a living organism), enabling it to offset deviations in its course toward a particular goal; (2) in programmed instruction information received by the student immediately after each of his responses to the programmed material; (3) knowledge obtained from testing or programmed materials that may be used by the programmer in making subsequent revisions; (4) the interchange of information on the part of human beings in a communication or problem-solving situation; (5) (audiovis, instr.) the pick-up of sound produced by an audio-system speaker, by a microphone attached to that speaker, and the recycling through the same speaker of the sound, which thus grows ever louder.

Field Test   —Testing of any training course on a representative sample of the target population to gather data on the effectiveness of instruction in regard to error rates, criterion test performance, and time to complete the course.

Field Theory —A theory that attempts to conceptualize those dynamic, interrelated psychological "fields" or systems in the environment that can exert various pressures on and influence decision-making and related behavior and interaction patterns in terms of such patterns.

Field Training —A method of training employees under actual working conditions.

FLES —An acronym formed from "foreign languages in the elementary school"; includes the teaching of any foreign language within or in conjunction with the curriculum of the elementary school.

Floppy Disk —A small, flexible, magnetized disk for storing data. The most common medium of storing data for microcomputers (home computers). Also called a diskette.

FORTRAN —An automatic symbolic coding language used in programming computational applications; an acronym formed from FORmula TRANslator.

Frame —In programmed instruction each portion of material to which the student makes a response. A frame is also called an exercise step, or an item of information. A frame may vary in size from a single incomplete sentence, question, or instruction to perform some response, up to a sizable paragraph.

Front-end Analysis —A basic tool of instruction management in planning, controlling, financing, or coordinating. It consists of the systematic examination and determination of (1) the nature, characteristics, functions, duties, activities, or responsibilities of a job; (2) the knowledge, skill, or experience that is essential for performance; and (3) the environmental conditions, safety, equipment, tools, and related factors. (See Job Analysis.)

Future Shock —A. Toffler's term for the shattering stress, confusion, and disorientation individuals may experience when being subjected to excessive social, cultural, demographic, ecological, information, and value changes in a short period of time.

Futuristics —Term referring to the dynamic, exploratory, and eclectic thinking, methods, and processes involved in the probabilistic assessment of future social, economic, technological advances and changes.

General Educational Development Test (G.E.D.)	—A comprehensive test used primarily to appraise the educational development of adults who have not completed their formal high school education; through achievement of satisfactory scores, adults may earn a high school equivalency certificate, qualify for admission to college or to more advanced educational or employment opportunities, or meet qualifications for admission to college or to more advanced educational or employment opportunities, or meet qualifications for admission to licensing examinations for certain occupations; tests are administered at official G.E.D. centers approved by state departments of education and, also to military personnel on active duty, through the U.S. Armed Forces Institute.
Generalization	—Learning to respond to a new stimulus that is similar, but not identical, to one that was present during original learning; for example during learning a child calls a beagle and a spaniel by the term "dog." A child who has generalized would respond "dog" when presented with a hound as a stimulus.
Genius	—(1) A person of exceptionally high mental ability, frequently evidenced by superior powers of invention or origination or by exceptional performance in some special skill, such as music, art, or mechanics; (2) exceptional ability as defined above. (No specific level of ability has been universally accepted as indicative of genius, although an IQ of 140 or more has sometimes been used as an arbitrary standard.)
Geography	—The science of the earth, including a study of land, water, air, the distribution of plant and animal life, man and his industries, and the interrelations of these factors.
Grant	—(1) Strictly and originally a gift of real property from the sovereign power to a natural or legal person for use in purposes likely to benefit the general public; (2) a contribution by a governmental unit to another unit, often by a larger unit to a subordinate one, ordinarily to aid in the support of a specified function (for example, education), but sometimes also for general purposes; (3) an appropriation of funds made by a foundation to a recipient; the amount and purpose of the funds and the period of time during which they are expendable are usually specified.

Group Discussion —A technique and process of solving problems of mutual concern by means of an organized, but still informal, face-to-face meeting in which normally six or more participants exchange all the ideas or opinions they have about the available facts, discuss the merits, or make suggestions under the guidance or chairmanship of a leader. (See Brainstorming.)

Group Job Descriptions —Computer-generated composite job descriptions of tasks performed by a group. They provide task statement, percent performing task, average percentage of time spent by job incumbents who perform the task, average percentage of time spent by all job incumbents, and cumulative sum of the average percentage of time spent by all job incumbents.

Group Pacing —A procedure in which students progress together toward the same objectives; often employed where self-pacing is not practical for administrative reasons. (See Self-Pacing.)

Guidance —(1) The process of assisting an individual to understand himself and the world about him and to gain a knowledge of the implications of this understanding for educational progress, career development, and personality fulfillment; (2) a form of systematic assistance (aside from regular instruction) to pupils, students, or others to help them to assess their abilities and liabilities and to use that information effectively in daily living; (3) the act or technique of directing the child toward a purposive goal by arranging an environment that will cause him to feel basic needs, to recognize these needs, and to take purposeful steps toward satisfying them; (4) a method by which the teacher leads the child to discover and make a desired response of his own will.

Guidance, Career —An interpersonal relationship in which a counselor or other qualified professional attempts to help an individual select and prepare for a career that is suitable for his aptitude, needs, or interests.

Guided Interview —Usually a task-centered interview whereby the interviewer attempts to gain specific information through questioning the person being interviewed without a certain subject rather than allowing for free discussion. Also referred to as "structured interview."

Halo Effect —A bias in ratings arising from the tendency of a rater to be influenced in his rating of specific traits by his general impression of the person being rated.

Hardware —The physical components of a system (usually electronic or electrical devices) that are utilized in educational processes, including computers, terminals, audiovisual devices, teaching machines, and the like. (See Software.)

Harvard Case Method —A nondirective and permissive participative training method and process of working toward the acquisition of creativity and independent thinking in applying management ideas, principles, and methods through the evaluation and discussion of a series of case studies that are presented to a class or group by a teacher or expert who acts as a guide rather than a lecturer during the learning process.

High School —The school division following the elementary school, composed of grades 9 to 12 or grades 7 to 13, and sometimes including grades 13 and 14.

History —(1) A systematically arranged, written account of events affecting a nation, social group, institution, science, or art, usually including an attempted explanation of the relationships of the events and their significance; (2) the science or field of study concerned with the recording and critical interpretation of past events; generally divided into ancient history, medieval history, and modern history, with many subdivisions, such as United States history.

Honor Society, National—An organization established under the auspices of the National Association of Secondary School Principals and designed to honor outstanding scholastic achievement by senior high school students; members are elected from the junior and senior classes, usually by secret vote of the faculty; no more than fifteen percent of a graduating class is eligible, and members must be chosen from the upper one-third of the class.

Human Engineering —A field of specialization that, by combining the theories and methods of psychology and engineering design, deals with (1) the study of people at work; (2) the design of physical equipment and facilities for human use according to the capacities, abilities, strength, or dimensions of their operators; and (3) the training or conditioning of workers for the most effective use of these equipments and facilities. Its main purpose is to (*a*) maximize efficiency, production, and quality; (*b*) create safe and comfortable working conditions; (*c*) increase job satisfaction; and (*d*) improve employee relations in the working environment. Frequently referred to as "ergonomics."

Human Existence Theory —A concept that is helpful to trainers. (1) It helps explain why certain individuals fail in group training settings; (2) it indicates why some participants rate you as an instructor "outstanding" and others rate you "lousy"; (3) it captures our interest as we try to pin our loss or a recalcitrant trainee to a specific category; (4) it provides a key as to how to obtain more homogeneous grouping of participants whether they be supervisors, managers, or top-level bosses.

Humanistic Education —A laboratory-type of small-group training, designed to create in the participants (normally executives, managers, and supervisors) an understanding of or "sensitivity" toward the causes, processes, and effects of (1) their own attitudes and behavior; (2) the attitudes and behavior of others; and (3) basic techniques of communication in various interpersonal situations, such as supervision, training, guidance, or counseling.

Humanities —(1) A term used currently by many schools and colleges in the United States to designate comprehensive courses in literature, language, art, philosophy, religion, and history, thus distinguishing the humanities from social science and the natural sciences; (2) whatever concerns man as distinct from physical nature, especially as expressed most adequately in the great or classic achievements of humanity in literature and art; (3) as used in the Renaissance period, the term designated the "more human letters" of recently revived Greek and Latin writers in contrast to the theological letters of the medieval schoolmen; (4) frequently has been used to designate courses in, or the study of, classical languages (Latin and Greek) and classical literature and art; (5) today the term "humanities" includes also the masterpieces of modern literature, art, and science, as being equally "creation of the free spirit of man."

Idiom —An expression of which the meaning does not appear directly from the ordinary signification of the words in the combination but is attached to them by conventional usage, so that the expression can seldom be literally translated into another language.

Illiteracy —(1) Strictly complete inability to read and write; (2) more broadly inability to read and write sufficiently well to meet the needs of adult life; a relative term usually implying comparison of the individual's ability to read and write with the average ability found at his social or economic level; (3) failure to learn to read through lack of educational opportunity.

In-Company Training —A formal process by which new employees, who may already have some general knowledge, but no experience, are oriented, introduced, instructed, developed, or otherwise prepared for the methods, processes, and responsibilities of their jobs.

Independent Study —An instructional technique in which learners carry on their learning activities without formal classes, but consult with an instructor or instructors as they complete individual study projects.

Individually Prescribed Instruction —(Sometimes called individually paced instruction.) A course of study or program fitted to the individual learner's background, abilities, and training needs in which the learner selects his/her own materials and proceeds at his/her own pace.

Industrial Arts —(1) Those occupations by which changes are made in the forms of materials to increase their value for human use; (2) an area of education dealing with socioeconomic problems and occupational opportunities, involving experience with a wide range of materials, tools, processes, products, and occupants typical of an industrial program concerned with orienting individuals through study and experience to the technical-industrial side of society for the purpose of enabling them to deal more intelligently with consumer goods, to be more efficient producers, to use leisure time more effectively, and to act more intelligently in regard to matters of health and safety, especially as affected by industry; (3) the study of industrial, technical, social, economic, occupational, cultural, and recreational nature and influences through research, experiment, design, invention, construction, and operation with industrial materials, processes, products, and energies for the purposes of acquainting the student with technological culture and aiding him in the discovery and development of his native potential; (4) organized study of the knowledge or practice within that subcategory of the economic, institution of society known as industry; (5) curriculum area in general education in which students may create, experiment, design, and plan while dealing with issues related to technology.

Industrial Education —A term used to designate various types of education concerned with modern industry, industrial arts, technical education and apprenticeship training, and vocational-industrial education in both public and private schools.

Initial Education —Education, training, or experience that employees acquire prior to having been appointed to their respective position in an organization.

In Loco Parentis —A Latin phrase meaning "in place of the parent." In contemporary educational parlance this refers to the school's position in determining the amount of supervision given a student away from home.

Input —The event, situation, condition, signal, or cue to which a response must be made.

In-Service Training —That portion of "post-entry education" by which new employees are oriented, introduced, instructed, developed, or otherwise prepared for the methods, processes, and responsibilities of their jobs about which they may already have some general knowledge (because of previous education or training) but no experience.

Instruction, Programmed —Instruction utilizing a workbook, textbook, or mechanical and/or electronic device programmed to help pupils attain a specified level of performance by (1) providing instruction in small steps; (2) asking one or more questions about each step in the instruction and providing instant knowledge of whether each answer is right or wrong; and (3) enabling pupils to progress at their own pace, either individually through self-pacing or as a team through group pacing.

Instruction, Student-Centered —A characteristic of *programmed instruction* which, as an example, strives to take into consideration all pertinent student personality factors, such as differences in aptitude, background, knowledge, and motivation.

Instruction Techniques Test —This test measures knowledge of learning principles, instruction techniques, teacher-learner relationship, learning aids, and learning environment.

Instructional Design Model	—The rules and strategies for deciding what type of instruction and instructional materials to present in an independent or group learning situation.
Instructional Material	—Any device with instructional content or function that is used for teaching purposes, including books, textbooks, supplementary reading materials, audiovisual and other sensory materials, scripts for radio or television instruction, programs for computer-managed instruction, instruction sheets, and packaged sets of materials for construction or manipulation.
Instructional Media	—The means used to present information to the student. Devices and other materials that present a complete body of information and are largely self-supporting rather than supplementary in the teaching-learning process.
Instructional Program Development	—The process of (1) analyzing training task data and (2) designing, developing, and validating a program of instruction within the context of the Instructional Development Model.
Instructional Strategy Diagnostic Profile	—An experimental guide to enable instructional developers and evaluators to predict the effectiveness of and prescribe improvements for existing instructional materials.
Instructional System	—An integrated combination of resources—students, instructors, materials, equipment, facilities, techniques, and procedures—performing efficiently the functions required to achieve specified learning objectives.
Instructional Systems Development (ISD)	—A deliberate and orderly process for planning and developing instructional programs which ensure that students learn the knowledge, skills, and attitudes essential for realistic and successful job performance. The system depends on a description and analysis of the tasks necessary for performing the job. Lesson objectives and tests must be clearly stated before instruction begins. Evaluation procedures must determine whether the objectives have been reached, and must specify the methods for revising the process, if necessary, based on empirical data. (See also Chapter VIII.)
Instructional Television Programming	—Lesson-planned programs, developed and conducted largely in educational institutions, often with the option for credit.

Instructor	—(1) A teacher with the responsibility of instructing trainees or students in their progress toward specific educational or training objectives; (2) one who imparts knowledge with a verified response; (3) in colleges and universities, a teacher holding a rank below that of an assistant professor.
Instructor Guide	—A publication designed to provide the administrator of instructional materials with information about the objectives of the materials, the procedures involved in their development, suggestions for their optimal use, and descriptions of what might be expected from the materials based on their previous effectiveness.
Intelligence	—(1) The ability to learn and to criticize what is learned; (2) the ability to deal effectively with tasks involving abstractions; (3) the ability to learn from experience and to deal with new situations; (4) as commonly used in measurement and testing, a degree of ability represented by performance on a group of tests selected because they have proved their practical value in the prediction of success in academic work and in some vocations; (5) (mil. ed.) the product resulting from the collection, evaluation, analysis, integration, and interpretation of all information concerning one or more aspects of foreign countries or areas, which is immediately or potentially significant to the development and execution of plans, policies, and operations.
Interaction	—Any form of personal communication or contact between two or more persons in which the attitude or behavior patterns of the participants may be stimulated or influenced to some extent. (1) (philos.) A relation between more or less independent entities in which reciprocal influences of one upon the other are possible; (2) in philosophy of education, the view that the growth of personality and character of education is a product of continuously related forces of nature and nurture; that deliberate education is the effort to stimulate and direct this process (Dewey); (3) in experimentation the condition resulting when the effect of one factor or condition is dependent on the presence or absence of another factor or condition (for example, if the effect of the size of type on reading rate is dependent on style of type used, there is an interaction between size and style).

Interview —An interactional process of collecting data about a person through questioning or conversing.

Intrinsic Programming —A programming method characterized by relatively lengthy items, multiple-choice responses, and consistent use of branching. If, after reading the information section of each item, students select the correct response, they are sent to an item presenting new information. If they select an incorrect alternative, they are sent to an item that provides information as to why their choice was incorrect.

Ivory Tower —A figure of speech referring to the state of mind of an individual, usually a scholar, who supposedly is not aware of what is going on in the world outside his field of particular interest.

Ivy League —An association of eastern colleges and universities organized for athletic contests, primarily football; composed of Brown, Columbia, Cornell, Dartmouth, Harvard, Princeton, the University of Pennsylvania, and Yale.

Job —(1) All of the duties and tasks performed by a jobholder (an individual employee is normally assigned only one job until he is promoted or transferred to another job); (2) in labor relations a group of all positions, responsibilities, activities, or operations that may be assigned to and carried out by an employee or group of employees in an organization; (3) in electronic data processing, a unit of work to be accomplished by the computer.

Job Analysis —(1) The basic method used to obtain salient facts about a job involving observation of workers, conversations with those who know the job, analysis of questionnaires completed by job incumbents, and/or a study of documents involved in performance of the job; (2) a detailed listing of duties, tasks, and skills necessary to perform a clearly defined, specific job; (3) in management a basic tool in planning, controlling, financing, or coordinating. It consists of the systematic examination and determination of (*a*) the nature, characteristics, functions, duties, activities, or responsibilities of a job; (*b*) the knowledge, skill, or experience essential for performance; and (*c*) the environmental conditions, safety, equipment, tools, and related factors. (See Human Engineering.)

Jenkins Job Attitude Survey	—This test is designed to identify and evaluate personality characteristics that might be related to accident-proneness in employees. Special attention is given to variables like attentiveness, judiciousness, independence, personal-social sensitivity, presumptuous self-assurance, social orientation, and attitude toward pain.
Job Description	—A relatively detailed official statement of the methods, procedures, duties, responsibilities, equipment, tools, and other functions that are specifically related to a particular unit of work. It is generally used for purposes of selection, placement, training, compensation, promotion, and transfer.
Job Design	—An aspect of managerial planning and human engineering that is concerned with the contents and functions of individual jobs and how these relate to (1) the capabilities of workers; (2) routine activities; and (3) all other jobs in other units of the organization.
Job Evaluation	—(1) The rating of jobs to determine the relationships of all jobs in the organization and thereby to compile a complete picture of the organizational job structure; (2) the art, not an exact science, of systematically analyzing the various characteristics that make up the degree of difficulty of a job, and through analysis establishing a fair and just wage structure; (3) a systematic and objective process of analyzing and determining the nature and characteristics of jobs and occupations, and their relationship to organizational effectiveness.
Job Inventory	—The instrument used for conducting an occupational or position survey. It consists of items of identification and background information on personnel selected for the survey, and duty and task statements applicable to the career field or utilization field.
Job Performance Requirements	—The tasks required of the human component of a system, the conditions under which these tasks must be performed, and the quality standards for acceptable performance. Job performance requirements describe what people must do to perform their jobs.
Job Relations Training	—A type of human relations training program designed to teach supervisors (1) a certain amount of general knowledge that is needed in dealing with employees as individuals; (2) some basic

techniques of meeting individual problems through the recommended steps of (*a*) getting all the facts; (*b*) evaluating and making decisions; (*c*) taking the necessary steps toward the solution of the problem; and (*d*) checking the results.

Job Specification —A brief, but detailed description of the minimum characteristics, abilities, qualities, training, or other related requirements for a certain job or occupation that should be possessed by an employee to perform that job effectively.

Job Standardization —(1) The establishment of a prescribed method for performing an operation or procedure; (2) the specifying of its minimum requirements for satisfactory performance.

Johari Window —A graphic learning instrument consisting of four quadrants which, when used in leadership training groups, may help participants acquire or increase their knowledge of personality and group dynamics through examining personality and interpersonal reality areas that are (1) known to self and others; (2) known to self, but not known to others; (3) known to others, but not known to self; and (4) not known to self and others. This concept was developed by Joe Luft and Harry Ingram.

Keller Method —In higher education the instructor devises a training method in which learning materials, instruction, guidance, and tutoring suit the individual abilities and personal needs and interests of each learner involved.

Knowledge —Knowledge is not directly observable. It involves the use of mental processes, which enable a person to use symbols. A person knows something when he or she shows that he/she has used the symbols associated with it. (See Skills.) (1) The accumulated facts, truths, principles, and information to which the human mind has access; (2) the outcome of specified, rigorous inquiry which originated within the framework of human experience and functions in human experience; (3) the product of the operation of man's intellect, either within or apart from human experience; (4) the recall of specifics and universals, or the recall of a pattern, structure, or setting. For measurement purposes the recall situation involves mostly bringing to mind the appropriate material, with major emphasis on the psychological processes of remembering the problem in a knowledge test situation (finding in the problem or task the appropriate signals, and cues that will most effectively bring out whatever relevant knowledge is filed or stored).

Laissez-faire Leadership—A type of leadership whereby the leader (1) allows his followers to set their own objectives, to make their own decisions, and to create, develop, and proceed in their own direction with minimum or no control or supervision; (2) gives or is merely available to give necessary materials, information, guidance, or instruction; and (3) passively stands by as some sort of observer or mediator without actually participating or being involved in the activity of his group. Although there may be circumstances, such as a group of highly capable, motivated, and creative individuals, with whom such approach could prove beneficial in tapping imagination and resourcefulness, many authorities in management and in the various behavioral sciences feel that the probability for disorganization, instability, nonparticipation, low output, failure, or even chaos is just too great.

Language —(1) A code for conveying the thoughts and feelings of one individual to another, which has been accepted and is mutually understood by both; may be (*a*) oral, through the articulation of vocal sounds into words and then the grouping of words into statements; (*b*) written, through an arrangement of symbols roughly approximating the sounds that one makes in speaking; or (*c*) gestural, through body movements; (2) (data processing) any system of characters used to represent instructions and/or data so that the instructions and data are understandable to both computer and operator.

Law of Association —In education a hypothesis stating that learning by associating materials to be learned with other previously learned materials tends to produce more success in learning than attempting to learn new materials only.

Law of Effect —In education a hypothesis stating that learning is influenced positively when it brings satisfaction and negatively when it brings annoyance or frustration.

Law of Exercise —In education a hypothesis stating that learning is the result of positive involvement by the learner in a learning situation.

Law of Intensity	—A vivid, dramatic, or exciting learning experience teaches more than a routine or boring experience.
Law of Organization	—Organized teaching produces organized learning and it is remembered longer.
Law of Primacy	—In education a hypothesis stating that whatever is learned first may create the most lasting impression in the learner.
Law of Readiness	—Students learn best when they are ready to learn, and they will not learn much if they see no reason for learning.
Law of Recency	—In education a hypothesis stating that whatever is learned most recently may be remembered most successfully by the learner.
Law of Success	—Nothing succeeds like success. Teachers can help students experience some personal satisfaction from each learning activity and achieve some success in each class presentation.
Lead Time	—In PERT the time scheduled between the completion of an event and the completion of the event(s) preceding it on a path in a network. In inventory control the lead time starts as of the date an order is released and ends with the first receipts. There are often several different lead times to consider in inventory control, such as the processing lead time (time for an order to be processed), delivery lead time (time for an order to be delivered), replenishing lead time. In a fixed interval reorder system, the replenishing lead time, which begins when an order to replenish stock is released and lasts until the item is delivered to stock, ready for filling customer demand. Since replenishment orders are released only at regular intervals in this type of system, one review period (the interval between the regular reviews) must be added to the replenishment lead time to get the total lead time that must be considered in setting reorder points. In a fixed order system, when a replenishment order can be released at any time, the lead time is exactly the time required to deliver the item to stock (i.e., the replenishment lead time is equal to the total lead time). (See PERT.)
Leader	—An individual who, by virtue of his power, influence, authority, office, status, prestige, know-

ledge, personal qualities, or group acceptance, formally or informally exercises the right, function, and responsibilities of leading, directing, or controlling others. (See Leadership.)

Leadership —The act of inspiring an organization in its entirety and carrying it on toward the realization of its established objectives and goals through the qualities of vision of the future, understanding of the capacities, emotions, and ideas of the workers and groups of employees who are vitally concerned with making the future. This same statement can be applied to an individual as well as to an organization. A complex quality and system of interpersonal relationships, which consists of all the theories, methods, acts, and processes of planning, initiating, organizing, directing, influencing, guiding, motivating, and controlling the attitudes, behavior patterns, and activities of individuals and/or groups toward the attainment of some particular interests, goals, or objectives by any available means. (1) The ability and readiness to inspire, guide, direct, or manage others; (2) the role of interpreter of the interests and objectives of a group, the group recognizing and accepting the interpreter as spokesman.

Learner Analysis —The identification of the intended audience for an instructional product and of the significant traits, aptitudes, and proficiencies of these learners. Includes consideration of factors such as the learner's subject-matter competencies, background experiences, instructional preferences, maturity level, and communication skills.

Learner-centered Instruction —An instructional process in which the content is determined by learner's needs. The instructional materials are geared to the learner's level, and the instructional design makes the learner actively participate. The instructional system development process produces learner-centered instruction.

Learner-controlled Instruction —An instructional environment in which the student can choose from a variety of instructional options for achievement of the terminal objectives. Students can vary their rate of learning, the media used, and so forth.

Learning —(1) A change in the behavior of the learner as a result of experience. The behavior can be physical and overt, or it can be intellectual or attitudinal; (2) usually a need-oriented, psychological, and cognitive experience by which an individual's or group's behavior, attitudes, knowledge, habits, or skills are acquired, modified, intensified, or abandoned; (3) change in response or behavior (such as innovation, elimination, or modification of responses) involving some degree of permanence caused, partly or wholly, by experience, such "experience" being in the main conscious, but sometimes including significant unconscious components, as is common in *motor learning* or in reaction to unrecognized or subliminal stimuli. This includes behavior changes in the emotional sphere, but more commonly refers to the acquisition of symbolic knowledge or motor skills; does not include physiological changes, such as fatigue, or temporary sensory resistance or nonfunctioning after continued stimulation.

Learning Center —A learning environment that has been specifically developed to foster individualized instruction and that emphasizes employment of media to augment textbooks and manuals.

Learning Curve —In learning, a graphic representation of the relationship between progress and elapsed time.

Learning Lab —A teaching environment for students with special learning problems that usually contains specialized self-instructional equipment and materials and may have a specialized staff.

Learning Plateau —A period in the learning process during which minimum or no progress takes place.

Learning Resource Center (LRC) —Many libraries are now more than collectors, repositories, and lenders of books. They offer a wide range of services and equipment to facilitate the flow of information to the general public. Libraries have become "learning resource centers," with audiovisual, computer, and other high-tech equipment to speed the flow of information. In addition to the traditional books, magazines, and newspapers, LRCs now maintain computer banks of information, records, tape recordings, filmstrips, videotapes, and a myriad of other electronic and mechanical methods for storage and retrieval of information. In the well-equipped LRC, a student may view a movie, listen to an instructor's tape-recorded lecture, or participate in a computer-assisted learning program.

Learning Task Analysis —(1) An identification of the main skills to be acquired by the learner and the breakdown of these skills into their basic components; (2) an indication of the performance and knowledge requirements for a particular skill.

Lesson
—(1) A short period of instruction devoted to a specific limited topic, skill, or idea; (2) the materials to be studied before or during such a period; (3) what is learned during such a period of instruction.

Liberal Education
—(1) In the philosophy of Aristotle, the education a man needs when growing up in order to bring his manhood and freedom to perfection—education cultivating his soul's powers to perform "leisure" activities judged desirable for their own sake, such as contemplation of scientific and philosophic truth, rather than activities of "occupation" or "recreation," judged desirable for the sake of something else to which they lead; (2) in the Middle Ages, the education then thought most effective for cultivating such powers—education in the *seven liberal arts;* (3) in the philosophy of John Dewey, liberating education—whatever education actually accomplishes, liberation for the students being educated, as judged by observable consequences in the quality of their future experience, rather than by any supposition that certain subjects of study always possess more power of liberation than others; (4) in contemporary nonphilosophic usage, any education accepted as relatively broad and general, rather than narrow and specialized, and as preparation for living rather than for earning a living, such as that offered by academic high schools or by liberal arts colleges.

Linguistic Approach
—An approach to beginning reading instruction, distinguished by the systematic control of the introduction of sound and letter relationships. Use of a sight vocabulary and picture clues to meaning, as in traditional basal reader approaches, are not aspects of most linguistically based programs for beginning reading.

Linear Programming
—A programming method in which set sequences of frames require a response from the student at each step. The steps are so designed that errors will be minimal for even the slower students in the target population. Each student does each frame in the program. Progress will be different for each student going through the same program only in the rate at which he/she

proceeds through the sequence.

Logic
—(1) The science or art of reasoning; reasoning by inference from reliable propositions; system of principles of reasoning applicable to all scientific activities; convincing by reasoning. A system or method of reasoning whereby principles and criteria of truth and validity are formulated, examined, interrelated with, and/or applied toward the solution of problems. In general, scientific (or systematic) study of the general principles on which validity in thinking depends; deals with propositions and their inferential interrelations; (2) the science of inference and proof; (3) the science of implication; (4) in computer operation the process of determining by deductive reasoning the means for obtaining a desired result from a given set of conditions.

Mass Media
—The instruments of communication that reach a large number of people at once with a common message, for example, books, magazines, television, radio, motion pictures, etc., in contrast to the means employed for limited communication, as with a specific student or group of students.

Massed Practice
—During learning the process of providing all practice sessions at a specific point in the learning period, normally at the end of instruction. This is generally considered inferior to distributed practice. (See Distributed Practice.)

Master of Arts (M.A.)
—(1) The degree now usually given in the United States to university students who have completed certain requirements embracing at least one year's work above the baccalaureate degree; (2) historically a degree granted to advanced students in the medieval universities in Europe who majored in the faculty of arts rather than in higher faculties of theology, law, and medicine.

Materialism
—(1) Historically the view that only matter is real and that in the last analysis, all reality (including mind, idea, and purpose) is reducible to matter in motion; (2) modern materialism asserts an emergent and behavioral theory of mind, a conception of matter as developed by modern science, an optimism regarding scientific method and its control of nature, and a synoptic view of man and the universe, implicit in contemporary science; it rejects vitalism, general

theology, dualism, reductionism, terminal skepticism, supernaturalism, and contemporary fainthearted naturalism.

Mathematics, Applied —(1) School mathematics in which the topics are selected for and the teaching aimed at some particular use of mathematics, as, for example, *consumer mathematics, business arithmetic,* and *trade mathematics;* (2) topics in mathematics that are relevant to the theory of other disciplines that are studied for this reason.

Mathetics —A programming method that stresses the analysis and arrangement of subject matter and the systematic application of scientific training techniques. Four technical phases of mathetics are the task analysis, prescription of behavior (statement of objectives), characterization of the prescription (detailed analysis of behavior to be taught and strategy to be used), and exercise writing.

Matriculation —The formal process, completed by registration, of being admitted as a student to the rights and privileges of membership in a college or university. (In some institutions admission implies only that certain courses may be pursued; candidacy, that certain or all requirements preliminary to approval for pursuit of a degree have been met; matriculation, usually that all such requirements have been met.)

Measurement, Criterion-Referenced —The process of determining, as objectively as possible, a student's achievement in relation to a fixed standard, which is based on objectives.

Measurement, Norm-Referenced —The process of determining a student's achievement in relation to other students' "grading" on the curve involves norm-referenced measurement, since an individual's position on the curve (grade) depends on the performance of other students. Generally norm-referenced measurement is not appropriate in Instructional Systems Development.

Media —Any intervening substance through which a force acts on objects at a distance or through which impressions are conveyed to the senses. That through or by which anything is accomplished. Vehicle of ideas and information; intermediate agency, channel, or instrument of information; communications. In industrial and public relations and in advertising, the media are channels of communication (as bulletins, bulletin boards, letters, periodicals, booklets, public address systems, meetings, radio, and similar aids).

Media, Visual Aids —Any form of graphic material, such as a film, display, or photograph, used for educational or publicity purposes.

Medium —(Pl. Media) A means of effecting or conveying something. Medium is a general term roughly compatible in many ways with tools, instruments, vehicles, means, and so forth.

Microform —Any arrangement of images reduced in size, as on microfilm or microfiche.

Middle School —A school administrative unit typically between the primary elementary unit and the last, or secondary, unit in the school system. In one form of organization, it includes in one school children of approximate ages ten to fourteen from the conventional grades 5 to 8, making possible a primary school for kindergarten through grade 4, and a four-year high school for grades 9 through 12. The middle school is viewed as serving a transitional function from childhood to adolescence and seeks to overcome the rigidity of departmentalization, the pressures of intraschool competition, and the tensions of older adolescent functions commonly found in the conventional junior high school.

Mirror Script —Handwriting produced by writing from right to left, so that what is written becomes legible when read from the reflection in a mirror; may be a sign of abnormality, or may occur as a result of forcing a left-handed person to use the right hand.

Modem —A telephone hookup that allows two computers to "talk" (communicate) with each other.

Modern Languages —A term collectively applied to the study of pronunciation, grammar, composition, and reading of foreign languages in contemporary use, as contrasted with that of the ancient language commonly called the "classical languages."

Modular Scheduling —A course is divided into small units of instruction called modules. Each module supports one or more training objectives. Students are pretested and counseled on objectives to determine which modules of instruction they require. Students receive only those modules that pretesting and counseling indicate they need.

Module
—(1) A self-contained unit; (2) the material used to teach a performance or knowledge; it includes module objectives, a teaching outline, training materials (actual or by reference), training aids, and tests; the teaching outline recommends procedure and pacing, and identifies lesson objectives, aids, and materials; (3) an independent set of instructional materials; the same module may appear unchanged in more than one Plan of Instruction (POI).

Montessori Method
—The method developed by Dr. Maria Montessori, an Italian psychiatrist and educator, for education of children from birth to maturity, with special emphasis on the years of early childhood and featuring special techniques and materials to develop the child's senses and intellect, along with a new philosophical viewpoint regarding the nature of children. Includes emphasis on (1) the ability of the child's "absorbent mind" to absorb his culture and to select pertinent parts, unconsciously before age three, consciously thereafter; (2) "intrinsic motivation" through use of the child's innate curiosity and delight in discovery; (3) teaching through daily living activities concerned with care of self and environment; (4) indirect preparation, that is, activities that prepare the sensorimotor pathways for the future (for example, scrubbing as preparation for writing); (5) "didactic materials" in graded series; and (6) liberty within limits, that is, freedom to choose between things that are in themselves good.

Moral
—(1) A term used to delimit those characters, traits, intentions, judgments, or acts that can appropriately be designated as right, wrong, good, bad (in this meaning moral is opposed to amoral); (2) a term also used to designate the right or good over/against the wrong or bad, in relation to some criterion of obligation (in this meaning moral is an antonym of immoral).

Motion Study
—A scientific observation and analysis of the physical movements made by a worker in the performance of an operation or task.

Motivation
—Any direct or indirect, positive or negative inducement influence, suggestion, or other stimuli that can mobilize and direct the attitude and behavior of an individual or group toward the accomplishment or abandonment of some specific goal, objective, or condition. (1) (psych.)

broadly considered the process of arousing, sustaining, and regulating activity, a concept limited to some aspect such as the energetics of behavior or purposive regulation; (2) the practical art of applying incentives and arousing interest for the purpose of causing a pupil to perform in a desired way. Usually designates the act of choosing study materials of such a sort and presenting them in such a way that they appeal to the pupil's interests and cause him to attack the work at hand willingly and to complete it with sustained enthusiasm. Also designates the use of various devices such as the offering of rewards or an appeal to the desire to excel.

Multimedia Approach —The correlated use of more than one type of instructional medium as a vehicle for presenting the instructional materials. Characteristically an instructional package that employs a multimedia approach (use of textbooks, films, slides, and so forth) to present various segments of the entire package.

Multitrack Course —A course that employs more than one track or channel of instruction. Course goals are the same on all channels, but course content, degree of instruction, and presentation all vary to accommodate students of different aptitudes and levels of previously acquired skills and knowledge.

Naturalism —(1) The philosophic point of view that considers mental phenomena, and particularly moral values, as natural phenomena of natural sciences; (2) the educational point of view that stresses, as the goal of education, the development and expansion of what is natural in man, as opposed to discipline and the cultivation of an imposed set of standards and values; (3) (art) a style in which some aspect of reality is projected with very little interpretation, intensification, or modification on the part of the artist; in the mid-nineteenth century, a style that attempted to report reality as it appeared, without idealization, and that deliberately sought the commonplace for subject matter (Gustave Courbet was representative of this style).

New Technology Training —Training designed to introduce the knowledge, skills, abilities, and attitudes necessary to keep abreast of new developments in the immediate or related occupational fields of employees already with an organization.

Objective —Aim, end in view, or purpose of a course of action or a belief; that which is anticipated as desirable in the early phases of an activity and serves to select, regulate, and direct later aspects of the act so that the total process is designed and integrated. Objectives specify precisely what behavior is to be exhibited, the conditions under which behavior will be accomplished, and the minimum standard of performance. Objectives describe only the behaviors that directly lead to or specifically satisfy a job performance requirement. Many terms have been used to describe the various levels of objectives, but basically they are all objectives and should describe behavior, conditions, and standards.

Objective (adjective) —(1) Impersonal, impartial, free of bias or idiosyncrasy; (2) pertaining to the object itself as it exists independently of the knowing mind; (3) relating to that which is reliably known through public demonstration or verification.

Objective Test —Any test that personal feelings, judgments, bias, or intuition of persons administering, evaluating, or taking it are ideally reduced to a minimum.

Objectivity —An appraisal procedure is objective (that is, it has objectivity) if it elicits observable response that can be recorded and reported in a precise, specified way. Objectivity seeks to remove personal opinion by reducing the impact of individual judgment.

Occupational Analysis —(1) The basic method used to obtain salient facts about a job, involving observation of workers, conversations with those who know the job, analysis of questionnaires completed by job incumbents, and/or a study of documents involved in performance of the job, such as job descriptions; (2) a detailed listing of duties, tasks, and skills necessary to perform a clearly defined, specific job; (3) in management a basic tool in planning, controlling, financing, or coordinating. It consists of the systematic examination and determination of (*a*) the nature, characteristics, functions, duties, activities, or responsibilities of a job; (*b*) the knowledge, skill, or experience that is essential to have for its performance; and (*c*) the environmental conditions, safety, equipment, tools, and related factors. (See Human Engineering.)

Occupational Survey —The procedure for the identification of the duties and tasks that comprise one or more shred-outs, prefixes, specialties, career field ladders, or utilization fields; for the collection, collation, and analysis of information concerning such duties and tasks.

Omnibus Test —An intelligence test that is made up of questions, problems, or tasks from several different areas of learning.

On-the-Job Training —An effective and economical practice of training (or coaching) new employees on the actual job or work site by the supervisor, an experienced fellow employee, or an instructor who is specifically employed for such purpose. The form of training that places an inexperienced worker directly on the job and, by instruction and supervised use of tools, equipment, and materials, trains him for his specific job. Such training may sometimes be supplemented by classroom instruction.

Open Classroom —An instructional technique utilizing a classroom setting to provide maximum freedom for the pursuit of learners' interests. Such layout emphasizes a number of specialized interest areas rather than formal seating arrangements.

Opinion —(1) In popular usage a belief, judgment, idea, impression, sentiment, or notion that has not been conclusively proved and lacks the weight of carefully reasoned judgment or certainty of conviction; taken broadly it represents probability rather than knowledge; (2) the official view of an attorney general or other administrative official; rationale for a judge's decision.

Opinion Survey —A diagnostic method and process designed to determine the opinions, concerns, values, and interests of employees toward their job, trainees toward their training, the supervisor, the organization, policies, and so forth. Whether being given as a test, survey, questionnaire, or interview, it usually gives relatively accurate feedback that may be used to improve training or management.

Outdoor Education —An approach to teaching and a process through which learning experiences in all areas of the educational curriculum are provided and in which natural, community, and human resources beyond the traditional classroom are utilized as a motivation for learning and a means of broad curriculum enrichment and vitalization. Direct firsthand learning opportunities involve the teacher and student in ecological explorations of the environment to develop and/or improve the knowledge, understanding, attitude, behavior, appreciations, values, skills, and stewardship responsibility of the learner. Education in, for, and about the physical and biotic environment is emphasized in order to achieve a wide variety of educational goals.

Overlearning —Process or result of longer practice than it is judged to be necessary to learn a required skill or knowledge.

Parts of Speech —In the study of traditional grammar, a classification of the words of a language in terms of function and use; for example, English is classified into eight parts of speech: noun, pronoun, verb, adverb, preposition, adjective, conjunction, and interjection. Modern grammar classifies the parts of speech according to distribution.

Pedagogical Techniques —(1) Demonstration Method—A method of instruction in which the instructor explains and shows the student the precise action necessary to perform skills or processes. (2) Discussion Method— A method of instruction in which the instructor uses questions to cause students to participate actively in a learning situation by exchanging ideas, questions, and experiences to reach conclusions that will support learning objectives. (3) Individually Prescribed Instruction—A course of study or program fitted to the individual learner's background, abilities, and training needs in which the learner selects his/her own pace. (4) Investigation and Report—In this learning system, the student is assigned to investigate and report on specific assigned topics and issues that are related to a central problem or subject. This pedagogical technique provides excellent training in data collection and presentation, and it offers an opportunity to evaluate the learner's progress. (5) Lecture—One of the most commonly used and formal teaching techniques. Lectures are used in presenting an address, a topic, or a class by an instructor, leader, or expert. Usually such presentations are made to a large group of employees/students. (6) On-the-Job Training—The student/employee receives his/her training while actually performing a job or task. This teaching method allows the instructor to tell, show, observe, and correct the trainee in an actual job situation. (7) Peer Instruction—A method of instruction in which a student who has completed training acts as an instructor to another student in the skill or process to be learned. This process continues with each trainee becoming, in turn, an instructor for the next student. (8) Programmed Instruction—A student-centered method of instruction that presents the information in planned steps or increments with the appropriate responses immediately following each step. The student is guided step-by-step to the successful completion of the assigned task or training exercise. (9) Role-Playing—Role-playing is a teaching technique involving "acting"; that is, the student/trainee assumes a new identity to facilitate the learning of material or skills. For example in a history class, students may assume the persona of the individuals being studied in an attempt to understand better the specific historical milieu. (10) Simulation—Simulations are used to imitate a real situation. However the simulation is carefully controlled by the instructor, and it is carried out in a controlled environment. For example the aircraft industry uses simulators to train pilots on new equipment without the hazard of actual in-flight variables. (11) Question-and-Answer—When utilizing this teaching technique, the instructor employs thought-provoking questions to involve the student. At the optimum questions ought to stimulate thinking and reflection, rather than calling on the student for a yes-or-no answer or one repeated from rote memorization. (12) Workshop/Seminar—The workshop/seminar involves an interchange of knowledge and skills between people in mutual functional areas or a group of persons meeting together for the purpose of studying a common subject under the guidance of an instructor/expert.

Pedagogy   —(1) The art, practice, or profession of teaching; (2) the systematized learning or instruction concerning principles and methods of teaching and of student control and guidance; largely replaced by the term "education."

Percentile   —(1) One of the 99 point scores that divide a ranked distribution into groups or parts, each of which contains 1/100 of the scores or persons; the points are located to coincide with the obtained score below which in each division 1/100 of the cases fall; (2) (for example, P1, P10, P37, P90) a point on a scale of test scores or other measures below which a given percentage of the measures fall and above which the complementary proportion of measures fall; designated by the percentages of cases lying below it; thus 37 percent of the measures fall below P37 (37th percentile) and 63 percent above it.

Performance —The carrying out of an act to completion; actual accomplishment of a task to some preset standard of completeness and accuracy. An actual accomplishment distinguished from potential ability, capacity, knowledge, skill, or aptitude.

Performance Measurement —The process of determining if the student's performance on a given task reaches the criterion level set as the standard for that specific task.

Performance Method —A training method that provides learners with the opportunity to develop and apply, under controlled conditions and close supervision, the principles and skills that have been explained and demonstrated to them previously. (See On-the-Job Training.)

Personality —(1) The total psychological and social reactions of an individual; (2) the synthesis of his subjective, emotional, and mental life, his behavior, and his reactions to the environment. The unique or individual traits of a person are connoted to a lesser degree by personality than by the term "character."

PERT —Acronym for *Program Evaluation and Review Technique*. PERT is a tool or concept designed to facilitate management of complex projects. PERT was first introduced in 1958 as a system for monitoring development of the Polaris Ballistic Missile, a primary weapon of the United States' nuclear-powered submarines, and is widely credited with saving years in making the Polaris operational. The tool was devised, and is now used throughout industry, to help management control large, complicated projects. The concept deals explicitly with the network of relationships among the various phases of a total program production. A computer-implemented planning and control system, it is designed to help top management with planning, research, problem-solving, decision-making, and control of organizational processes.

Phenomenon —(1) A fact, occurrence, circumstance, or circumstances that are open to observation; (2) (philos.)

an immediate object of awareness in experience. Kant distinguishes between phenomena, things as we see them, and noumena, things as we apprehend them by pure reason, as they really are. (Comte founded positivism on the acceptance of phenomena, positive facts, and the rejection of speculation about their causes and origins.)

Philosophy —(1) An integrated personal view that serves to guide the individual's conduct and thinking; (2) the science that seeks to organize and systematize all fields of knowledge as a means of understanding and interpreting the totality of reality; usually regarded as comprising logic, ethics, aesthetics, metaphysics, and epistemology; (3) a habit of mind in the exercise of which one tends not to take the conventional and customary for granted but always to see possible alternatives (Dewey); (4) in military usage a body of beliefs or principles that give to the person who entertains them a certain bias for doing certain things and not doing others, or for doing something in a particular way.

Philosophy of Education —A careful, critical, and systematic intellectual endeavor to see education as a whole and as an integral part of man's culture, the more precise meaning of the term varying with the systematic point of view of the stipulator; any philosophy dealing with or applied to the process of public or private education and used as a basis for the general determination, interpretation, and evaluation of educational problems having to do with objectives, practices, outcomes, child and social needs, materials of study, and all other aspects of the field.

Philosophy of John Dewey —A pragmatic philosophy of education, formerly known as instrumentalism but now generally called experimentalism, that avoids the metaphysical and holds that both knowledge and value are instrumentally determined; broadly naturalistic, humanistic, and biologically derived; strongly oriented toward democracy; educational ideas follow those of Rousseau, Pestalozzi, Froebel, and others. Dewey profoundly influenced the progressive education movement in the United States.

Phonetics —(1) The science of speech sounds; (2) the analysis of words into their constituent sound elements.

Physics —The branch of *physical science* that is concerned with matter and energy, including the study of

291

phenomena associated with mechanics, heat, wave motion, sound, electricity, magnetism, light, and atomic and nuclear structure.

Plan —The basic element that denotes the mental condition, previous to physical movement, of determining a method of proceeding with the program of instruction or task to be accomplished.

Plan of Instruction (POI) —A qualitative course-control document designed for use primarily within an instruction of learning, or a school, for course planning, organization, and operation. Generally every block of instruction within a course (criterion objectives, duration of instruction, and support materials and guidance factors) is included in the Plan of Instruction.

Planning —(1) The action that is undertaken to meet future needs most effectively on the basis of evidence, which is, to a large extent, obtained from past experience; (2) an orderly and systematic process of thinking aimed at producing a pattern that is to be followed for a specific action; (3) the procedure for predetermining a course of action intended to accomplish a desired result; (4) a systematic, step-by-step method and process of defining, developing, and outlining possible courses of action to meet existing or possible future needs, interests, or problems.

Political Science —(1) A field of social studies having for its purpose the ascertaining of political facts and arranging them in systematic order as determined by the logical and causal relations that exist among them; concerned with political authority in all its forms, and dealing with them historically, descriptively, comparatively, and theoretically; (2) a division of social studies concerned with government, its origin, development, geographical units, forms, sources of authority, powers, purposes, function, and operations.

Position Description —Description of a job organized on the basis of duties and responsibilities and for the purpose of delineating authority, establishing chains of command and providing equitable salary. Usually an official statement setting forth in detail the methods, procedures, duties, responsibilities, supervisory relationships, and other pertinent factors that are specifically related to a particular position in an organization. Some position descriptions include standards for the position, prerequisites, both educational or through experience, and organizational levels for such position.

Postgraduate Education —Formal education for graduate students. Usually identified with higher education beyond the baccalaureate degree, but also applicable in some secondary schools where students holding the high school diploma may enroll for additional secondary school courses past requirements for graduation.

Post-test —A test given to a student upon completion of a course of instruction to measure learning achieved.

Pragmatism —(1) The philosophical position, founded in the United States by Charles S. Pierce and continued by John Dewey, and given a different, more psychological interpretation by William James, which holds that the meaning of an idea consists in the conduct it designates, that all thought distinctions consist in possible differences in practice, that thinking is a functional process for guiding action, and that truth is a social value which ideas earn as they are verified by competent inquirers in the open forum of thought and discussion; (2) sometimes loosely and erroneously thought to be the doctrine that a narrowly practical interest or view should predominate, that ends are denied or reduced to the status of means, that an idea which works or is personally satisfying is therefore true.

Preparatory School —A school to prepare students for entrance to another educational institution; usually refers, in the United States, to a private secondary school preparing students for college.

Prerequisites —Behaviors (knowledge, skills, attitudes) established as entry requirements for a particular course of instruction, training pattern, or job.

Pretest —A test given to a student or trainee prior to entry into a course or unit of instruction to determine the technical skills and knowledge (entering behavior) he or she possesses in a given subject. It can be used to identify portions of the instruction the student can bypass. In training the assessment done prior to instruction that determines the level of knowledge, skill and/or aptitude that a learner brings to instruction.

Professor —A teacher of the highest academic rank in an institution of higher education. Within the staff different grades are usually recognized, as full professor (designated as professor), associate professor, and assistant professor, in descending order.

Proficiency Test —A standardized and commercially available examination that is constructed to measure an applicant's or a student's job knowledge and/or proficiency for purposes of selection, promotion, or training. Its validity is usually determined on the basis of content or concurrent validity.

Program —Instructions given to a computer to solve a problem or perform a task. Also called Software.

Program Evaluation and Review Technique (PERT) —A tool or concept designed to facilitate management of complex projects. PERT was first introduced in 1958 as a system for monitoring development of the Polaris Ballistic Missile, a primary weapon of the United States' nuclear-powered submarines, and is widely credited with saving years in making the Polaris operational. The tool was devised, and is now used through-out industry, to help management control large, complicated projects. The concept deals ex-plicitly with the network of relationships among the various phases of a total program production. A computer-implemented planning and control system, it is designed to help top management with planning, research, problem-solving, decision-making, and control of organizational processes.

Programmed —A sequence of planned steps or increments that lead the student or trainee to mastery of the subject, while minimizing uncontrolled error. The student is required to respond actively to each step and is given immediate feedback as to correctness of his or her response. The distinguishing characteristic of programmed materials is the testing procedure to which they are subjected. Empirical evidence of the effectiveness of each teaching sequence is obtainable from the performance records of students. (See Intrinsic Programming; Linear Programming; Mathetics.)

Programmed Instruction —A student-centered method of instruction that presents the information in planned steps or increments, with the appropriate response immediately following each step. The student is guided step-by-step to the successful completion of the assigned task or training exercise.

Programmed Instructional Material —Instructional material, such as texts, tapes, films and filmstrips, slides, and scripts for live presentations prepared specifically to employ techniques of programming.

Programmed Instructional Package	—All the components of a specific unit of programmed instruction, including the programmed instructional materials, learning aids, instructor guide or manual, pretests and post-tests, validation data, description of intended student population, and objectives.
Programmed Text	—A publication prepared in one or more of the programmed instruction formats. Applies the concepts of programmed instruction. (See Linear Programming; Mathetics.)
Programmer	—(1) (programmed instruction) The person responsible for the design of items and sequences in a program; may be either a psychologist working with a subject-matter expert who delineates the content or a subject-matter specialist trained in programming techniques; (2) the individual who develops the step-by-step operations that are to be performed by the computer to solve a problem; (3) (data processing) a person who creates, evaluates, and/or corrects programs used in electronic data processing.
Prompt	—A stimulus added to the terminal stimulus to make the correct response more likely while the student is learning. It may be pictorial or verbal. It may vary in strength, that is, provide a model of the response that the student copies (for example, "Watch me and then do the same.") or provide a cue or hint of a weaker sort (for example, "The opposite of black is ..."). (See Input.)
Psychology	—The study of adjustments of organisms, especially the human organism, to changing environment.
Psychomotor Learning	—Pertaining to the manipulative or motor skill area. In psychology, tests designed to measure the various effects of or the relationship between sensory and motor abilities and processes.
Puberty	—(1) The period of life or stage of development at which the reproductive organs mature and become capable of functioning and the secondary sex characteristics develop; (2) the physiological stage marking the beginning of adolescence.
Public Education	—Usually the educational programs sponsored by the state, by countries, by school districts, etc., for the pupils in the elementary and secondary schools; may include adult or vocational education. (Sometimes used in contrast with private and parochial education and sometimes

to differentiate elementary and secondary education from higher education.)

Questionnaire —A method and practice of investigating, examining, and evaluating situations, trends, practices, or values among individuals and groups through a set of questions of various degrees of complexity, direction, and depth designed to obtain immediate feedback.

Quotient, Educational (EQ) —(1) The quotient obtained by dividing educational age by chronological age and multiplying by 100; (2) shows a pupil's achievement as compared with the average achievement of pupils of his own age.

Quotient, Ratio Intelligence (IQ) —A measure for expressing level of mental development in relation to chronological age, which is obtained by dividing the mental age (as measured by a general intelligence test) by the chronological age and multiplying by 100. The chronological age is often fixed at a certain maximum, most commonly sixteen years, when growth of intelligence due to maturation has been assumed to cease, so that a testee whose actual age was greater than this would still be assigned an age of sixteen years. Maximum chronological age for different tests varies from about fourteen to eighteen years. Formerly a commonly used scale, now largely replaced by a standard score scale, the deviation intelligence quotient.

Readability Formula —(1) A technique for determining the difficulty of reading materials, generally taking into account vocabulary and sentence length, although additional aspects are included in different formulas; (2) a style of writing, popularized by Rudolph Flesch and imitators, formerly employed to provide easier reading, especially for the less educated.

Reason —A term used for a function of knowing, a faculty of knowledge, or an object of comprehension; (1) as a function of knowing, reason may refer to a process of drawing inferences by combining concepts or propositions to reach truth discursively; or of intuiting truths immediately and nondiscursively; or of judging well in discriminating good from evil, truth from falsity, beauty from ugliness; or of grasping natural knowledge (as distinguished from revealed knowledge grasped by faith); or of discovering within itself, by reflection, innate ideas whose meaning, and first principles, whose truth, can be established apart from experience; or of comprehending directly the reality underlying appearances or the absolute underlying accidents; or, in a problematic situation, of solving the problems and thereby resolving the situation; or reason may refer to the whole constellation of higher mental processes; (2) as a faculty of knowledge, reason may refer to a special faculty with power to perform one of the foregoing functions, or to a general faculty with power to perform several of them, or to all the higher mental capacities; (3) as an object of comprehension, reason may refer to the principles of orderliness that make things understandable; to the ratio or relationship constituting a mathematical progression; or to the theoretical explanation that enlightens men's minds by leading them to understand something (in contrast to its efficient cause or a logical demonstration concerning it); or to the legitimate motive, or justification, for doing something; or to the intelligence or order pervading minds collectively, nature, or the universe, and thereby fitting whatever it pervades to be comprehended by functions or faculties of men's reasons.

Reflex (fact. anal.) —To reverse the direction of measurement of a test or factor by interchanging positive and negative ends of a variable or factor and to make the corresponding changes in the signs of the correlations and factor loadings.

Reinforcement —The strengthening of the probability of the recurrence of a particular response in a stimulus situation that is the same as or similar to the situation that originally induced the response.

Relating Training to Occupational Needs (RETONE) —A process model designed in the U.S. Federal Government to increase and strengthen communication linkages between the vocational educators and the actual or potential employers and their program graduates. Its purposes and objectives include the following: (1) providing a mechanism whereby existing and proposed occupational information systems at the state and local levels can be strengthened (retoned) through a process of interaction between the vocational education and CETA administrators and the employing organization(s); (2) improving the congruence of vocational education programs to current job practices as perceived by the employers of vocational education and manpower program graduates; and (3) removing some of the barriers to employment of trainable youths and adults.

Relativity, Theory of —(Philos.) The doctrine that the actual nature and meaning of any thing or situation are relative to its connection with other things or situations and that its nature and meaning may be discovered only by consideration of its position and relations within the system of which it is a part.

Reliability —Dependability of a testing device, as reflected in the consistency of its scores when repeated measurements are made of the same group. When a test is said to have a high degree of reliability, it means that an individual tested today and tested again at a later time with the same test and under the same conditions will get approximately the same score. In short, a test is reliable if it gives dependable, repeated measures.

Renaissance —A movement or period of vigorous artistic and intellectual activity; the transitional movement in Europe between medieval and modern times, beginning in the fourteenth century in Italy and lasting into the seventeenth century; marked by a humanistic revival of classical influence expressed in a flowering of the arts and literature and by the beginning of modern science.

Report Card —Formal, written notification to parents and/or guardians reporting achievement or progress of a student in various aspects of the school program; may include such items as subject-matter achievement, pupil's attitudes, effort, and attendance.

Research —Systematic search for knowledge. Careful search; a close searching. Studious inquiry; usually critical and exhaustive investigation having for its aim the revision of accepted conclusions, in the light of newly discovered facts. A continued process of scientific investigation prior to and during development, aimed at discovering new scientific facts, techniques, and natural laws. Systematic study and investigation undertaken to establish or increase knowledge of facts or principles. Careful, critical, disciplined inquiry, varying in technique and method according to the nature and conditions of the problem identified, directed toward the clarification or resolution (or both) of a problem. (Philosophical dimensions or aspects of research have to do with locating hidden assumptions, presuppositions, and value judgments implicit in the treatments of problems; with criteria of evaluation and of admissible evidence; with selection of methods appropriate to various investigations; and with the basis for selection and interpretation of data, etc.).

Research, Applied —Work aimed at specific application of scientific laws, principles, and phenomena. In contrast with basic research, the prospect of practical application results is a primary reason for "applied research." Often the methods to be used are clear before work is begun. Research concerned with the development and practical application of knowledge, material, and/or techniques directed toward a solution to an existing or anticipated organizational product or service.

Research, Basic —The theoretical or experimental study directed toward the increase of knowledge. It may result in the discovery of new scientific phenomena, principles, techniques, or significant data that add to the store of scientific knowledge. Immediate practical application is not necessarily a direct objective. A searching for new relations within a total structure of thought and understanding (for example, a theory of learning) and for a correlation of discoveries in a way that is in agreement with the total of observed properties or behaviors; an assumed relation stated as a hypothesis gives specificity and direction to the search.

Response —Any activity that is induced by a stimulus. In instruction it designates a variety of behaviors that may involve a single word, selection among alternatives (multiple choice), the solution of a complex problem, the manipulation of buttons or keys.

Response, Covert —An international response that the student presumably makes, but that is neither recorded nor otherwise available to an observer (for example, a student "thinks" a response).

Response Mode —The manner in which a student responds, for example, writing a sentence, selecting an answer from a group of choices, repairing a piece of equipment, and so on.

Response, Overt —A student's oral, written, or manipulative act that is, or can be, recorded by an observer.

Retraining —A management method and process of preparing employees already with the organization for new skills, which are created by various internal (organizational) or external (economic, social, technological, or other) needs.

Role-Playing —(1) The assuming, either overtly or in imagination, of the part or function of another or others; a tool in the philosophical analysis of personality and society, the concept of role-playing now has important theoretical and practical applications in psychotherapy, group dynamics, and education; (2) a method for developing insights into human relationships by acting out certain behavior in situations that are similar to real life; (3) an instructional technique involving a spontaneous portrayal (acting out) of a situation, condition, or circumstances by selected members of a learning group. (See also Figure 29.)

Safety Education —An organizational training program designed to make employees familiar with the common hazards at work and the ways to prevent or lessen the probability for the occurrence of on-the-job hazards, injuries, and unsafe working habits and conditions. Its principal components include thorough job instruction training, job methods training, job relations training, and on-the-job training. (1) Education for effective living in relation to the physical and health hazards of modern society; current school programs deal with safety as related to the following areas: home, school, traffic (including school transportation), fire, industry, rural, civil defense, and recreation; (2) (ind. arts) instruction in the safe use of tools and machinery and in preventive maintenance, inspection, and safe operation of automobiles, small engines, and outboard motors.

Scenario —An outline or synopsis of the environment of the problem area to be examined or analyzed.

Scheduling —A process of planning, arranging, and controlling a program in terms of time, place, personnel, and sequence of operations and activities.

School —(1) An organizational group of pupils pursuing defined studies at defined levels and receiving instruction from one or more teachers, frequently with the addition of other employees and officers, such as principal, various supervisors of instruction, and a staff of maintenance workers; usually housed in a single building or group of buildings; (2) a division of the school organization under the direction of a principal or head teacher (to be distinguished from the school building, which may house more than one school); (3) a major subdivision of a university, offering a curriculum to which admission can be had usually only after some study in a college of arts and sciences and which leads to a technical, professional, or graduate degree; (4) occasionally used to designate a group of subjects organized to a definite end, as a school of civil engineering in a college of engineering; (5) a common body of beliefs and assumptions held by authoritative scholars in philosophy, theology, science, economics, etc., for example, the Montessori school, the Freudian school.

School Planning Evaluation and Control System (SPECS) —Training system with purposes to (1) collect information about the goals, methods, and controls and outcomes of particular school situations; (2) aid school personnel with program budgeting and cost accounting; (3) facilitate overall organizational and system control; (4) provide for citizen participation in identifying educational goals; and (5) provide a procedure for identifying and resolving discrepancies between actual district outcomes and the board goals and expectations of its citizenry.

Science —(1) Activity carried on as an effort to make the diversity of our sense experiences correspond to a logically uniform system of thought; in this activity experiences are correlated with a previously constructed theoretic structure of thought and understanding in an effort to make the resulting coordination in agreement with all observed properties or behavior; (2) in the personal experiences of an individual, science is an activity by means of which the person seeks to relate his current sense experiences to his total structure of understanding in a manner that is in agreement with all his pertinent observations of properties and behaviors; such activity is believed to be inherent in the behavior of individuals at all levels of maturity; the individual gains, through practice, in his ability to correlate his current experience with his previously conceived structure of understanding however naive or sophisticated that structure may be; (3) organized knowledge gained through science as activity, frequently used with a qualifying adjective to indicate a special branch of study, for example, *biological science, physical science, or social science.*

Science, Applied —(1) Utilized or practical knowledge of facts, laws, and/or proximate causes, gained and verified by exact observation and logical thinking; also the application of universal knowledge; (2) any branch of science employed for a particular purpose, pursued for some end outside its own domain, whether in a distinctly utilitarian way or as an aid to some other branch, as applied mathematics or applied biological science.

Science, Basic —General facts and principles that are fundamental to the study of specialized fields of science.

Science, Pure —Sometimes science concerned with concrete problems of data rather than with fundamental principles, as distinguished from abstract or theoretical science.

Scrambled Book —A form used to present an intrinsically programmed text. In such a book, the student reads a portion of material and selects an answer to a multiple-choice question based on the material. The answer selected determines the page within the book to which the student is then directed for comment, shuffled so that the student cannot detect the right answer pages by their relative placement. (See Intrinsic Programming.)

Self-Pacing —A procedure in which students can progress through an instructional program at their own rate. This procedure enables slower students to take as much time as they need. Faster students can finish a course more quickly. (See Group Pacing.)

Seminar —An instructional technique common in, but not limited to, higher education, in which a group of students engaged in research or advanced study meets under the general direction of one or more leaders for a discussion of problems of mutual interest.

Sensitivity Analysis —In quality control projective method and process designed to estimate, predict, or evaluate probable variance or deviation in a range of hypothetical or projected quantitative or qualitative values or data. Sometimes also referred to as "parametric."

Sensitivity Interpersonal —An imaginative projection of one's self into the mental, psychological, and behavioral processes of another person, in order to understand, gain insight into, sympathize with, or predict what such person might do, without actually feeling what such a person feels. A social awareness. Sometimes also called "empathy."

Sensitivity Training —A laboratory-type of small-group training designed to create in the participants (usually supervisors or higher level), an understanding of or "sensitivity" toward the causes, processes, and effects of (1) their own attitudes and behavior; (2) the attitudes and behavior of others; and (3) basic techniques of communication in various interpersonal situations, such as training, supervision, guidance, or counseling.

Sensor Base Computer —In data management a computer designed and programmed to receive and generate real-time data from transducers, sensors, and other data sources that monitor a physical process.

Setting Analysis —In training, the identification of those environmental factors relevant to the design of instructional products.

Shaping —A technique that reinforces successive approximations, starting with behavior that is already present (for example, questions the capability for audiovisual presentations).

Simulation —(1) In learning and training, making the practice and materials as near as possible to the situation in which the learning will be applied; for example, microteaching wherein student teachers actually teach a small group in a laboratory setting; (2) an initiative type of data processing in which an automatic computer is used to implement an information model of some entity, such as a chemical process; information enters the computer to represent the factors entering or affecting the real process, and the computer then produces information that represents the results of the process, with the processing done by the computer representative of the process; (3) the use of role-playing by the actors during the operation of a comparatively complex symbolic model of an actual or hypothetical social process; usually includes gaming and may be all-man, man-computer, or all-computer operations. A technique whereby job-world phenomena are mimicked in an often low-fidelity situation in which costs may be reduced, potential dangers eliminated, and time compressed. The simulation may focus on a small subset of the features of the actual job-world situation.

Simulator —A generic term including whole-task simulators, part-task trainers, procedure trainers, and so on. Simulator and simulator training device may be used interchangeably.

Situation Test —A test that measures the reaction or response of individuals to real-life or simulated situations or problems.

Situational Variables —All changeable ideas, elements, traits, characteristics, or processes that exist in the physical or social environment of organizations.

Skill —An inherent or learned ability to apply one's knowledge and/or experience to one's job, vocation, or profession.

Skills —Skills involve physical or manipulative activities. They often require knowledge for their execution. All skills are actions having special requirements for speed, accuracy, or coordination. (See Knowledge.)

Slide Projector —A training device designed to project slides or transparencies mounted in small frames. It may be silent, or cassettes, cartridges, records, or tapes may be used for audiovisual presentations.

Slide Viewer —A training device equipped with a built-in glass or a rear projection screen for viewing slides. It may be silent, or cassettes, cartridges, records, or tapes may be used for audiovisual presentations.

Small-Group Discussion —A technique and process of solving problems of mutual concern by means of an organized, but still informal, face-to-face meeting in which participants exchange all the ideas, feelings, or opinions they have about available facts, under the guidance or chairmanship of a chosen or appointed leader.

Social Anthropology —A branch of anthropology that studies the patterns of communication, interaction, division of work, family, customs, norms, habits, ideas, and related social behavior of man in groups, societies, or cultures throughout the world.

Social Studies —Those portions of the subject matter of the social sciences (particularly history, economics, political science, sociology, and geography) that are regarded as suitable for study in elementary and secondary schools and are developed into courses of study, whether the subject matter and the aims are predominantly social; not to be confused with the social sciences or with subjects having a social aim but not social content (as in the case of courses in English, art appreciation, and personal health), nor to be confined to too narrow or rigid a combination of studies.

Society —(1) An enduring, cooperating social group (generally of human beings) so functioning as to maintain and perpetuate itself; (2) any group, but especially a nation, consisting of human beings who may be similar or different in race and culture, who have more or less clearly recognized common interests, and who cooperate in the pursuit of those interests.

Sociology —(1) The science or study of human social grouping and behavior, regarded generally and collectively, and dealing particularly with the origins, development, purposes, functions, problems, adjustments, and peculiarities of human society; (2) the study of human beings living together in groups.

Software —The programs and routines used to extend the capability of automatic data processing equipment. The programs developed and maintained in conjunction with a computer for the purpose of developing and performing routine programming operations. (1) All nonhardware elements of a computer-based system, including written computer programs, flow charts, subroutines, and other items related to information systems; also the package of programming support or utility routines that is provided (or available with) a given computer, generally including an assembler, a compiler, an operating system (or monitor), debugging aids, and a library of subroutines; (2) the educational stimuli or messages, such as a televised lecture, a teacher-prepared audiotape, or a programmed textbook, which provide the content of instruction to the student.

Sound-Slide Program —An audiovisual instructional program that uses 35mm slides and recorded sound. Sometimes this program is referred to as slide/tape, and in the case when the recording is a part of the slide frame, as sound-on-slide.

Special Education —The education of pupils (for example, the deaf, the blind and partially seeing, the mentally subnormal, the gifted) who deviate so far physically, mentally, emotionally, or socially from the relatively homogeneous groups of so-called normal pupils that the standard curriculum is not suitable for their educational needs, and their variation presents unusual management problems to the school through its interference with the learning of others; carried on in special classes, through special curricula, and/or in special schools.

Specialist —A person who has studied and worked intensively in one field of knowledge and has attained a high degree of understanding and proficiency. In teacher education there are specialists in subject matter as well as in fields related to the science and practice of education, such as educational philosophy, educational psychology, methods of teaching, curriculum, and administration. In public school systems, there are often specialists in art, music, and physical education.

Speech —A system of communication by means of symbolic vocal sounds.

Statistics —(1) A value of measure that describes or characterizes a particular series of quantitative observations, or that characterizes the universe from which the observations were drawn, or that is designed to estimate the corresponding value in that universe; (syn. characteristic, statistical constant; ant. parameter); (2) a summary value based on a sample; (3) a term sometimes used to designate any statistical item, observation, score, measure, or similar datum (a usage that results in ambiguity).

Step —A portion of material to which the student makes a response. It is a stage in the instructional process that represents progress in the student's mastery. A subject to be taught is broken down into frames, items, or segments (steps). It is assumed that students cannot take later steps in a given sequence before taking the earlier step, and that each segment or item represents a step forward. (See Frame.)

Stimulus —The event, situation, condition, signal, or cue to which a response must be made. Any physical, psychological, or social idea, phenomenon, or event that is capable of causing changes in the attitudes and/or behavior of a person or a group.

Storage —In electronic data processing, the memory unit of a computer in which information is entered, retained, and made available for use.

Subsystem —A major functional subassembly or grouping of items or equipment that is essential to the operational completeness of a system. A human, technical, man-machine, or automated unit or group of units within an organizational system that performs an essential complementary function and that can be separated and dealt with independently as a complete entity for purposes of planning, maintenance, coordination, or control.

Summative Testing —In training, testing of learners at the close of a program of instruction that measure the degree of performance attained in relation to the total behavioral objectives of the program.

Summum Bonum —The ultimate goal. Justice, truth, wisdom, beauty, charity, and virtue are indicative of the many values that have competed for supremacy over all others as the summum bonum, the chief end and aim of existence.

Supervisory Job Instruction Test —This test is designed to measure knowledge of learning principles, teacher-learner relationship, learning aids, and learning environment.

Supplemental Training —Training to provide the knowledge, skills, abilities, and attitudes necessary to improve or maintain present level of proficiency on the job. Sometimes referred to as "refresher training."

Survey Test —The survey test is a criterion-referenced test used prior to the development of an instructional system. It is administered to a sample of prospective students to determine what skills and knowledge should be included in the course of instruction.

Syllabus —A condensed outline or statement of the main points of a course of study, books, or other educational or training documents.

Syntality —The sum of all traits, attitudes, abilities, interests, drives, behavior patterns, activities, or tendencies of the individual members of a group by which that group can consistently be defined and recognized. Syntality is to a group as personality is to the individual.

Synthesis —A method, process, or result of investigating, comparing, and establishing logical relationships among different data, facts, ideas, and viewpoints.

System Safety Engineering	—A scientific method for investigating all the facts necessary to assure the harmonious relationship between personnel, facilities, and equipment in a defined environment to prevent unexpected or inadvertent hazardous or injury and damage-causing conditions to occur.
Systems Analysis	—The scientific study and analysis of all related aspects of an organizational or management system to determine the necessary steps for continuation, improvement, or correction.
Systems Approach	—An integrated, programmed complex of instructional media, machinery, and personnel whose components are structured as a single unit with a schedule of time and sequential phasing; purpose is to ensure that the components of the organic whole will be available with the proper characteristics at the proper time to contribute to the total system, and in doing so fulfill the goals that have been established.
Systems Research	—A systematic, objective, creative, and logical method of inquiring into and analyzing all related aspects of biological, social, or organizational systems within the framework of the scientific method and systems theories. The methodology used includes (1) definition of needs or goals; (2) collection of pertinent data; and (3) classification, analysis, and evaluation of data, with purposes to determine a solution on the basis of such data, apply the proposed solution, and provide the necessary verification and follow-up. Although "systems analysis" has also been used for reference, this is a broader and more inclusive concept.
Target Population	—The persons (group) for whom the instructional or training materials are designed. Samples from this population are used in evaluating instructional materials during their development.
Task Analysis	—A descriptive method of tasks in terms of manageable units small enough to be studied for possible elimination, combination, rearrangement, and simplification. A detailed inventory of what needs to be done. The behavior to be taught and learned. A detailed inquiry into the actions that need to be taken in the performance of a specific task or job. It involves making an inventory of what has to be done. Such an inventory would include not only information about the knowledge and motor actions that are required, but also the skills and attitudes that are necessary.

Task Description —A written description (in column, outline, decision table, or timeline format) that describes the required job behavior at the highest level of generality, and provides an overview of the total performance.

Task Inventory —A detailed list of all the steps comprising a specific job or jobs. Reduction of the components of a task to its basic behavioral elements, usually for purposes of determining the best methods of training to perform it, but also to understand better the learning process.

Teacher —(1) A person employed in an official capacity for the purpose of guiding and directing the learning experiences of students in an educational institution, whether public or private; (2) a person who, because of rich or unusual experience or education, or both, in a given field, is able to contribute to the growth and development of other persons who come in contact with him; (3) a person who has completed a professional curriculum in a teacher education institution and whose training has been officially recognized by the award of an appropriate teaching certificate; (4) a person who instructs others.

Teacher Certification —The procedure by which the state department, or an agency thereof, authorizes the issuance of licenses or certificates that permit the individual holder to teach in the public schools of that state.

Teacher Education —(1) All the formal and informal activities and experiences that help to qualify a person to assume the responsibilities of a member of the educational profession, or to discharge his responsibilities of a member of the educational profession more effectively; (2) the program of activities and experiences developed by an institution responsible for the preparation and growth of persons preparing themselves for educational work or engaging in the work of the educational profession. Also called "teacher training."

Teachers College —(1) A degree-granting college specializing in the preparation of teachers and other education workers; (2) a college within a university that is responsible for the professional preparation of teachers.

309

Teaching	—(1) Narrowly the act of instructing in an educational institution; (2) broadly management by an instructor of the teaching-learning situations, including (*a*) direct interaction between the teacher and the learner, (*b*) the pre-active decision-making process of planning, designing, and preparing the materials for the teaching-learning conditions, and (*c*) post-active redirection (evaluation, redesign, and dissemination); (3) collectively that which is taught, such as the teachings of a religious leader or an educational institution. The art of awakening the natural curiosity of both young and not-so-young minds. Syn. instruction.
Teaching, Diagnostic	—The process of prescribing for pupils learning opportunities based on individually determined needs and objectives.
Teaching Machine	—A device that presents a program. The machine usually controls the material to which the student has access; contains a response mechanism; contains provision for knowledge of results; and may score and tabulate results either by revealing the correct answer after the student responds or by advancing to the next item, signaling correct completion of the previous item. Some machines score responses and tabulate errors.
Teaching, Objective	—(1) Teaching in which the presentation and treatment of the subject are clearly defined and based as much as possible on factual material, with a minimum of subjective feelings and personal bias, and in which the evaluation of pupil achievement is made largely on a nonsubjective basis; (2) teaching based on concrete experiences and perceptions of sense or form rather than on abstractions and verbalization.
Technical	—(1) Of or pertaining to that aspect of an art or science requiring practical, applied, mechanical, or scientific skills or knowledge; (2) qualified or skilled in the practical, mechanical, or applied aspects of an art or science; (3) of, or pertaining to, or characteristics of a specialized field or activity; (4) of, pertaining to, or providing knowledge of any of various subjects that involve practical, applied, mechanical, or industrialized skills or knowledge.
Technology	—(1) The systematic scientific study of technique; (2) the application of science to the solution of practical problems; (3) a systematic body of facts and principles comprehensively organized

for a practical purpose; may include the principles of effective teaching; (4) the science or systematic knowledge of the industrial arts, especially as applied to manufacturing; (5) the material culture resulting from the combination of logic, mathematics, and science.

Technology, Educational —The application of scientific principles to the designing and implementing of instructional systems, with emphasis on the precise and measurable educational objectives (learner-centered rather than subject-centered orientation); strong reliance on educational theory to guide educational practice; validation of educational practices through empirical analysis; and the extensive use of audiovisual equipment in instruction.

Training —(1) The special kind of teaching and instruction in which the goals are clearly determined, are usually readily demonstrated, and call for a degree of mastery that requires student practice and teacher guidance and appraisal of the student's improved performance capabilities; (2) a process by which a group of persons gains unity by virtue of its members learning to do certain things together; (3) in a derogatory sense, a process of helping others to acquire skills or knowledge by rote, without reference to any greater framework of knowledge or comprehension.

Tutorial —A method of teaching initiated in Great Britain where a teacher meets individually with a student for an intensive discussion of some topic, often based on material that the student has prepared prior to the meeting.

Validity —The extent to which a test actually measures the characteristics it is intended to measure. Derived validity: the extent to which test scores correlate with criterion scores that possess direct validity. Direct validity: the extent to which the tasks included in a test represent faithfully and in due proportions the kinds of tasks that provide an operational definition of the achievement or trait in question.

Chapter XVII
Selected Suggestions for Further Reading

Abernathy, Elton, *The Advocate: A Manual of Persuasion,* New York: David McKay Co., 1964.

Alexander, William M., *Are You a Good Teacher?,* New York: Rinehart & Co., 1959.

Allen, Myron S., *Morphological Creativity: The Miracle of Your Hidden Brain Power,* Englewood Cliffs, N.J.: Prentice-Hall, 1962.

Anderson, D. C., *Evaluating Curriculum Proposals: A Critical Guide,* New York: Halsted Press, 1981.

Argris, C., *Role-Playing in Action,* New York State School of Industrial and Labor Relations Publications, no. 816, Ithaca: New York State School, 1971.

Arnold, John E., *Problem-Solving–A Creative Approach,* Washington, D.C.: Industrial College of the Armed Forces, 1976.

Auer, Jeffrey J.; Eisenson, Jon; and Irwin, John V., *The Psychology of Communication,* New York: Appleton-Century – Crofts, 1973.

Bair, Medill, and Woodward, R. G., *Team Teaching in Action,* Boston: Houghton Mifflin Co., 1974.

Baker, Samm S., *Your Key to Creative Thinking,* New York: Harper & Row, 1972.

Barzun, Jacques, *Teacher in America,* Boston: Little, Brown & Co., 1955.

Beardsley, Monroe C., *Thinking Strait,* Englewood Cliffs, N.J.: Prentice-Hall, 1970.

Benedict, J. A., and Crane, D. A., *Producing Multi-image Presentations,* Tempe: Audiovisual Services, Arizona State University Press, 1973.

Benne, Kenneth D., and Tozer, Steven, eds., *Society as Educator in an Age of Transition,* National Society for the Study of Education, Eighty-Sixth Yearbook, Part 2, Chicago: University of Chicago Press, 1982.

Berlo, David K., *The Process of Communication,* New York: Holt, Rinehart, & Winston, 1970.

Black, John W., and Moore, Wilbur E., *Speech Code: Meaning and Communication,* New York: McGraw-Hill, 1975.

Blair, G. M.; Jones, R. S.; and Simpson, R. H., *Educational Psychology,* 2d ed. New York: Macmillan, 1972.

Bloom, Benjamin S., *Taxonomy of Educational Objectives,* New York: Longmans-Green, 1976.

Bluem, William A., *Television in the Public Interest,* New York: Hastings House, 1981.

Boatright, Mody C., *Accuracy in Thinking,* New York: Rinehart & Co., 1980.

Bolado, Victor H., *Management Terminology,* Great Neck, New York: Todd & Honeywell, 1983.

Bossing, N. L., *Progressive Methods of Teaching in Secondary Schools,* Boston: Houghton Mifflin Co., 1972.

Boy, Angelo V., and Fine, Gerald J., *Client-Centered Counseling in the Secondary School,* Boston: Houghton Mifflin Co., 1974.

Bradford, Curtis, and Moritz, Hazel, *The Communication of Ideas,* Boston: Heath & Co., 1971.

Braun, Ernest, and Macdonald, Stuart, *Revolution in Miniature: The History and Impact of Semiconductor Electronics,* Cambridge: Cambridge University Press, 1988.

Braun, Ernest, and Macdonald, Stuart, *Revolution in Miniature: The History and Impact of Semiconductor Electronics,* Cambridge: Cambridge University Press, 1981.

Bremeck, Cole S., *The Discovery of Teaching,* Englewood Cliffs, N.J.: Prentice-Hall, 1972.

Bridges for Ideas, Visual Instruction Bureau, Austin: University of Texas Press.

Briggs, Thomas H., and Justman, Joseph, *Improving Instruction Through Supervision,* New York: Macmillan, 1972.

Brown, J. W., and Lewis, R. B., eds., *AV Instructional Technology Manual for Independent Study,* 4th ed. New York: McGraw-Hill, 1973.

Brown, James W.; Lewis, Richard; and Hancleroad, Fred, *AV Instruction: Technology, Media, and Methods,* New York: McGraw-Hill, 1983.

Bryant, Donald D., and Wallace, Karl R., *Fundamentals of Public Speaking*, 3d ed. New York: Appleton–Century–Crofts, 1970.

—— *Oral Communication*, 3d ed. New York: Appleton– Century–Crofts, 1972.

Burns, Richard W., and Craik, Mary B., "Factors for Consideration in Program Selection," *Teaching Aids News*, vol. 3 (July 1974): 1–5.

Burton, William H., *Guidance of Learning Activities*, New York: Appleton–Century–Crofts, 1962.

Burton, William H., and Brueckner, Leo J., *Supervision: A Social Process*, 3d ed. New York: Appleton-Century-Crofts, 1975.

Butler, F. A., *Improvement of Teaching in Secondary Schools*, 3d ed. Chicago: University of Chicago Press, 1974.

Byrne, Richard H., *The School Counselor*, Boston: Houghton Mifflin Co., 1973.

Cabot, Hugh, and Kahl, Joseph A., *Human Relations*, Cambridge: Harvard University Press, 1973.

Carpenter, C. R., and Greenhill, L. P., *Instructional Television Research, no. 2*, Pennsylvania: Pennsylvania State University, 1978.

Castell, Aubrey, *A College Logic*, New York: Macmillan, 1969.

Chase, Stuart, *The Proper Study of Mankind*, New York: Harper & Row, 1978.

Chauncey, Henry, and Dobbin, John E., *Testing: Its Place in Education Today*, New York: Harper & Row, 1973.

"Checklist for Selecting Programs," *NSPI Journal*, July 1973: 4.

Clark, Harold F., and Sloan, Harold S., *Classrooms in the Military*, New York: Columbia University Press, 1974.

Clement, R. W., "Evaluating the Effectiveness of Management Training Progress During the 1970s and Prospects for the 1980s," *Human Resources Management*, Winter 1981: 8–13.

Cook, Floyd A., *School Problems in Human Relations*, New York: McGraw-Hill, 1967.

Costello, Lawrence F., and Gordon, G. N., *Teach with Television*, New York: Hastings House, 1971.

Crawford, Claude C., *How to Teach*, Los Angeles: South California Book Depository, 1968.

"Criteria for Assessing Programmed Instructional Materials: 1962 Interim Report of the Joint Committee on Programmed Instruction and Teaching Machines," *Audiovisual Instruction*, February 1973: 84–89.

Dale, Edgar, *Audiovisual Methods in Teaching*, rev. ed., New York: Dryden Press, 1974.

de Kieffer, R. E., and Cochran, Lee W., *Manual of Audiovisual Techniques*, 2d ed., Englewood Cliffs, N.J.: Prentice-Hall, 1973.

de Leon, Peter, *Scenario Designs: An Overview*, Santa Monica, Calif.: Rand Corp., 1973.

Dell, Helen Davis, *Individualizing Instruction: Materials and Classroom Procedures*, Chicago: Science Research Associates, 1974.

Delva, Daines, *Designing Instruction for Mastery Learning*, Provo: Brigham Young University Press, 1982.

Deterline, William, *An Introduction to Programmed Instruction*, Englewood Cliffs, N.J.: Prentice-Hall, 1972.

DeTouzos, Michael L, and Moses, Joel, *The Computer Age: A Twenty-year View*, Cambridge: MIT Press, 1979.

Dick, Walter, and Reisner, Robert A., *Planning Effective Instruction*, Englewood Cliffs, N.J.: Prentice-Hall, 1989.

D'Ignazio, Fred, *Messner's Introduction to the Computer*, New York: Julian Messner, 1981.

DiLauio, T. J., "Training Needs Assessment: Current Practices and New Directions," *Public Personnel Management*, November–December 1979: 351–59.

Doll, Ronald C., *Curriculum Improvement: Decision-Making and Process*, 8th ed., Needham Heights, Mass.: Allyn & Bacon, 1992.

Duff, John Carr, *Creative Teaching in Colleges and Universities*, New York: New York University Press, n.d.

Durost, Walter N., and Prescott, George A., *Essentials of Measurement for Teachers*, New York: Harcourt Brace Jovanovich, 1972.

Edgar, Thomas, *The Invaluable By-Product: Creativity*, Phi Delta Kappa, February 1975: 273–76.

Educational Developmental Laboratories, Reading Newsletter no. 26, Huntington, N.Y.: November 1972.

Erickson, Carlton, W. H., *Administering Audiovisual Services*, New York: Macmillan, 1969.

Espich, J. E., and Williams, B., *Developing Programmed Instructional Materials: A Handbook for Program Writers,* Belmont, Calif.: Fearon Publishers, 1977.

Evans, James L.; Coulson, John E. ed., *Program Learning and Computer-based Instruction,* New York: John Wiley & Sons, 1972.

Flesh, Rudolf, *The Art of Clear Thinking,* New York: Harper & Row, 1971.

Fox, J. H.; Bish, C. E.; and Ruffner, R. W., *School Administration,* New York: Prentice-Hall, 1977.

Freeley, Austin J., *Augmentation and Debate,* San Francisco: Wadsworth Publishing Co., 1981.

Frye, R. A., *Graphic Tools for Teachers,* 2d ed., Austin, Texas: E & I Printing Co., 1973.

Fulmer, Daniel W., and Bernard, Harold W., *Counseling: Content and Process,* Chicago: Science Research Associates, 1974.

Galanter, Eugene, ed., *Automatic Teaching: The State of the Art,* New York: John Wiley & Sons, 1979.

Garner, W. Lee, *Programmed Instruction,* New York: Center for Applied Research in Education, 1969.

Garrett, Henry E., *Statistics in Psychology and Education,* 5th ed., New York: David McKay Co., 1978.

Gilbert, Thomas, "Mathetics: The Technology of Education," *The Journal of Mathetics,* Vol. 1, no. 1, January 1972.

Gilmer, Ben S., *Education for Creativity,* Southern Bell Management Information Bulletin, February 1972.

Glasser, William, *Schools Without Failure,* New York: Harper & Row, 1969.

Glasser, William, *The Quality School,* New York: Harper & Row, 1985.

Glueck, W. F., *Personnel: A Diagnostic Approach,* 3d ed.

Goetting, M. L., *Teaching in the Secondary School,* New York: Prentice-Hall, 1972.

Plago, Tex.: Business Publications, 1982.

Grace, Nathaniel *Handbook of Research on Teaching,* Chicago: Rand-McNally, 1973.

Grace, W. J., and Grace, J. C., *The Art of Communicating Ideas,* New York: Davin-Adair Co., 1972.

Granbard, Steve R., and Holton, Gerald, *Excellence and Leadership in a Democracy*, New York: Columbia University Press, 1972.

Green, Edward J., *The Learning Process and Programmed Instruction*, New York: Holt, Rinehart & Winston, 1973.

Green, J. H. C., *Speak to Me*, New York: Odyssey Press, 1972.

Griffith, B. L., and MacLennan, D. W., eds., "Improvement of Teaching by Television," Proceedings of the Conference of the National Association of Educational Broadcasters at the University of Missouri, Missouri: University of Missouri, 1974.

Gropper, George L., "Does Programmed Television Need Active Responding?" *AV Communication Review*, Spring 1976.

Grubb, Ralph E., and Selfridge, Lenore D., *Computer Tutoring in Statistics*, Watson Research Center, IBM, Yorktown Heights, N.Y.: March 1974.

Grunlund, Norman, *Stating Objectives for Classroom Instruction*, 3d ed. New York: Macmillan, 1985.

Guilford, Joy P., *Psychometric Methods*, 2d ed. New York: McGraw-Hill, 1974.

Gullahorn, John T., "Teaching by the Case Method," *The School Review*, Winter 1959: 448–59.

Guthrie, Edwin R., and Powers, Francis F., *Educational Psychology*, New York: Ronald Press Co., 1980.

Gwynn, John M., *Theory and Practice of Supervision*, New York: Dodd-Mead, 1971.

Haas, Kenneth B., and Ewing, C. H., *Tested Teaching Techniques*, New York: Prentice-Hall, 1981.

Haas, Kenneth B., and Packer, Harry Q., *Preparation and Use of Audiovisual Aids*, 3d ed. New York: Prentice-Hall, 1975.

Haemer, K. W., *Making Your Meaning Clear*, New York: American Telephone & Telegraph Co., 1979.

Haiman, Franklyn S., *Group Leadership and Democratic Action*, Boston: Houghton Mifflin Co., 1971.

Hammock, Robert C., *Supervising Instruction in Secondary Schools*, New York: McGraw-Hill, 1975.

Hance, Kenneth G.; Ralph, David C.; and Wiksell, Milton J., *Principles of Speaking*, Belmont, Calif.: Wadsworth Publishing Co., 1972.

Harless, J. H., "Mathetics: The Ugly Duckling Learning to Fly." Paper presented to the Fourth Annual Convention of the National Society for Programmed Instruction, St. Louis, Mo., April 1976.

Harless, J. H., "The Two Meanings of Mathetics." Paper presented to the National Programmed Learning Conference, Leicestershire, England, April 1976.

Harris, Chester W., ed., *Encyclopedia of Educational Research*, 3d ed. New York: Macmillan, 1970.

Haskey, Lawrence D., and McLendon, Jonathon C., *This Is Teaching*, Chicago: Scott, Foresman & Co., 1972.

Hayakawa, S. I., *Language in Thought and Action*, 2d ed. New York: Harcourt Brace Jovanovich, 1975.

Hendershot, Carl, *Programmed Learning: A Bibliography of Programs and Presentation Devices*, Bay City, Mich.: Carl Hendershot.

Highet, Gilbert, *Man's Unconquerable Mind*, New York: Columbia University Press, 1974.

—— *The Art of Teaching*, New York: Vintage Books, 1975.

Hodnett, Edward, *The Art of Working with People*, New York: Harper & Row, 1979.

Hook, J. N., *Guide to Good Writing*, New York: Ronald Press Co., 1972.

Horn, Nicol, Razar, and Kleinman, *A Reference Collection of Rules and Guidelines for Writing Information*. Mapped Materials. Cambridge, Mass.: Information Sources, 1981.

Hovland, Carl I.; Irving, Janis L.; and Kelley, Harold H., *Communication and Persuasion*, New York: Yale University Press, 1973.

Huff, Darrell, *How to Lie with Statistics*, New York: W. W. Norton & Co., 1974.

Hullfish, H. Gordon, and Smith, Philip C., *Reflective Thinking: The Method of Education*, New York: Dodd, Mead & Co., 1971.

Hunter, Beverly, *My Students Use Computers: Learning Activities for Computer Literacy*, Alexandria, Va.: Human Resources Research Organization, 1983.

Hunter, M., *Mastery Teaching*, El Segundo, Calif.: TIP Publications, 1982.

Jacobs, Maier, and Stolurow, *A Guide to Evaluating Self- instructional Programs*, New York: Holt, Rinehart & Winston, 1975.

Johnson, Earl A., and Eldon, Michael R., *Principles of Teaching*, Boston: Allyn & Bacon, 1978.

Jones, Arthur J., *Principles of Guidance*, New York: McGraw-Hill, 1973.

Kanner, J. H.; Runyon, R. P.; and Desidenato, Otelle, *Television in Army Training*, Department of the Army, 1978.

Kealey, Robert J., *Curriculum in the Catholic School*, Washington, D.C.: National Catholic Association Press, 1986.

Kearsley, G., and Compton, T., "Assessing Costs, Benefits, and Productivity in Training Systems," *Training and Development Journal*, January 1981: 52–61.

Kelley, Earl C., *Education for What Is Real*, New York: Harper & Row, 1977.

Kemp, J. E., *Planning and Producing Audiovisual Materials*, 2d ed. San Francisco: Chandler Publishing Co., 1979.

Kilpatrick, W. H., *Foundation of Method*, New York: Macmillan, 1936.

Kinder, James A., *Audiovisual Materials and Techniques*, 2d ed. New York: American Book Co., 1969.

Kirkpatrick, D. L., "Techniques for Evaluating Training Programs," *Journal of the American Society of Training Directors*, December 1979: 3–4 and 21-26; January 1970: 13–18 and 28–32.

Klomoski, P. K., ed., *Programmed Instruction*, Vol. 4, no. 2. New York: Columbia University Press, 1974.

Knowles, Malcolm S., *The Modern Practice of Adult Education*, New York: Association Press, 1970.

Laird, Dugan, *Approaches to Training and Development*, Reading, Mass.: Addison-Wesley, 1978.

Lane, Howard A., and Beauchamp, Mary, *Human Relations in Teaching*, New York: Prentice-Hall, 1965.

Laux, Dean M., *A New Role for Teachers*, Phi Delta Kappa, February 1975: 265–68.

Leifer, M. S., and Newstrom, J. W., "Solving the Transfer of Training Problems," *Training and Development Journal*, August 1980: 42–46.

Lewis, Phillip, *Educational Television Guide Book*, New York: McGraw-Hill, 1971.

Lincoln, Richard E. Unpublished Material, Denton, Texas, 1981.

Lindgren, Henry C., *Educational Psychology in the Classroom*, New York: John Wiley & Sons, 1972.

Lumsdaine, A. A., and Glaser, Robert, *Teaching Machines and Programmed Learning*, Washington: National Education Association, 1970.

Lundell, Kerth T., "The Behavior Change Process," *NSPI Newsletter*, Vol. 11, no. 6, 1972.

Lysaught, J. P., and Williams, C. M., *A Guide to Programmed Instruction*, New York: John Wiley & Sons, 1963.

MacLinker, J., *Designing Instructional Visuals: Theory, Composition, Implementation*, Austin, Texas: University of Texas Instructional Media Center, Division of Extension, 1968.

Magoun, F. Alexander, *The Teaching of Human Relations*, Boston: Beacon Press, 1969.

Margulies, Stuart, and Elgen, Lewis D., *Applied Programmed Instruction*, New York: John Wiley & Sons, 1962.

Markle, David G., "In Which It Is Demonstrated That a Program That Works May Well Be Worthless," *Improving Human Performance*, Fall 1973.

Markle, Susan Meyer, *Good Frames and Bad: A Grammar of Frame Writing*, 2d ed. New York: John Wiley & Sons, 1979.

—— "The Lowest Common Denominator: A Persistent Problem in Programming," *Programmed Instruction*, Vol. 2, no. 3, February 1973.

Markle, Susan Meyer, and Tiemann, Phillip W., *Really Understanding Concepts: Or in Frumious Pursuit of the Jabberwock*, Chicago: Tiemann Associates, 1969.

—— "Conceptual Learning and Instructional Design," *Journal of Educational Technology*, Vol. 1, no. 1, 1970.

Marksberry, Mary Lee, *Foundation of Creativity*, New York: Harper & Row, 1973.

Maslow, A. H., *Motivation and Personality*, New York: Harper & Row, 1954.

May, Mark A., *The Role of Student Response in Learning from the New Educational Media*. A report by the U.S. Department of Health, Education, and Welfare, August 1966: 8–9.

McBurney, James H., and Hance, Kenneth G., *Discussion in Human Affairs*, New York: Harper & Row, 1980.

McBurney, James H.; O'Neill, James M.; and Mills, Glen E., *Argumentation and Debate*, New York: Macmillan, 1959.

McGregor, Douglas M., *The Human Side of Enterprise in Readings in Leadership,* West Point, N.Y.: U.S. Military Academy, 1964.

McLagan, P. A., *Helping Others Learn: Designing Programs for Adults,* Reading, Penn.: Addison-Wesley Publishing Co., 1978.

Mealira, L. W., and Duffy, J. F., "An Integrated Model for Training and Development: How to Build on What You Already Have," *Public Personnel Management,* 1981: 336–43.

Mednick, S. A., *Learning,* Englewood Cliffs, N.J.: Prentice-Hall, 1974.

Meredith, J. C., *CAI Author/Instructor,* Englewood Cliffs, N.J.: Educational Technology Publications, 1971.

Mickalar, Donald F., and Yager, Edwin C., *Making the Training Process Work,* New York: Harper & Row, 1979.

Miller, Harry, *Teaching and Learning in Adult Education,* New York: Macmillan, 1964.

Miller, John P., and Seller, Wayne, *Curriculum Perspective and Practice,* White Plains, N.Y.: Longmans-Green, 1985.

Minor, E., and Frye, H., *Techniques for Producing Modern Visual Instructional Media,* 2d ed. New York: McGraw-Hill, 1970.

Moore, Robert Hamilton, *Effective Writing,* 2d ed. New York: Rinehart & Co., 1959.

Morse, W. C., and Wingo, G. M., *Psychology and Teaching,* Chicago: Scott, Foresman & Co., 1972.

Mort, Paul R., and Vincent, William S., *Modern Educational Practice,* New York: McGraw-Hill, 1970.

Mouly, George J., *Psychology for Effective Teaching,* New York: Holt, Rinehart & Winston, 1970.

Mourer, O. Hobart, *Learning Theory and Behavior,* New York: John Wiley & Sons, 1970.

Mudd, Charles S., and Sellars, Malcolm O., *Speech Content and Communication,* San Francisco: Chandler Publishing Co., 1972.

Muhlback, Captain George W., "Appraisal of the Case Method," *Instructors Journal,* July 1974: 2–13.

Munn, Norman F., *Psychology: The Fundamentals of Human Adjustment,* Boston: Houghton Mifflin Co., 1976.

Mursell, J. L., *Successful Teaching,* New York: McGraw-Hill, 1972.

National Training Laboratories, *Reading Book,* Washington: National Education Association, 1964.

Newell, G. E., "How to Plan a Training Program," *Personnel Journal,* May 1976.

Nichols, Ralph G., and Lewis, Thomas O., *Listening and Speaking,* Dubuque, Iowa: W. C. Brown, 1954.

Nixon, J. E., "The Mechanics of Questionnaire Construction," *Journal of Educational Research,* Vol. 47, no. 7, (March 1974): 481–87.

Ofiesh, G. D., and Meier, Henry W. C. *Trends in Programmed Instruction,* Washington, D.C.: National Education Association, 1974.

Osborn, Alex F., *Applied Imagination,* 3d ed. New York: Charles Scribner's Sons, 1973.

Parnes, Sidney J., *Instructor's Manual for Semester Courses in Creative Problem-Solving,* Buffalo, N.Y.: Creative Education Foundation, 1973.

Pennington, Dempsey F., Jr., *Mathetical Lesson Preparation,* New York: TOR Education, 1971.

PHSP 2196. *Designing Good Slides: An Instructive Communication.* Atlanta, Georgia: U.S. Department of Health, Education, and Welfare. Center for Disease Control, June 1981.

Peterson, Houston, *Great Teachers,* New Brunswick, N.J.: Rutgers University Press, 1966.

Popham, James W., *Criterion-referenced Measurement,* Englewood Cliffs, N.J.: Prentice-Hall, 1978.

Reeder, Ward G., *A First Course in Education,* New York: Macmillan, 1978.

Reid, Loren, *Speaking Well,* Columbia, Mo.: Artcraft Press, 1972.

—— *Teaching Speech in the High School,* Columbia, Mo.: Artcraft Press, 1972.

Remmers, Hermann H., et. al., *A Practical Introduction to Measurement and Evaluation,* New York: Harper & Row, 1970.

Resnick, Lauren B., *Education and Learning to Think,* Washington, D.C.: National Academy Press, 1987.

Rogers, Carl R., *On Becoming a Person,* Boston: Houghton Mifflin Co., 1971.

Rountree, Derek, *Basically Branching,* London, England: Macdonald & Co., 1966.

Ruch, F. L., *Psychology and Life,* Chicago: Scott, Foresman & Co., 1948.

Rummler, Geary A., "The Economics of Lean Programming," *NSPI Journal*, Vol. 4, no. 10 (December 1975): 8.

Sands, Lester B., *Audiovisual Procedures in Teaching*, New York: Ronald Press Co., 1956.

Sanford, William P., and Yeager, William H., *Principles of Effective Speaking*, New York: Ronald Press Co., 1973.

Schifferes, Justus J., *The Older People in Your Life*, New York: Washington Square Press, 1972.

Schorling, Raleigh, *Student Teaching*, New York: McGraw-Hill, 1959.

Sedik, J. M.; Magnus, A. K.; and Rakow, J., "Key Elements to an Effective Training System: *Training and Development Journal*, July 1980: 10–12.

Severin, Werner, "The Effectiveness of Relevant Pictures in Multiple-Channel Communications," *AV Review*, Winter 1977: 386–401.

Silvertone, David M., "Successful Listening," *Teaching Aid News*, February 1974.

Smith, Kellogg, and Stapleford, *Effective Writing*, Garden City, N.Y.: Doubleday & Co., 1973.

Smith, Mary H., ed., *Using Television in the Classroom*, "Midwest Program on Airborne Television Instruction," New York: McGraw-Hill, 1971.

Smith, R. G., "Controlling the Quality of Training," *Technical Report 65–6*, Alexandria, Va.: George Washington University, Human Resources Research Office, June 1965.

Snyder, Benson R., *The Hidden Curriculum*, New York: Knopf, 1971.

Spalding, Eugenia K., R.N., "What Is a Teacher?," *Hospital Progress*, October 1973: 1–6.

Stanley, Julian C., *Measurement in Today's Schools*, Englewood Cliffs, N.J.: Prentice-Hall, 1982.

Stasheff, E., and Bretz, R., *The Television Program: Its Direction and Production*, New York: Hill & Wang, 1978.

Staton, T. F., *How to Instruct Successfully*, New York: McGraw-Hill, 1970.

Stokes, Maurice S., *An Interpretation of Audiovisual Learning Aids: An Educational Monograph*, Boston: Meador, 1966.

Sullivan, M. W., *Programmed Grammar*, New York: McGraw-Hill, 1974.

Supek, D. J., *Motivation to Learn: From Theory to Practice*, Englewood Cliffs, N.J.: Prentice-Hall, 1988.

Tate, Merle W., *Statistics in Education*, New York: Macmillan, 1965.

Taylor, Clavin W., "Clues to Creative Teaching," *The Instructor*. A series of ten articles, September 1973 to June 1974.

Taylor, Jack W., *How to Create New Ideas*, Englewood Cliffs, N.J.: Prentice-Hall, 1971.

Thorndike, Robert L., and Hagen, Elizabeth, *Measurement and Evaluation in Psychology and Education*, 2d ed. New York: John Wiley & Sons, 1971.

Tracey, William R., "Program Reviewers Checklist," *NSPI Journal*, January–February 1965: 6–7.

Torrance, Paul E., *Education and the Creative Potential*, Minneapolis: University of Minnesota Press, 1963.

Travers, Robert M. W., *Educational Measurement*, New York: Macmillan, 1955.

—— *Essentials of Learning*, New York: Macmillan, 1973.

Trow, W. H., and Smith, E. A., *Filmstrip Techniques for Individual Instruction*. AMRL-TR-65-78. Wright Patterson AFB, Ohio: Aerospace Medical Research Laboratories, 1975.

Underwood, B. J., and Schulz, R. W., *Meaningfulness and Verbal Learning*, Chicago: J. B. Lippincut Co., 1960.

Utterback, William E., *Group Thinking and Conference Leadership*, New York: Rinehart & Co., 1970.

Wagner, Russell H., and Arnold, Carroll, C., *Handbook of Group Discussion*, Boston: Houghton Mifflin Co., 1970.

Walter, Otis M., and Scott, Robert L., "Listening Analytically," *Thinking and Speaking*, 1972.

—— *Thinking and Speaking*, 3d ed. New York: Macmillan, 1973.

Walton, Mary, *Deming Management at Work*, New York: Putnam, 1990.

Weaver, Andrew T., and Ness, Ordean G., *An Introduction to Public Speaking*, New York: Odyssey Press, 1971.

Weiss, Harold, and McGrath, J. B., Jr., *Technically Speaking*, New York: McGraw-Hill, 1973.

White, Eugene E., *Practical Speech Fundamentals*, New York: Macmillan, 1970.

Whorf, Benjamin L., *Language: Thought and Reality*, Cambridge: MIT Press, 1966.

Wilds and Zachert, *Programmed Instruction: Teaching Gynecologic Cander,* Georgia: Medical College of Georgia, 1967.

Wiles, Kimball, *Teaching for Better Schools,* Englewood, N.J.: Prentice-Hall, 1959.

Williamson, Edmund G., *Counseling Adolescence,* New York: McGraw-Hill, 1970.

Wittich, Walter A., and Schuller, Charles F., *Audiovisual Materials–Their Nature and Use,* 3d ed. New York: Harper & Row, 1972.

Wood, Dorothy A., *Test Construction: Development and Interpretation of Achievement Tests,* Columbus, Ohio: Charles E. Merrill Books, 1970.

Wrenn, Gilbert C., *The Counselor in a Changing World,* Washington, D.C.: American Personnel and Guidance Association, 1972.

Wynn, Richard, *Simulation: Terrible Reality in the Preparation of School Administrators,* Phi Delta Kappa, Vol. 46, no. 4 (1964): 170–73.

Wynne, John P., *Theories of Education,* New York: Harper & Row, 1968.

Yoakum, G. A., *Modern Methods and Techniques of Teaching,* New York, Macmillan, 1978.

Zemke, Ron, and Zemke, Susan, "30 Things We Know for Sure About Adult Learning," *Training,* June 1981: 45–46; 48 & 52.

Zirbes, Laura, *Spurs to Creative Teaching,* New York: G. P. Putnam's Sons, 1959.